A History of Hispanic Theatre in the United States
Origins to 1940

A History of Hispanic Theatre
in the United States

Origins to 1940

Nicolás Kanellos

UNIVERSITY OF TEXAS PRESS   AUSTIN

First edition, 1990

Requests for permission to reproduce material from this work
should be sent to Permissions, University of Texas Press, Box 7819,
Austin, TX 78713-7819.

⊗ The paper used in this publication meets the minimum require-
ments of American National Standard for Information Sciences—
Permanence of Paper for Printed Library Materials, ANSI
Z39.48-1984.

Library of Congress Cataloging-in-Publication Data

Kanellos, Nicolás.
    A history of Hispanic theatre in the United States : origins to
1940 / Nicolás Kanellos.—1st ed.
        p.   cm.
    Bibliography: p.
    Includes index.
    ISBN 0-292-73049-7 (alk. paper). — ISBN 0-292-73050-0 (pbk. : alk.
paper)
    1. Hispanic American theater—History.   I. Title.
PN2270.H57K36   1990
792'.08968073—dc20   89-14645
                                                                    CIP

For my loving but impatient wife, Cristelia Pérez, who kept pushing me to finish this labor of love.

Contents

Acknowledgments

It has been sixteen years since I first began to research this topic, and in that time I have received assistance and encouragement from many individuals and institutions. Over this period I was fortunate to receive fellowships that made possible a good deal of the traveling and release from teaching duties needed to work in archives in Spain, Mexico, Puerto Rico, and some eight states on the three coasts of the United States: Ford Foundation/ National Research Council Fellowship, Lilly Faculty Open Fellowship, National Endowment for the Humanities Summer Fellowship, and summer fellowships from the University of Houston and Indiana University. On the road I was greatly assisted by the archivists at the numerous special collections that have preserved a treasure house of documents: Antonio Pasarell Archives, University of Puerto Rico; Bancroft Collection, University of California, Berkeley; Barker Texas History Center, University of Texas; Nettie Lee Benson Latin American Collection, University of Texas; Center for Research Libraries, Chicago; Biblioteca Nacional, Mexico City; Chicano Studies Library, University of California, Berkeley; Federal Theatre Archives, George Mason University; Houston Metropolitan Archives, Houston Public Library; Columbia University; Huntington Library, Pasadena, California; Library of Congress; Los Angeles County Museum; New York Public Library; Secretaría de Relaciones Exteriores, Mexico City; San Antonio Conservation Society; Sociedad de Autores, Mexico City; and the University of South Florida, Tampa. I am also indebted to the following for allowing me to use their private or personal archives: Lalo and Susie Astol, Belia Areu Camargo, *El Diario—La Prensa*, Pedro González González, William Lansford, Lydia Mendoza, Elsa Ortiz Robles, Tony Pizzo, and Rafael Trujillo Herrera. My special thanks go to two librarians who not only gave me the keys to the collection so that I could work into the early morning hours but also gave me food and lodging: Richard Chabrán and Oscar Treviño. I also would like to acknowledge Mildred Boyer, my professor at the University of Texas, who taught me how to research and write on theatre, and Américo Paredes, for pointing me in the direction of the Spanish-language newspapers. And my very special thanks and love go to my dear friend Tato Laviera, who came in to greet me in his freshly cleaned white outfit only to end up helping me in the dark, dank, and dirty storage room where bound copies of *La Prensa de Nueva York* had laid forgotten for two decades. There were many other friends, too numerous to name here, who put me up and otherwise assisted me in these labors that were quite often physically and intellectually taxing. In particular, Francisco Blasco was infected by this obsession and became a more than able research assistant and a tireless and enthusiastic coordinator of my touring exhibitions, Two Centuries of Hispanic Theatre in the Southwest, funded by the state humanities councils of Arizona, California, New Mexico, and Texas, and Two Centuries of Hispanic Theatre in the United States, funded by the National Endowment for the Humanities. I would like to express my thanks to these humanities agencies for their support and to the staff of the museums that housed our exhibitions in Albuquerque, Chicago, El Paso, Houston, Los Angeles, Miami, New York, San Antonio, San Francisco, Tempe, and Tucson. My special thanks go to Rolando Hinojosa for proofreading and suggestions; to Tomás Ybarra-Frausto for collaborating with me on related research projects; Rodolfo Cortina, Francisco Lomelí, Arturo Rosales, María Herrera-Sobek, Rosaura Sánchez, Arturo Ramírez, Joe Rodríguez, Félix Padilla, and Jorge Huerta for inviting me to speak on this topic at their institutions; and especially to Jorge Huerta for all the years of encouragement. My partner in publishing ventures at Arte Público Press, Julián Olivares, has been an invaluable proofreader and critic. Thank you, Delia Ruiz, for all the word processing, and Marina Tristán, for carrying on at Arte Público Press for me while I was writing this book. And of course this work would never have reached its happy terminus without the constant love and encouragement of my wife, Cristelia Pérez.

Introduction

Until the early 1970s, studies of Hispanic theatre in the United States concentrated almost exclusively on folk drama, with the bulk of published research relating to the Mexican shepherd plays, or *pastorelas*. It was unusual for a scholar to explore the development of professional Spanish-language theatre in the United States, for it was simply assumed that such a theatre did not exist. Today there is still a singular absence of the Hispanic background and contribution in books on the history of the American stage and particularly in those on the origins of theatre in the American West. No one mentions, for example, the theatre houses that bore Spanish names and that were already functioning when the first minstrels arrived from the East. Neither do they make note of the professional and amateur Spanish-language companies that represented the only available theatrical entertainment for Mexicans and Anglos alike in various parts of the Southwest. Moreover, even the greatest flourishing of Hispanic theatre and its relationship to the movie industry in Hollywood during the 1920s have never before been written about in this country. To be sure, there are a handful of dissertations, theses, and published scholarly articles that study the development of theatre in Texas and California and the Federal Theatre Project in Florida; they represent a mere beginning to the research of this important cultural expression in the United States. But until now, except for this present effort, there has been no systematic attempt at locating long-forgotten texts and survivors of what, unfortunately, has become an underground or forgotten tradition, a forgotten part of a our national history and culture.

The appearance in 1965 of a farmworkers' theatre, El Teatro Campesino, finally attracted attention from scholars despite the fact that the Campesino's style of labor theatre was down-to-earth, improvised, and far from the lights and glamour of Broadway. Many of the Chicano players that emerged to follow Luis Valdez and El Teatro Campesino acknowledged a deep-rooted tradition in the Southwest. And El Teatro Campesino took the lead, not only in reviving the neighborhood parishes' Guadalupe plays, but also in fashioning its performance style after the Mexican tent theatres, commonly known as *carpas* or *maromas*. El Teatro Campesino developed one-act plays modeled on the *revistas*, or revues, that were performed in these *carpas* and also incorporated into their works the beloved comic character of that tradition, the *peladito*.

Since 1965 a flurry of scholarly interest has developed on the history of Chicano theatre. Much of the work, however, concentrates on the analysis of contemporary pieces, often identifying them as Brechtian, guerrilla, and agitprop or psychodrama. Very rarely has Chicano theatre been examined from within the context of a Hispanic or Mexican theatrical past, except for an occasional mention of somewhat removed origins in Aztec dance-drama, seventeenth-century missionary theatre, or the primitive works of colonizers and soldiers opening up New Mexico. Since the early 1970s, because of the activity of such companies as the Puerto Rican Traveling Theatre and the Teatro Repertorio Español in New York, the Cuban immigrant theatre in Miami, and the individual successes of such playwrights as the late Puerto Rican Miguel Piñero and the Cuban Iván Acosta, there has been some renewed interest in researching the background of Hispanic theatre in the East. But to date there has been even less scholarship published on this topic than on Hispanic theatre in the Southwest.

It is the purpose, therefore, of this book to provide a basic starting point for further studies and to begin to set the historical record straight, not only as it pertains to theatre, but also as it relates to the general cultural makeup, sophistication, artistry, and other contributions of Hispanics in the United States. The Hispanic tradition in the United States is not one that can be characterized exclusively by social dysfunction, poverty, crime, and illiteracy, as the media would often have us believe. Rather, if we focus on theatre, we can draw alternative characterizations: the ability to create art even under the most trying of circumstances, social and cultural cohesiveness and national pride in the face of racial and class pressures, cultural continuity and adaptability in a foreign land. All of these can be accounted for in the trajectory of Hispanic theatrical development. The theatre without a doubt was the most popular and culturally relevant artistic form in Hispanic communities throughout the United States.

In the chapter that follows, attention will first be drawn to the origins of the Hispanic professional stage in the Southwest, followed by chapters dedicated to the most important centers of Hispanic theatrical activity: Los Angeles, San Antonio, New York, and Tampa. A final chapter discusses theatrical manifestations outside these great urban communities. Each chapter in itself is organized around that most identifiable and stable dramatic element: the theatre house itself. Each of the important theatre houses of these cities is studied in chronological order. Where this becomes most difficult, however, is in New York, where the sheer number of theatre houses available for rental made for great mobility of the Hispanic companies and also retarded Hispanic ownership and/or management of theatre houses, contrary to the reality experienced by Hispanics in Los Angeles and Tampa, for example. Another reason that theatre houses are used to provide the main structure for these chapters is that there were far too many theatre companies to study in any orderly or logical fashion; they also metamorphosed often, changing names and personnel, and they traveled far and wide. There has been an attempt, where sufficient documentation exists, to trace the development of individual personalities, such as Leonardo García Astol, Beatriz ("La Chata") Noloesca, Manuel Noriega, Marita Reid, etc.

Particular attention is given in each chapter to the one or two outstanding contributions of each city to Hispanic theatrical culture. In Los Angeles, for instance, without a doubt this contribution was the development of a cadre of professional playwrights and the production of their locally based dramatic material. In San Antonio, among other contributions, there was the tent theatre and its nurturing of a nascent Mexican American culture. The role of the mutual aid societies in Tampa's Hispanic community was unique not only to Hispanic theatre in the United States but also in the history of theatre in the whole Hispanic world. And, finally, New York was a model for solidifying diverse Hispanic nationalities on the stage.

Because of the dearth of scripts, promptbooks, publications, and preserved Spanish-language newspapers, we shall not be able to benefit from too many excerpts from the plays written in the United States or from the types of anecdotes and real-life episodes that would otherwise enrich our recounting of this history. We have had to rely on the imperfect record of the few Spanish-language newspapers that have been preserved, and most of these have tremendous gaps in their runs. We are fortunate, however, that a few actors and directors have survived into their eighties and have been able to inform us of their personal experiences via interviews and open their personal archives in order to enrich this book with illustrations. In an attempt to make this history come as alive as possible, I have maintained verbatim quotes in Spanish from interviews and from newspapers and other documents; my English translations of these are to be found in the endnotes. Finally, I have not provided a general bibliography; there simply are no other books on this topic. However, the endnotes contain ample references to all published mentions of the topic and to the handful of extant scholarly studies. So without further delay, let us raise the curtain on Act One.

1. Origins

The origins of the Spanish-language professional theatre in the United States are to be found in mid-nineteenth-century California, where troupes of itinerant players began touring from Mexico to perform melodramas accompanied by other musical and dramatic entertainments for the residents of the coastal cities that had developed from earlier Franciscan missions—San Francisco, Los Angeles, San Diego. These three cities were more accessible from Mexico than was San Antonio, Texas, because of the regularity of steamship travel up and down the Pacific Coast. Of particular importance to the development of these coastal cities, however, was first the trade in hides and later mining.

There is evidence that plays were being performed as early as 1789. The documentary evidence comes first from Monterey, California. A play manuscript dated in that year, *Astucias por heredar un sobrino a su tío*, written by Fernando de Reygados and copied by Mariano Guadalupe Vallejo (1807–1890), exists today in the Bancroft Collection of the University of California.[1] The three-act cloak-and-dagger drama manuscript from Monterey, with stage directions written in the margins, is accompanied by a cover letter, dated 1875, that states that this was the first drama staged in California and that it had had numerous titles. Given that the play was performed, even copied, passed on, and retitled so often, it is indeed tempting to infer that at least one theatrical troupe was touring the California settlements at the turn of the nineteenth century. Vallejo also adds that Spanish soldiers, "los voluntarios de Cataluña," took part in one of the performances of the play, and this would also place the performance before Mexican independence from Spain in 1821.

What is certain is that records of professional theatrical performances became more numerous some decades later. Again Monterey is the site, and it is mentioned by J. E. Lawrence, writing in the *Golden Era* on May 13, 1846, with reference to the work *Adam and Eve* (one of the plays of the *pastorela* cycle?) at the house of Rafael González, the same residence that DeWitt Bodeen claims housed a regular troupe of Spanish players and musicians during the 1840s.[2] On October 6, 1847, the *Californian* reviewed a production of *Morayma*, author unknown, for private subscription, as part of a regular series being presented in Monterey. The same article goes on to state that officers of both the American army and navy were in attendance. This, added to the fact that the performance was reviewed by an English-language newspaper, indicates that the shows were frequented by Anglo-Americans as well as by the Mexican and other Hispanic residents of the area. That this Monterey performance was professional in nature is surmised from the following: it represented one of a series supported by paid subscriptions; it was elaborately staged ("The scenery of the theatre was well done, the dresses of the different performers very handsome and appropriate, and the acting in general good"); and the performance was most likely held in the entertainment establishment (unnamed in the *Californian* review) owned by a Monterey innkeeper, José Abrego (1813–1878), whose son was a cast member. Mr. Abrego was the proprietor of a commercial billiards hall that may have housed these presentations.[3] Finally, had the performance been produced by an amateur group, it would clearly have been identified as such, as in the case of the performance of the comedy *Un novio para la niña* on June 4, 1865, at the New Almaden Mine by "la compañía de aficionados" (the company of amateurs) (*La Voz de Méjico*, June 3, 1865).

By the 1840s in Los Angeles at least one semiprofessional theatre house existed in "which the Mexicans and the native Californians, of the place amused themselves," according to J. E. Lawrence writing in the *Golden Era*.[4] He was probably referring to the Coronel Theatre, for none other is known at that time. It has been well documented that don Antonio F. Coronel opened a theatre in his home on July 4, 1848; it was an addition to his house that included a covered stage with a proscenium. According to Lawrence, it had a drop curtain and "a tolerable supply of scenery had been painted by a low comedian and pantomimist," and it seated three hundred. The only part of the theatre that was covered by a roof was the end where the stage was. Coronel, married to Mariana Williamson, was the mayor of Los Angeles in 1853 and 1854 and his theatre housed paid professional productions in English and Spanish. In the Coronel papers at the Los Angeles County Museum of Natural History there is an extensive collection of plays in Spanish as well as *pastorelas*, at least one of which was written by Coronel himself.[5] According to S. W. Earnest, another theatre, don Vincente Guerrero's Union Theatre, existed from 1852 to 1854 and housed legitimate drama in Spanish, often directed by Rafael Guerrero on Saturday and Sunday evenings; admission was seventy-five cents (1947: 351). Two other early theatres that housed productions in Spanish and English were also the products of Anglo-Hispanic marriages: Stearn's Hall (also called Arcadia or Teutonia Hall) was opened in July 1859 by the very Hispanicized don Abel Stearns and used as a theatre until 1875, and the Temple Theatre, built and administered by don Juan Temple in 1859 and finally razed in 1892; it had raised seats, private boxes, and a stage measuring forty-five by twenty-five feet (ibid.: 361, 366). Later in the 1860s and 1870s the Hispanic community would also frequent the Teatro de la Merced, Teatro Alarcón, and Turn Verein Hall. And, according to broadsides in the Coronel collection, in the 1880s and 1890s Spanish-language performances were also held at the Grand Opera House. The first of these theatres, the Teatro de la Merced, was built by William Abbott and named after his wife, Mercedes García, in 1870. The structure, which is still standing today, was built adjacent to the Pico House Hotel in hopes of attracting audiences and included an entrance direct from the hotel into the theatre hall, which was located on the second floor. On the ground level there was a store, and the top floor over the theatre served as living quarters (ibid.: 372–373). The Merced housed a thirty-five-by-twenty-five-foot stage and could accommodate four hundred spectators (ibid.: 44). In 1873 and 1875 the theatre was remodeled, lighting and ventilation were improved, and a balcony was constructed, but the building ceased serving as a theatre in 1894 (ibid.: 5). A 1911 account of the theatre during the years 1874 and 1877 has preserved for posterity some rather negative impressions of this somewhat short-lived theatre:

> The auditorium was a long, narrow, badly lighted, illy ventilated room on the second floor. It had a small stage at the inner end, a

fairly high ceiling, and had been finished with some regard to ornament, but was old and shabby when I first saw it. As a revenue producer it could not have been much of a factor, for Merced Theatre was dark most of the time. If something was pulled off there once a month, it was a good average. Los Angeles was so far away from any line of travel, so difficult and expensive of access, that no regular troupes came through, and if anything in the dramatic or musical way appeared it was furnished by local talent, or by some remnant of a stranded company endeavoring to make a stake to get out of the country.[6]

Of the Teatro Alarcón nothing is known, except that there were reports of Hispanic dramatic performances there, its impresarios were señores Guerrero and Vásquez, and Professor Velazco was the director of the orchestra (*La Crónica*, August 3, 1878). Could this be the Vicente Guerrero who had owned the Union Theatre? It is likely. Whether or not the theatre was named for the great Mexican playwright Juan Ruiz de Alarcón is unknown.

The Turn Verein was constructed in 1871 by the German society as a theatre-gymnasium and consisted of a large two-story structure with a fifty-by-twenty-six-foot hall that housed a twenty-by-fifteen-foot stage. Before 1874 the stage was used mostly by the amateur German dramatic association (Earnest 1947: 54). From 1874 until it was demolished in 1887, it served as a professional house, according to the *Los Angeles Times* (May 23, 1887).

By the 1860s the professional stage in California had become so established and important to the Spanish-speaking community that companies that once toured the Mexican Republic and abroad began to settle down as resident companies in California. Such was the case of the Compañía Española de la Familia Estrella, which later came under the directorship of its leading man, renowned Mexican actor Gerardo López del Castillo.[7] The company was typical of those that toured Mexico in that it was composed of Mexican and Spanish players, principally organized around a family unit that staged Spanish melodrama and occasionally a Mexican or a Cuban play, and held most of its performances on Sunday evenings. Prices varied somewhat depending upon which theatre troupe was performing and in what theatre. For the Estrella family's performances, Tucker's Academy charged one peso for orchestra and family circle seating and four reals for patio benches ("bancos de patio"). A decade later, a company such as Mariano Luque's, performing at the Opera House and the California Theatre in Los Angeles, usually charged eight to ten dollars for lower box seats, six dollars for upper boxes, one dollar for dress circle and orchestra, fifty cents for reserved seats, and fifty cents for family circle. Each program was a complete evening's entertainment that included a three- or four-act drama, song and dance entertainment, and a one-act farce or comic dialogue to close the performance. The full-length plays that were the heart of the program were mostly melodramas by peninsular Spanish authors such as José Zorrilla, Mariano José de Larra, and Manuel Bretón de los Herreros and, for the most part, represent texts which were readily available then as now. The origin of a few other plays such as *El terremoto de la Martinica* is unknown.[8]

There is ample indication that the productions were seen as wholesome entertainment appropriate for the family and that a broad segment of the Hispanic community, not merely the elite, subscribed and attended. Judging from *La Voz de Méjico*'s (April 3, 1862) reaction to a disparaging review in San Francisco's French newspaper, *Le Phare*, criticizing the attendance of "cowboys" at a previous performance, other elements than merely those of the Hispanic bourgeoisie were proudly welcomed. The writer goes on to state in praising the Hispanic stage and the Compañía Española that most "American" theatrical presentations in San Francisco were by minstrels and no one had ever censured them, thus snubbing Anglo and, presumably, French inferior tastes. But, for the most part, there seems to have been an unexpected degree of integration of Anglos and others in the audiences for the Hispanic shows. Furthermore, it is obvious that the actors were seen as upstanding members of the community, at times even leaders, as was the case with Gerardo López del Castillo.

López del Castillo, the leading man and later director of the Compañía Española, was a native of Mexico City and had been a professional actor since age fifteen. He is known as the first Mexican actor to take companies on tour outside of Mexico,[9] and by the time he had arrived in California he was already well known throughout Mexico, the Caribbean, and Central and South America (Mañón 1932: 241). An intensely patriotic individual, López del Castillo used theatrical performances to raise funds for Zaragoza's and Juárez's liberation forces and interrupted his theatrical career on various occasions to serve Mexico as a soldier (ibid.). He is also regarded as a great motivator and protector of a national dramatic art for Mexico (María y Campos 1964: 21–23). By 1849 he was so well regarded that he was chosen to inaugurate the new theatre, El Pabellón Mexicano, with a production of *El paje* by Eugenio García Gutiérrez (Mañón 1932: 241).

In June 1859, López del Castillo was in Hermosillo, Sonora, associated with the Estrella family company and married to Amalia, daughter of Donato Estrella, the director of the company (Gipson 1967: 353–354).[10] Donato Estrella also served as the comic actor and musical director of the troupe. The leading lady, María de los Angeles García, born in Murcia, Spain, had become an actress in Mexico City at an early age and had performed at the Teatro Principal in 1844 (Mañón 1932: 92). Other members of the troupe included Manuel Mancera, Rafael Rodríguez, Juan Samartín, their wives, and Jacinto Dávila, a character actor.

By 1862, the Estrella company had made San Francisco its home, from which it continued to tour the area and, at least once, traveled down the coast to Mazatlán, according to *El Nuevo Mundo* (December 30, 1864). Previous to making San Francisco its home base, the troupe has been recorded as performing in Hermosillo for three seasons (1859, 1860, and 1861), which also leads one to believe that the company may have been performing in San Francisco and Los Angeles during these years as well. Part of the reason for the Estrella family's decision to settle in San Francisco rather than continue to tour year-round on a circuit that included the Mexican cities of Mazatlán, Ures, and Hermosillo and Tucson, Arizona, may have been the growing hostilities in northern Mexico from the French and the danger of Apache attacks on the stagecoach line in Arizona when American troops were withdrawn to fight in the Civil War. In fact, in 1864 French troops occupied the port of Mazatlán and in 1865 the French navy captured the port of Guaymas, Sonora.

From March to May 1862, the company performed regularly on Sundays at Tucker's Music Academy, closing its season with a special performance at the Metropolitan Theatre as part of a grand fundraising event organized by López del Castillo for the wounded, widowed, and orphaned in the Franco-Mexican War. What is noteworthy about this benefit performance is the participation of Anglo-American and Italian singers, Miss Lizzie Parker, Mr. John Gregg, and Signor E. Grossi, performing operatic arias, according to *La Voz de México* (August 7, 1862), thus leading us to assume once again that audiences for Hispanic theatre were not solely made up of native Spanish speakers. On another occasion, according to the December 7, 1864, *El Nuevo Mundo,* Anglo-American minstrels performed in honor of López del Castillo, which further indicates a level of integration or at least mutual appreciation of Anglo and Hispanic artists at that time.

According to the imperfect record of newspapers that have survived from the period, on March 30, 1862, the first performance of the Compañía Española took place, according to *La Voz de Méjico*. At this time there is no way to ascertain how far in advance of this date the Estrella family was performing in San Francisco. The plays noted in *La Voz de Méjico* were *Fuego del cielo*, March 30, 1862; April 3, the three-act melodrama *Es un angel o lucha de amor maternal*; April 5, *La aventura* in four acts by the Cuban writer Gertrudis Gómez de Avellaneda; *El prisionero* in two acts and Bretón de los Herreros's *Por poderes* in one act; April 12, Bretón de los Herreros's five-act *comedia de costumbres ¿Quién es él?*; April 17, Antonio Auset's three-act play *Trampas inocentes* and *Por los celos de una monja* in one act; April 24, Victor Hugo's *Angelo, tirano de Padua*; May 1, Tomás Rodríguez Rubí's *Borrascas del corazón* and the *juguete cómico La ley del embudo*; May 8, Gertrudis Gómez de Avellaneda's drama *La hija de las flores* and the *juguete Las citas de medianoche*; May 15, Luis Olona's *Las elecciones* and the one-act *Malas tentaciones*; May 22, Olona's two-act comedy *Alza y baja* and García Gutiérrez's *juguete Un novio al vapor*; August 7 at the Metropolitan Theatre, Ventura de la Vega's one-act *No hay que tentar al diablo* and the one-act *Bárbaro y silvestre*.

Presumably after closing, the troupe toured in California; it did receive an invitation from Los Angeles and perform there (*La Voz de Méjico*, April 24, 1862). It should be noted that throughout 1862, López del Castillo continued to participate in civic affairs in San Francisco, where he was serving as president of the Junta Patriótica Mexicana de San Francisco, according to *La Voz de Méjico* (September 18, 20, 1862) and *El Eco del Pacífico* (March 10, 1863). Thus, the company could not have traveled too far.

The bits and pieces of newspapers place the Estrella family and López del Castillo on stage in San Francisco again in June 1863, able to perform, it seems, only after the steamship *Orizaba* had brought the company a reinforcement in the person of Mexican actor José de Jesús Díaz.[11] The fragmented record shows performances by what had become Castillo's Compañía Española at the American Theatre during 1863 and 1864. A decade earlier, in 1851, the American Theatre had been constructed, with two thousand seats, and was one of two premier theatres in San Francisco;[12] the other was Tom Maguire's Jenny Lind, which (if this is what the Spanish-language newspapers were referring to as Maguire's New Theatre) was also used by the Hispanic companies in the 1860s. The American, however, was only in use until 1868, when it burned down. Only the following performances at the American were noted in *La Voz de Méjico*: July 5,

1863, Tomás Rodríguez Rubí's four-act drama *La trenza de sus cabellos* and the *juguete cómico Cuerpo y sombra;* July 26 the three-act *Flor de un día* by Francisco Camprodón and *Bárbaro y silvestre* again; August 25, Part Two of Camprodón's *Flor de un día, Espinas de una flor* in three acts.

When the López del Castillo company returned to San Francisco and how much longer it resided there are not certain. What is certain is that López del Castillo, reunited with his wife and theatrical company, had a long performance season the following year at Los Angeles' Temple Hall. According to Earnest (1947: 34), during their run from November 21, 1865, to May 7, 1867, the following plays were staged: Victor Hugo's *Tyrant of Padua,* Juan de Ariza's *God, My Arms and My Right* and *Lázaro el mudo,* Antonio de Leiva's *La hija de las flores, The Bandit's Heart, The Printer's Devil,* and *The Troubadour.* Bills were advertised in the *Los Angeles News* sometimes in English, sometimes in Spanish. The *Los Angeles News* praised Amalia Estrella del Castillo's performance on two occasions:

> Mr. and Mrs. Castillo will rank with the best performers in the state. Mrs. Castillo's imposing and attractive form, handsome features and graceful and charming ease with which she moves through all her representations is alone well worth the price of admission. When fond of looking at a beautiful woman in the theatrical costume, we would advise you to purchase a ticket. (January 26, 1866)

> Señora Estrella del Castillo took . . . the difficult role of "María" in "Troubadour" which she played with happy effect, her rich voice adding greatly to the natural beauty of the piece in the song, "Grace of God." In this piece Señora Castillo exhibited genuine talent in all parts of the play, successively as a shepherdess, dancing girl, accomplished young lady of the world, and a maniac bereft of reason. (February 27, 1867)

After these notices, the written record provides no further news of the Castillo family in California.

In 1874, López del Castillo surfaced again in Mexico City, actively promoting the creation of a national dramatic literature. He performed in 1874 and 1875 at the head of a company in the Teatro Nuevo México (María y Campos 1964: 21–22) and later directed a company that included Amelia and Donato Estrella at the newly founded Liceo Mexicano in 1876.[13] He risked his career in 1876 to perform Alberto G. Bianchi's political play *Martirios del pueblo*, the same play that had resulted in the author's imprisonment (María y Campos 1964: 46). Of the elderly López del Castillo, María y Campos wrote:

> El público ovacionaba al gran cómico, comediante nacionalista, en la escena y fuera del teatro, que tuvo en su época, su público, y que murió pobre, pero sin abandonar la escena nacional, para la que vivía, ambicionando que fuera comprendida y estimada en lo que era y valía. Su gallarda actitud causaba risas, a pesar de lo bien intencionada y patriota. Aspiraba a lo más noble y justo, a un México para los mexicanos.[14]

As mentioned above, Los Angeles' Hispanic theatre probably predated San Francisco's and the *angeleno* Hispanic community even owned and operated many of its own theatres. Although it is certain that the Los Angeles theatres were very active from the 1850s through the 1880s, the sporadic newspaper documentation only records the performances of three companies: Vicente Guerrero's stock company at the Union Theatre, with notices of *Don Juan Tenorio, Los dos virreyes de Nápoles, El zapatero y el rey*, all by Spaniard José Zorrilla, and Molière's *El médico a palos*; the Familia Máiquez at the Temple Theatre in 1859, en route by steamer from San Francisco and Santa Barbara, and again in 1860 and 1862; and the López del Castillo troupe in 1865. Two broadsides (item 865) in the Antonio F. Coronel Collection document the presence of two additional troupes: an unnamed variety acts company directed by Gregorio E. González in 1886 and the Arcaraz Spanish Opera Company in 1892. It is also probable that at least four other companies noted by Gipson as performing in Tucson during the 1880s and early 1890s also made their way to Los Angeles: the Aguilar–Cuello Zarzuela company, the Villaseñor company, the Compañía Cepeda y Cadena, and the Compañía Dramática Artega. It must also be assumed that all of the above worked full seasons in Los Angeles. Furthermore, given the extensive collection of plays and theatrical material in Antonio Coronel's archive at the Los Angeles County Museum, it must be assumed that his theatre was also housing performances by itinerant companies if not a stock company. One of the great problems in documenting theatre of this period is the method by which theatres and companies advertised by distributing handbills and posters. They rarely purchased ads in the newspapers and, in turn, the newspapers did not review their performances on a regular basis.

During the 1870s, three companies are documented as having performed in Los Angeles. The Señores Romero y Compañía were only noted once in Los Angeles (*La Crónica*, April 3, 1878) as having performed Zorrilla's *Los dos virreyes de Nápoles* and the *sainete Me conviene esta mujer*. Members of the troupe were Adelina Domínguez and the señores Romero, Angulo, Pozo, and Franco. There is, however, a more complete picture of two other companies: the Compañía Dramática Española directed first by José Pérez García and later by Pedro C. de Pellón, and the Compañía Dramática Española directed by Angel de Mollá. Both companies competed for use of El Teatro de la Merced, with Mollá moving in 1877 to the Turn Verein.

The José Pérez company was active in the south, including Hermosillo and Ures in Sonora, Mexico, and Tucson, Arizona, in its itinerary, with Los Angeles probably as its home base (Gipson 1972). The members of the company were doña Jesús de Terán, leading lady; José Pérez García, leading man and director; Pedro Castillo de Pellón, comic actor; Elena Mancera and Dolores Rodríguez, dancers. Documentation of the company's performances begins on February 27, 1876, with its performance of *Lázaro el mudo* through the September 15, 1876, performance of *Arturo o amor de madre* in two acts and *Maruja* in one act. The remainder of the performances noted in *La Crónica* were March 12, Juan de Ariza's three-act historical drama *Antonio de Leiva o el gran batallón de Pavia* and the short piece *Amar sin dejarse amar*; March 19, Luis M. de Larra's *comedia de costumbres Oros, capas, espadas y bastos* and the short piece *Pescar y cazar*; March 25, the religious drama *El cura de Aldea* by Enrique Pérez Escrich and the one-act *Don Ramón*; on April 15 the first four acts of Zorrilla's *Don Juan Tenorio* and on April 16 the second three acts, as well as the one-act *Tres eran tres las hijas de Elena*; April 23, a repeat of April 16; April 30, Narciso Serro's three-act drama *El reloj de San Plácido o la mujer enterrada en vida* and *El loco por fuerza* in one act; May 5, the three-act *comedia Quevedo o la Buñolera o poderoso caballero es don Dinero*; May 10, Ventura de la Vega's drama *Arturo o el amor de madre* and the short piece *E. H.* (with señora Mollá from the Compañía Mollá playing the role of the *gracioso*, or fool); May 21, Eduardo Zamora y Caballero's *El filósofo del gran mundo o una coqueta del día*; May 28, Enrique Zumel's *comedia de costumbres* in three acts, *Riendas del gobierno*, and the one-act *El tigre de Bengala*, in which some local amateurs were allowed to participate; May 31 (under the directorship of Pedro C. de Pellón), Palau y Coll's *La campana de la Almudaina o el toque de agonía* with the *zarzuela La viuda y el sacristán*; June 10, the drama *Viva la libertad* and the short *La casa de campo;* July 1, the drama *La oración de la tarde* and the *juguete cómico No lo quiero saber.* Starting with the May 31 performance, Pedro C. de Pellón was the company's director, and the troupe began to alternate at La Merced with the Angel de Mollá company. After September 1876, we lose track of the Pellón company in Los Angeles. In March 1878, Pellón returned to Tucson and organized the town's first group of amateur actors, Teatro Recreo (Gipson 1972: 243). Included in the repertoire of his new company were some of the same plays that he had performed in Los Angeles.

Gipson had found that the Compañía Española de Angel de Mollá was a Los Angeles–based theatre that traveled to Tucson by stagecoach every two or three years between 1873 and 1882 (ibid.: 245). According to the fragmented newspaper record, the Mollá company performed at the Teatro de la Merced in Los Angeles from June 11, 1876, until March 7, 1877. The following were performed: June 3, 1876, *Los soldados de plomo* by Eduardo Equílaz and the *sainete,* or Spanish farce, *Las gracias de Gedeón;* June 24, Larra's *comedia de costumbres* in three acts *El amor y el interés* and the short *Potencia a potencia;* July 8, *Flores y perlas;* July 15, *Los soldados de plomo;* October 28, Larra's four-act play *Bienaventurados los que lloran* and the short *No más secreto;* December 23, Larra's *La cosecha o el fruto del libertinaje* and the *zarzuela Geroma la castañera;* December 30, Gaspar Núñez de Arce's *Deudas de la honra* and the one-act *La sospecha;* March 7, 1877, Zorrilla's three-act *Traidor, inconfeso y mártir.* From April 7, 1877, until January 2, 1884, the company performed at the Turn Verein: April 7, 1877, Antonio Guillén y Sánchez's *Malditas sean las mujeres;* April 14, the same; June 2, Gaspar Núñez de Arce's *Deudas de la honra;* May 26, 1883, the same plus the one-act *Como el pez en el agua;* June 6, Bretón de los Herreros's *El poeta y la beneficiada o una vieja como hay muchas* and *Pescar y cazar;* June 16, Pastorndo's five-act drama *Las dos madres;* June 30, Echegaray's *La esposa del vengador;* July 21, the two-act plays *No hay humo sin fuego* and *Me conviene esta mujer;* August 11, José María Tovar's *La vuelta del mundo o un episodio de la independencia;* Larra's *Los lazos de la familia* and *Me conviene esta mujer* on January 1, 1884; January 2, *La esposa del vengador.* After this date, no other performances by this troupe have surfaced.

One additional and interesting document refers specifically to the Mollá company: a poem dedicated to leading lady Laura Morales de Mollá by Antonio F. Coronel. It attests not only to her talent and beauty as an actress but also to the former Los Angeles mayor's devotion to the stage:

A Laura Morales de Mollá

EN SU BENEFICIO

Quién, hechicera Laura, te ha enseñado tanto hacernos gozar dicha serena?

Quién te dotó de este arte dedicado, que haces reír y gemir a tu manera?

De quién suelta, vagando en el tablado, a mover la piedad has aprendido, y después de tronar duros furores, a suspirar la voz de tus amores?

Alegras, cual te place, o entristeces; inflamas, cual te place, las pasiones; mueves, tiemplas, agitas, endureces, y derrites los tiernos corazones.

Aquel que te oye, el que sensible aprecia, los pródigos de tu arte portentoso, se extasía, se deleita, se enajena, y disfruta del más dulce reposo.

A. F. C.

Los Angeles, Junio 21 de 1883[15]

In Los Angeles, and generally wherever a professional Hispanic stage was sustained, there were numerous groups of amateurs and aspiring actors that performed at times in the very same halls that housed the touring professional companies. It was not uncommon, furthermore, for the small itinerant companies, which were basically family units and extended families, to hire some of the local amateurs to play minor roles in their melodramas. That amateur companies were active at this time is also evident from newspaper notices. The Teatro de la Merced in 1873, for example, hosted such a group of amateurs, the Compañía Dramática Española de Jóvenes Aficionados, directed by José María Fuentes, and charged reduced ticket prices of fifty cents for the gallery, one dollar for reserved seats, and five dollars for boxes at one performance of *El rey y el aventurero* (*La Crónica*, June 21, 1873), two separate performances of Zorrilla's *Vivir loco y morir más* and Francisco Fernández's *Los negros catedráticos* (*La Crónica*, August 3, 1873, and September 6, 1873), and one of *Como pez en el agua* and other miscellaneous pieces (*La Crónica*, December 12, 1873). At the June 2, 1877, performance by the Angel Mollá company at the Turn Verein, *La Crónica* noted that a señor Cardona of the above-mentioned amateur group had been playing one of the major roles in *Deudas de la honra*. It is also interesting that on April 29, 1873, *La Crónica* reported that the last performance by the Jóvenes Aficionados was attended by the

cream of Hispanic society as well as by some Americans, who, according to the newspaper, possibly wanted to familiarize themselves
with Spanish drama or just admire the young people who had nobly
decided upon a career in the arts. *La Crónica* also reported on April
22, 1882, that a group of Hispanic American young people, in order
to please the people who had been complaining about not having
seen a Spanish play in Los Angeles in a long time, would perform
that evening Mariano José de Larra's *No más mostrador o la varie-
dad corregida* at the Turn Verein.

If we compare the preceding data with the documentary evidence
that we have from Texas in the 1840s and 1850s, it immediately becomes obvious that the Texas Hispanic stage had not progressed as
much. An editorial published in San Antonio's *Bejareño* as late as
July 19, 1856, seems to indicate that there were no theatres in San
Antonio by this date and that if plays were indeed performed they
would have been performed by amateurs in buildings other than
theatres:

> Se nos asegura que varios jóvenes de esta ciudad están haciendo
> al presente los preparativos necesarios para establecer un nuevo
> teatro. El número de la población y la falta de diversión pública
> hace tiempo que reclaman un establecimiento de esa clase; pero
> dicho sea con verdad nos duele algún tanto ver que se desatien-
> dan algunas mejoras de una necesidad más apremiante y se dé
> lugar a otras que son secundarias. Nosotros creemos que lo que
> ha de invertirse en ese teatro, podría dedicarse muy bien a la con-
> strucción de un Hospital que bien lo necesitan las clases pobres y
> desvalidas de nuestra ciudad.[16]

During the same year, however, *El Bejareño* noted performances by
a "circo mexicano" (Mexican circus) (June 21 and July 19, 1856). A
decade later, on December 19, 1866, the San Antonio *Daily Herald*
reviewed the performance of a *pastorela* and on July 20, 1869, the
Daily Herald and the *Express* both reported on a Mexican Concer-
tant, Operatic and Glasseology Company, directed by Gregorio Par-
tida at Meunch Hall in San Antonio. On April 25 and May 5, 1871,
the *Daily Herald* reported on the performance of *La vuelta al mundo
o la bandera mexicana* and *La derrota del convoy o entrada de los
libres a Monterrey* by a Mexican dramatic troupe. In November
1871 and again on April 7, 1875, the *Herald* reported on a Spanish
theatrical company; on the latter date, a performance of *El cura de
aldea o la caridad cristiana* was reported as having been presented

at Turner Hall, Wolfram's Garden. It is not until the 1880s that there are regular notices of touring Hispanic theatrical companies in Texas, and the majority of these notices come from Laredo, not San Antonio. On February 19, March 5, and April 28, 1878, the *Herald* noted a señor C. Mendoza directing weekend performances of such plays and afterpieces as *El patriarca del furia o la boda de Felipe III, La trenza de sus cabellos,* and *El solterón y la niña* at San Antonio's Krish Hall.

On July 22, 1881, the newspaper *El Correo de Laredo* favorably compared the Compañía Hernández's performance of the drama *Los mártires de Japón o San Felipe de Jesús* with that of a local Laredo company's performance of *La América en triunfo* at a local tavern for "gente non sancta" (unholy people). The Laredo group was seen as a "compañía raquítica" (rickety company). In 1891 groups of aficionados like the Cuadro Drámatico of the Sociedad Hidalgo, directed by Santos Treviño, performed *Los mártires de Tacubaya* at the marketplace (*El Correo de Laredo,* September 20, 1891), and the newspaper also noted that many performances had been suspended because of wind, rain, and sickness.

As late as 1884, theatrical performances were still housed at the marketplace in Laredo, where the Compañía Dramática Mejicana would perform such plays as Spanish playwright José Echegaray's *El gran galeoto,* Blasco's *El anzuelo,* and short works like *Casa del campo* and *Heraclio y Demócrito* (*El Horizonte,* December 3 and 6, 1884). What is notable about the touring Compañía Dramática Mejicana, which was said to be on its way to San Antonio, is that its leading actors, Francisco Solórzano and Tomás Baladía, were well known in Mexico and would return later to Laredo and become the heart of a very vital theatrical movement there (Mañón 1932: 136). There is also some confusion about the marketplace used by this and other theatrical companies. *El Horizonte* called it a *salón,* or hall, while *El Correo de Laredo* referred to it simply as the marketplace ("plaza del mercado"). In all likelihood it was a marketplace with a roof but open to the elements, if one can so infer from the references to rain and wind. The only other reference to a Hispanic theatre house in Texas during this time is an isolated mention of the existence of a "Mexican theatre" in Austin in 1875, without any other information given about performances, ownership, or audiences (Manry 1979: 35).

Based on the documentary evidence or lack thereof, we can only conclude that Texas did not benefit from as active a theatrical circuit in the nineteenth century as did California, nor did a resident Hispanic theatre develop in Texas until much later. It is during the 1880s and 1890s that Texas began to develop a Hispanic stage and to attract large numbers of touring companies from Mexico, and only at the turn of the century and afterward did some of these companies begin to reside in Texas, mainly in Laredo and San Antonio. This will be covered in chapter 3.

On the other hand, Arizona is credited with having had a more active Hispanic theatrical life at mid-nineteenth century than Texas, largely because theatre was becoming more important in northwestern Mexico, with Hermosillo sporting its own theatre house and attracting companies from Mexico City by 1859 (Gipson 1972: 239). Among the first of the dramatic companies documented as traveling north from Sonora by stagecoach was the Marino Carrillo Gymnastic and Theatrical Company (probably a circus theatre), which performed the melodrama *Elena y Jorge* in 1871 in the Camp Lowell corral (ibid.: 239–240).[17]

The Compañía Dramática Española de Angel Mollá toured to Tucson every two or three years between 1873 and 1882, and the José Pérez García company came to play at the Cosmopolitan Hotel in Tucson in 1875 with a repertoire that included *El hombre negro, El bastardo de Castillo, La cosecha, Los lazos de la familia,* and *Hija y madre* (ibid.: 241–242). In 1877, the García and Aragón company, another *circo-teatro,* performed, among others, the plays *El médico a palos* and *Los dos payos* in Tucson's plaza. On June 8, 1880, the Carlos Portán company performed *La Malinche.* It was not until 1882 that the Teatro Cervantes, a remodeled grocery store, opened and hosted the Mollá company again. Gipson explains that the same year that the Teatro Americano opened, two other theatres also opened to house Anglo-American companies traveling from the east by railroad, which had just then reached Arizona (ibid.: 245–249). The combination of the railroad and the dramatic increase of new settlers from the East, the changing Mexican demographics from 67 percent of the population in 1878 to 43 percent in 1881, effectively killed the demand for Mexican/Spanish theatre. The Teatro Americano closed down in 1883, and only rarely did a Mexican dramatic company make it to Tucson thereafter until the turn of the century: the Aguilar–Cuello Zarzuela company on its way to Los Angeles and San Francisco in 1884, the Villaseñor company in 1886, Compañía Zepeda y Cadena in 1890, the Compañía Dramática Artega in 1892, and the Mexican Grand and Comic Opera in 1898.

In addition to the priority of the Hispanic professional stage in California and Arizona as opposed to Texas,[18] it is evident that regular theatrical circuits were established for the touring companies that traveled by steamship up and down the coast of upper and Baja California, across Baja into northwestern Mexico and up to Tucson, and across to San Diego and Los Angeles by stagecoach. Such conclusions are sustained by Gipson's research as well as such documentary evidence as a letter from the Mollá company which was published in the April 4, 1883, edition of *La Crónica* and which refers to the company's performing in Guaymas after having performed in Hermosillo. They are also sustained by performances of the Estrella company in the state of Sonora and the aforementioned departure of López del Castillo for performances in Mazatlán. The same departure, in which López del Castillo bid his wife farewell for a while, also attests to the resident nature of his company and its home base in San Francisco, where he was also a respected pillar of the community and served as the president of a civic organization. Finally, we have evidence that the Hispanic community had its own theatre halls, possibly as early as the 1840s in Los Angeles, and certainly, by the 1860s, the theatre houses, touring and resident companies, as well as amateur groups were all well in place and active. In a final note, one might also conclude that the Hispanic stage was a strong and important enough institution at that time to attract Anglos into the audiences and to be reviewed in the English- and French-language newspapers.

An unidentified touring company in Tucson in 1906.

Virginia Fábregas at Lyceum Hall, Los Angeles.

El Teatro de la Merced, Los Angeles.

Ad for *Don Juan Tenorio* at the Teatro Mexicano.

Newspaper illustration of roles played by María Teresa Montoya in Los Angeles, 1922.

Romualdo Tirado.

Adalberto Elías González.

Gabriel Navarro.

The Teatro Hidalgo band.

Los Angeles' Teatro California today. Photo by Francisco Blasco.

Rosalinda Meléndez (*left*) as shoeshine boy during the Depression.

Don Catarino.

Dueto Cinema souvenir postcard: *peladitos* performing between movie showings, Los Angeles.

Mason Theatre, Los Angeles.

Carlos Villalongín. Courtesy Nettie Lee Benson Latin American Collection, University of Texas at Austin.

El Teatro Nacional, San Antonio.

El Niño Fidencio (Francisco Vega).

The Niño Fidencio troupe.

Comic Lauro Guerra.

A melodramatic scene with Dorita Ceprano, Manuel and José Areu.

Souvenir postcard given at performances by Dorita Ceprano. Courtesy Nettie Lee Benson Latin American Collection, University of Texas at Austin.

Leonardo García Astol's "Don Lalo."

La Chata Noloesca, Enrique and José Areu.

Broadside, Carlos Villalongín Company performance of *Tierra baja* by Angel Guimará. Courtesy Nettie Lee Benson Latin American Collection, University of Texas at Austin.

Broadside announcing a Villalongín production. Courtesy Nettie Lee Benson Latin American Collection, University of Texas at Austin.

Program cover for the opening of the remodeled church hall, Inmaculado Corazón de María, which housed theatrical performances in San Antonio.

Chorines (the García sisters) of the Carpa García.

La Chata Noloesca (*right*) in *bataclán*.

La Chata Noloesca and Ramirín (Pedro González González) at the Teatro Hispano, late 1940's.

Interior of Casa Galicia hall, New York.

World War II vaudeville sketch at the Teatro Hispano.

The Teatro Hispano stock company in support of the Allies during World War II.

The Teatro Hispano, New York.

Edelmiro Borras (*left*) in blackface.

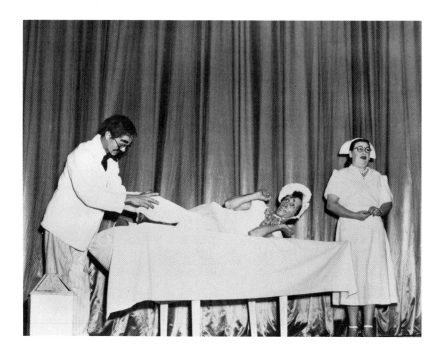

Belia Areu (*right*) in vaudeville sketch satirizing hospitals, at the Teatro Hispano.

Marita Reid in *Dispensa Perico*, by Pedro Muñoz Seca.

Broadside of Circo Escalante benefit performance for the Alfredo Grijalva defense fund in Arizona.

An aging La Chata Noloesca in vaudeville sketch satirizing cold winters in Spanish Harlem.

Broadside advertising the benefit performance of Josefina Rodríguez at the Centro Español, Ybor City.

Broadside advertising San Antonio's La Chata Noloesca and Ramirín at the Teatro Hispano, 1946.

Centro Asturiano, Ybor City.

Broadside advertising show with "Mary Reid," 1939.

Broadside advertising a play at the Mutualista Obrera in 1941.

Centro Español, West Tampa.

Centro Español, Ybor City.

Scene from *Los molinos de viento* at the Centro Asturiano. Courtesy Dorothea Lynch Collection, Special Collections and Archives, Fenwick Library, George Mason University, Fairfax, Virginia.

Scene from *El niño judío* at the Centro Asturiano. Courtesy Dorothea Lynch Collection, Special Collections and Archives, Fenwick Library, George Mason University, Fairfax, Virginia.

Audience at the Centro Asturiano. Courtesy Dorothea Lynch Collection, Special Collections and Archives, Fenwick Library, George Mason University, Fairfax, Virginia.

Teatro Juárez, Houston, which housed local amateur and itinerant professional companies. Also referred to as Mexican Hall, it was built ca. 1928. Photo by Thomas Kreneck, 1986.

Guadalupe Church hall (second floor), Houston, which housed itinerant companies. Courtesy Houston Metropolitan Archives, Houston Public Library.

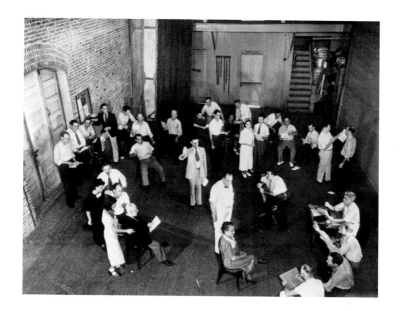

Manuel Aparicio (*standing behind chair*) directing *It Can't Happen Here* at the Centro Asturiano. Courtesy Dorothea Lynch Collection, Special Collections and Archives, Fenwick Library, George Mason University, Fairfax, Virginia.

Manuel Aparicio and Matilde López in *La malquerida*. Courtesy Dorothea Lynch Collection, Special Collections and Archives, Fenwick Library, George Mason University, Fairfax, Virginia.

María de los Angeles García. From Mañon, *Historia del Teatro Principal de México.*

Gerardo López del Castillo. From Mañon, *Historia del Teatro Principal de México.*

Manuel Noriega in 1902, Mexico City. From Mañon, *Historia del Teatro Principal de México.*

2. Los Angeles

The last decade of the nineteenth century experienced a tremendous increase in Mexican theatrical activity in the border states. More and more companies that had previously only toured interior Mexico were now establishing regular circuits extending from Laredo to San Antonio and El Paso, through New Mexico and Arizona to Los Angeles, then up to San Francisco or down to San Diego. It was the advent of rail transportation and the automobile that was bringing the touring companies even to smaller population centers after the turn of the century. Between 1900 and 1930 numerous theatres began to house Spanish-language performances all along this circuit. Along the Rio Grande Valley in Texas, for instance, Brownsville supported the Salón Hidalgo and the Teatro Estrella, San Benito the Teatro Juárez, Del Rio the Teatro Casino, Mercedes the Teatro Mercedes, East Donna the Teatro Chapultepec, Weslaco the Teatro Nacional. Kingsville had its Teatro Atenas and Corpus Christi its Teatro Melva. In New Mexico there were the Teatro Juárez in Las Cruces, the Salón Joya in La Joya, and the Salón Alianza Hispano Americana and Salón A. C. Torres, both in Socorro. In Arizona there were the Teatro Juárez in Sonora Town, Teatro Royal in Nogales, Teatro Mexicano in Superior, Teatro Amazu in Phoenix, Teatro Carmen in Tucson, and Teatro Yuma in Yuma. California's smaller towns boasted the Teatro México in Brawley, the Teatro Centenario in Ensenada, the Teatro Bonito in Belvedere, the Club Hispano Americano in Pittsburg, and many others.

By 1910 a few of the smaller cities had theatres with stock companies. Laredo attracted such impresarios as Francisco Solórzano, who had toured there earlier. During the next twenty years, the doors to other theatres would open in Laredo: Teatro Iris, Teatro García, Teatro Strand, Teatro Independencia, Teatro Variedades, Teatro Iturbide, Teatro Nacional.

Tent theatres, circus theatres, and smaller makeshift companies performed along the Rio Grande Valley as well but only occasionally ventured into the big cities to compete with the major drama and *zarzuela* companies. Touring the small towns (*pueblos*) on both sides of the border was called "puebleando." The Hernández-Villalongín troupe, organized around a family nucleus (as were the Estrella, Mollá, and Luque companies in nineteenth-century California), had been touring central and northern Mexico since 1849 but did not begin performing in the southwestern United States until the period 1900 to 1911 (Brokaw 1974: 25–26). By 1911 the company had begun to use San Antonio as its home base, where it leased the Teatro Aurora. Although San Antonio became the company's home, it continued to tour in Texas at least a few months each year.

Theatrical activities expanded rapidly when thousands of refugees took flight from the Mexican Revolution and settled in the United States from the border all the way up to the Midwest. During the decades of revolution, many of Mexico's greatest artists and their theatrical companies came to tour and/or take up temporary residence in the United States; some, however, would never return to the homeland.

Mexican and Spanish companies and an occasional Cuban, Argentine, or other Hispanic troupe began to tour throughout the Southwest, finding their greatest and most lucrative engagements in Los Angeles and San Antonio, but some also sallied forth as far north and east as New York, where there was also a lively Hispanic theatrical culture. Some companies even made the coast-to-coast tour via the northern route: New York, Philadelphia, Cleveland, Detroit, Chicago, and down into the Southwest to Los Angeles. Such was the route taken in 1924 by the Compañía Hispano-Mexicana de Zarzuela y Variedades F. Díaz de León after three seasons in New York, according to Los Angeles' *El Heraldo de México* (September 16, 1924). A correspondent for San Antonio's *La Prensa* on January 1 of the same year was proud to report warm audience receptions for the

F. Díaz de León company, even in the fierce Detroit winter: "No obstante la crueldad del invierno los hispanoamericanos concurren diariamente a las funciones que ofrece la Compañía Díaz de León, ya que muy rara vez se presenta la oportunidad a esas colonias de presenciar espectáculos en que se representan sus costumbres y en que toman parte actores de su misma raza."[1]

Another company that toured the United States from coast to coast was Spain's Compañía María Guerrero y Fernando Díaz de Mendoza, assisted by New York agent Walter O. Lindsay, who was testing the waters with Spain's leading lady in a trial run for other national tours by Hispanic companies that he would arrange (*La Prensa*, November 21, 1926). Lindsay engaged her at many large theatres that were rarely used by the regularly touring Hispano-Mexican companies: January 5 and 6 in Jerusalem Temple, New Orleans; January 8, Houston Auditorium; January 9, Municipal Auditorium, San Antonio; January 12, Grand Theatre, Douglas; January 14, Shrine Temple, Phoenix; January 15, San Bernardino Auditorium; the week of January 16, Mason Opera House, Los Angeles; the week of January 23, Columbia Theatre, San Francisco; then from San Francisco to San Diego, El Paso, St. Louis, Chicago, Detroit, Canton, Pittsburgh, Philadelphia, and New York.

The company of the famed Mexican actress Virginia Fábregas was of particular importance in its frequent tours because it not only performed the latest serious works from Mexico City and Europe but also because some of the troupe members occasionally defected to form their own resident and touring companies in the Southwest. Such was the case of Agustín Molinari, who by the time of his death in 1934 had succeeded in founding a theatrical dynasty in Los Angeles, with his children Raquel, Juan, and Agustín all following him onto the stage (*La Opinión*, October 10, 1934). There was also Bernardo Fougá, who became an important director in San Antonio and led a heroic struggle during the Depression to keep theatre alive there. Virginia Fábregas was also important in encouraging the development of local playwrights in Los Angeles by buying the rights to their works and integrating the plays into her repertoire. Incredible as it may seem for the times, Mrs. Fábregas's tours extended to the outer reaches of the Spanish-speaking world, including the Philippines and Guam.[2]

Many companies that toured offered a variety of theatrical genres, from *zarzuela* and operetta to drama, *comedia, revista,* and *variedades.* As the scores of companies throughout the Southwest adapted to changing tastes and economic conditions, the shifting of repertoires and the recruitment of new casts and musicians eventually brought about companies that could perform virtually anything, complementing a film with variety acts in the afternoon, producing a full-length drama in the evening or a *zarzuela* and a drama on Saturday and Sunday. In addition, to maintain a competitive edge in attracting audiences, the companies had to perform different works each day. The companies at times took names such as the Compañía de Comedias, Revistas y Variedades Peña-Mena, but this did not stop them from producing serious dramas like Brígido Caro's *Joaquín Murrieta*, even if the presentation of serious drama was not covered by the name of the troupe. As commercial ventures, the theatrical companies were driven by the tastes and interests of their audiences, and they would perform whatever it was that would please, be it comedy, drama, or variety acts.

The Mexican theatre in the Southwest before World War II is characterized by flexibility and adaptability to the varying tastes and economic conditions of the communities. An actor like Leonardo García Astol, for example, while initiated into serious drama and melodrama in his father's Compañía Azteca, had to conform, as time went on, to doing vaudeville sketches, creating the beloved character of a comic tramp, and, later, by working in radio drama and television in Spanish. Indeed, actors trained in the classical tradition or in the lyric tradition of *zarzuela* found themselves doing variety acts and vaudeville during the twenties and, especially, during the Depression. When vaudeville became popular, a number of Mexican performers were able to cross over into the Anglo-American circuits with their song and dance, and some performed actively in Canada. The Chautauqua circuit, for example, contracted Los Hermanos Llera, singers, for 125 performances across the United States (*La Prensa*, December 10, 1925). Acting and singing star Nelly Fernández had many successful tours with other Mexican performers throughout the United States and Canada, in part through the Pantages circuit, earning $1,000 per month during the Depression (*La Opinión*, August 8, 1933). *El Heraldo de México* in Los Angeles on June 6, 1925, advertised the Nelly Fernández–Rafael Díaz company in a Los Angeles show entitled *A Night in Mexico* at the Pantages Vaudeville Theatre there, clearly catering to an English-language audience in the most populous Mexican city of the United States.

The two cities with the largest Mexican populations, Los Angeles and San Antonio, naturally became theatrical centers, the former also feeding off the important film industry in Hollywood. In fact, Los Angeles became a manpower pool for Hispanic theatre. Actors, directors, technicians, and musicians from throughout the Southwest, New York, and the whole Spanish-speaking world were drawn here looking for employment. Naturally, Los Angeles became the center for the recruitment of talent in the formation of theatrical companies to perform either locally or on tour through the Southwest. Both Los Angeles and San Antonio went through a period of intense expansion and building of new theatrical facilities in the late teens and early twenties. Los Angeles was able to support five major Hispanic theatre houses with programs that changed daily. The theatres and their peak years were Teatro Hidalgo (1911–1934), Teatro México (1927–1933), Teatro Capitol (1924–1926), Teatro Zendejas (later Novel; 1919–1924), and Teatro Principal (1921–1929). Four other theatres—Princess (1922–1926), California (1927–1934), California International (1930–1932), and Estela (1930–1932)—were also important, and at least fifteen others housed professional companies on a more irregular basis between 1915 and 1935. These were the old Teatro México, Metropolitan, Cabaret Sanromán, Lyceum Hall, Empress, Leo Carrillo, Orange Grove, Mason, Million Dollar, Major, Paramount, Figueroa Playhouse, Alcázar, Philharmonic Auditorium, and Unique.

The documentary record of the first decade of the century is extremely broken and mainly shows performances in cabarets and clubs. It is in the second decade that a full-fledged theatrical movement is really in evidence, starting with the Teatro Hidalgo on September 10, 1911, and its performance of the *zarzuela El puñao de rosas*. The Hildago, owned and operated by a local business, Mayo and Company, was the longest lived Hispanic theatre, having hosted live performances well into 1934, when the documentary record again becomes obscure. Until 1919, the Hidalgo was probably the only permanent theatre house serving the Hispanic community, while other stages, like Lyceum Hall, Cabaret Sanromán, and the Empress Theatre, were still being leased to touring companies that were not performing at the Hidalgo.

It was on November 27, 1919, that the Teatro Zendejas joined the Hidalgo in offering daily productions, with two shows on Saturdays and Sundays, mainly *zarzuelas* and operettas. Two other theatres were opened on Main Street—the México in 1920 and the Principal in 1921—to initiate a decade of the greatest Hispanic theatrical activity in the history of the United States. As noted above, these houses were later joined by a number of others that experienced in the long run a lesser degree of success but certainly had achieved their moments of glory. The following will be a brief summary of the history of the more important houses: Teatro Hidalgo, the first Teatro México and the second one, the Teatro Zendejas, the Teatro Principal, and the Teatro California.

Teatro Hidalgo

As noted above, the Teatro Hidalgo was owned by Mayo and Company, which marketed tickets at the box office, by mail, and at its store at the following prices in 1918: fifty cents for orchestra, thirty-five cents for reserved seats, and twenty-five cents general admission. Booklets of ten discount tickets were also marketed vigorously. As was the custom, the playbills were changed daily and twice on weekends, with matinees on Saturdays and Sundays. Later in the 1920s, as movies began showing more frequently and became more important, as many as six or seven variety shows would be presented between daily showings of films.

As a sign that the Los Angeles theatre scene was heating up, the Hidalgo was remodeled in 1918, because, as Los Angeles' *La Prensa* noted on February 23, 1918, "En esta ciudad se hacía sentir ya la imperiosa necesidad de tener espectáculos de alta cultura y moralidad en nuestro idioma."[3] Thus the Hidalgo opened up after its remodeling with the Compañía Mexicana de Dramas y Comedias and its leading lady, Angélica Méndez, and a full bill of melodramas and three-act comedies. Theatre critic Gabriel Navarro, writing in *La Opinión* on August 8, 1933, stated that in 1919 the Hidalgo was owned by Japanese businessmen. Sometime toward the end of 1919, it is probable that this remodeling and reopening followed the sale by Mayo of the theatre to these businessmen. Navarro remembers that the theatre was filthy and in miserable conditions at that time.

On July 13, 1918, the Cuadro Novel debuted at the Hidalgo and experienced tremendous success for the next six months with its program of *zarzuelas* and *revistas;* so much success, in fact, that the Hidalgo raised the price of orchestra seats to seventy-five cents. The warm reception convinced the Novel to make Los Angeles its home base. On December 18, 1919, the Novel decided to give the Hidalgo competition; it bought or leased the Teatro Zendejas and rebaptized it Teatro Novel. Following the Novel's departure, on January 10, 1919, the Hidalgo booked in the famed Compañía María del Carmen Martínez with full-length dramas that were current on the stages in Mexico and Madrid—works by some of the most important Spanish playwrights like Jacinto Benavente, Carlos Arniches, Santiago Rusiñol, Joaquín Dicentá—and once again returned to a daily fair of serious drama and melodrama. Again the Hidalgo raised the price for orchestra tickets, this time to one dollar, but attendance soon began to fall, as reported in *El Heraldo de México* (January 25, 1919), and by January 25 *zarzuelas* were replacing straight drama on the bill. In February, Tuesdays became ladies' night, with "fashion shows as a

gift to the Fair Sex" ("funciones de moda en obsequio al Bello Sexo"),
Thursdays were for comedies, and Saturdays for "dramas emocio-
nantes." By February 22, the Hidalgo was advertising out-and-out
discounts and more Mexican plays like *Chucho el roto* and *La llo-
rona* were becoming part of the bill. By March 11, general admission
for a silent film and a *zarzuela* was ten cents. A glimpse at the margin of profit for the Teatro Hidalgo was offered by *El Heraldo de
México* on June 24, 1919, when the newspaper published the balance
sheet for the benefit performance by the María del Carmen Martínez
company for the Liga Protectora Mexicana:

Receipts

Ticket sales, minus war tax	$185.67

Expenses

Fee for the theatre company and Mayo Company	50.00
Expenses for the parade to advertise the performance	33.95
Printing of programs	7.00
50 percent of remaining receipts to Mayo Company	57.83
	$148.78
Money raised for the Liga	$ 36.89

After the sale of the Hidalgo to the new Japanese owners, the
theatre reopened on January 26, 1920, reorganized and with more
popular acts, including Justiniani, the magician, and a number of
companies that performed variety acts, *revistas,* and *zarzuelas*—
Compañía de Variedades Turich; Higares Novelty Compañía; Cuadro
de Zarzuela, Comedia y Variedades Multicolor; Compañía de Variedades Carmen Máiquez—which dominated the stage through December 1922. What typified these companies was their extreme flexibility in catering to popular, working-class audiences by mixing
theatrical genre (i.e., serious and light, lyric and realistic) and by
forefronting the comedians in their *revistas,* which became more
and more topical. It was not long before the high standards of morality and family entertainment began to give way in order to cater to
working-class, mainly male tastes. On November 16, 1921, *La Prensa*
published a scathing attack on the Compañía de Arte Nuevo's use of
offensive language and situations in its productions of *El amor que
se huye.* In blaring headlines, the theatre critic accused the Hidalgo
of loose morals ("EL TEATRO HIDALGO PUSO LA MORAL—POBRECITA—
POR EL SUELO"). In general, as shall be seen, this was to be an early
indication of trends that would develop in the 1920s: serious drama
ceding to *revista* and vaudeville, female costumes becoming more

revealing in the manner of French vaudeville (*bataclán*), and the *pelado*, or comic hobo, taking center stage in *revistas* built around his antics and lower humor.

But the *La Prensa* critic also used the occasion of his editorial to attack the Hidalgo on esthetic grounds: ad-libbings using inappropriate (old and dirty) props and costuming for the Viennese operetta *El conde de Luxemburgo*, mixing artists from different genres so that productions came out unevenly. "Una noche se representa una comedia, a la siguiente sigue una zarzuela, después se da un drama, y más tarde una opereta . . . quienes trabajan de tal manera son . . . 'aprendices de todo y oficiales de nada.'"[4] If this criticism were valid, then many of the companies of the time that continually varied their offerings must have sinned in this manner.

On December 8, 1921, the Hidalgo debuted its own stock company, the Cuadro Hidalgo, and thus was somewhat relieved from negotiating and booking with touring companies. Its somewhat limited repertoire, however, resulted in the management returning to booking the following companies through May 1924: Compañía Arte Moderno (September 8–December 3, 1922); Compañía de Operetas Hispano-Americana (December 4, 1922–February 2, 1923); Compañía de Arte Mexicano (February 5, 1923–June 19, 1924). For the most part these companies strung together an unending list of one-act *zarzuelas, revistas,* and minor works, along with variety acts and occasional dramas. What is noteworthy, however, is the proliferation of works by local playwrights on their programs. Although most of these works were one-act comedies and *revistas*, like Arturo Chacel's *Se solicita un marido* and Gabriel Navarro's *El gran visir*, full-length dramas dealing with topical subjects and Hispanic culture in California gradually made their way onto the Hidalgo's stage as well as into sister theatres. It is in 1924 and 1925 that the following plays by Los Angeles playwrights of Mexican origin became the biggest draws at the Hidalgo box office: Adalberto Elías González's *La muerte de Francisco Villa* and *La asesino del martillo o la mujer tigresa*, Eduardo A. Carrillo's *El rayo de Sinaloa* and *El proceso de Aurelio Pompa,* and Agustín Haro y T.'s *El gran recurso. Revistas* and one-acts increased their topicality and also attracted playwrights to experiment with these forms as vehicles for humor: *Los Angeles, la ciudad de los extras, Lo que pasa en México, Los Angeles cabaret, El pueblo quiere paz, La ley del petróleo, De cómico a periodista, Los poches de Los Angeles,* etc.

But the true master of the *revista* was Antonio Guzmán Aguilera (Guz Aguila), the comedian and prolific writer of *revistas* based on

Mexican pastoral themes and current events relevant to the Los Angeles audiences. Like the famous Mexican comics Roberto Soto, Leopoldo Beristáin, and Jesús Medel, Guz Aguila developed a repertoire of piquant *revistas* in which he could satirize all the aspects of daily life. During the 1920s Los Angeles seems to have become his home base. The Teatro Hidalgo hosted his troupe from June 11, 1924, to March 6, 1925, with its *zarzuelas*, dramas, and an interminable list of *revistas* like *Evite peligro, Alma tricolor, Los Angeles vacilador, Pierrot mexicano,* and even one dedicated to the four Mexican theatres located on Main Street, Los Angeles, *Los cuatro ases de la calle Main.*

For a short while after Guz Aguila's departure, there is no news of the Teatro Hidalgo. On April 1, 1925, word finally came that ownership of the theatre had passed into the hands of Meyer Trallis, who also owned the Capitol and the Principal theatres, where variety shows were emphasized.

Following the reopening of the Hidalgo, a number of vaudeville companies were booked to put on variety acts between films. From November 1925, companies made up of local professionals performed variety acts and a series of plays made up mostly of works written by local playwrights, like Adalberto Elías González, Eduardo A. Carrillo, José Pezantes Ganoza, Esteban V. Escalante, Brígido Caro, and others. It seems that it became common practice for the Los Angeles theatres to buoy up falling box office receipts and generally break the doldrums by staging very popular plays by the local playwrights. Included in this series were two familiar works dealing with the Mexican Revolution, *Sangre Yaqui* and *Hazañas, vida y muerte de Francisco Villa,* and one dealing with the persecution of a Mexican laborer, *El proceso de Aurelio Pompa.* The next variety company, México Alegre (January 26–July), continued to stage numerous works by local writers, including plays dealing with the themes of Mexican immigration like *El coyote* and *Los expatriados* and topical *revistas,* like *De Mexicali a Los Angeles.* The main reason that the new company did so was that the Teatro Hidalgo management decided to run a play-writing contest and produce the local plays. This dramatic work was produced despite the group's director, Arturo Rogelini, being known for his mastery of Afro-Cuban dances and having been promoted (*El Heraldo de México,* Janary 14, 1926) as producing *teatro bufo cubano* (Cuban musical farces). Whether he incorporated into his variety shows these Cuban pieces that were currently the rage in Havana, Tampa, and New York is not documented in the newspapers of the time. But what is certain is that he had inherited the chore of staging new plays by authors with whom he most certainly was not familiar.

The winner of the contest—and the winner of most others that would be held—was Adalberto Elías González with his *La desgracia del pobre*, staged on February 17. The attendance and newspaper coverage were so enthusiastic that the Hidalgo management decided to immediately sponsor another contest. Once again, on August 25, 1926, González was proclaimed winner, this time with his *La revista de papel*. But although González had won the first prize in the earlier contest, it was a competing work that became the hit of the season, with numerous repeat performances: Brígido Caro's dramatization of the life of the California bandit, *Joaquín Murrieta*.

The Hidalgo's management, however, went beyond sponsoring contests and producing local plays in order to develop material that was relevant to its audiences. In September 1927, the Hidalgo contracted the Salvadoran playwright Gustavo Solano to write works "de ambiente local" (with local color). And in September such *revistas* as Solano's *Al enfermo lo que pida* and *Se rifa una mujer encuerada* became part of the programs. The latter work captured much of the excitement of the times with five scenes dealing with hit songs, a great Mexican movie star, and life in Hollywood: "No Bananas Today," "Ramón Novarro," "En Hollywood," "El Enfocamiento," and "Se rifa una mujer encuerada." Perhaps it is appropriate to mention here that the Hidalgo had other strategies besides play-writing contests to encourage attendance by the working class. The Hidalgo resorted to sponsoring turkey raffles at its showings.

Through 1929, variety shows continued to occupy the Hidalgo's stage with companies that were occasionally reinforced by touring vaudevillians. When serious plays were produced, again locally written works held their own and continued to draw audiences. By January 1930, it seems, the public may have tired of the variety acts, for *La Opinión* reported on January 7 that the México Lindo company at the Hidalgo was going to forgo some of its usual repertoire to perform Spanish *zarzuelas*, comedies, and dramas. Los Pirríns, starring the comic don Catarino, followed with some *zarzuela* and drama, but mostly with an interminable list of musical-comedy *revistas* featuring don Catarino improvising and ad-libbing in every situation imaginable: as a doctor, nun, millionaire, count, milkman, army recruit, and so on. Along with his usual comic antics, Catarino created a few *revistas* that dealt comically with more serious subjects such as the Depression, Repatriation, drugs, exile: *Los efectos de la crisis, Regreso a mi tierra, El desterrado, Whiskey, morfina y marihuana.*

The year 1930 was, indeed, eventful for the Teatro Hidalgo. On

October 1 the theatre began showing its first talking films in Spanish. Whether this in itself presented competition to the live performances is not certain, but at times the paradox of having the live artists playing on stage and featured in a movie at another theatre on the same night did occur in the Mexican community of Los Angeles. The second singular event that year was the sale of the Hidalgo to a firm from Mexico. As reported on July 12 in *La Opinión*, the firm was reconditioning the theatre and making it more "decent" for the public. The newly cleaned Hidalgo had its grand reopening on July 3 with numerous Los Angeles artists performing as well as the company that would occupy the stage for the next few months: Los Pirríns. *La Opinión's* theatre critic commented that the Hidalgo was now as good as a new theatre, a proper place for the Mexican working class, which had abandoned other theatre houses that were featuring English-language talking films that the Spanish-speaking public did not understand. He also commented that it was important for them to support their own Mexican artists. That same year, the Teatro Hidalgo was closed down again and sold to an American firm that also owned the Estela and the Electric. According to *La Opinión* (November 21, 1930), the theatre was to reopen on November 27 strictly as a cinema, with the most modern equipment.

In the years 1931 and 1932 the Hidalgo changed performing companies more times than it ever did in its history. Variety acts were now clearly subordinated to films, and the works being performed were no longer advertised in the newspapers. As the Depression deepened, booking large drama and *zarzuela* companies was not financially feasible, nor did it make monetary sense to even advertise the featured acts in the newspapers. It was so much cheaper to rent films and draw audiences in to see their favorite movie stars talking and singing: Lupe Vélez, José Mojica, Dolores del Río, even Virginia Fábregas, Romualdo Tirado, and don Catarino. At the end of November 1932, the Hidalgo policy was officially instituted of having variety acts every day. In April 1932, perhaps because of competition with the other theatre houses, the Hidalgo returned to advertising its live performances, and the Compañía de Comedias, Revistas y Variedades Peña-Mena that was booked in once again began to feature plays and shorter works written by the Los Angeles playwrights. While other theatres like the Teatro California were failing, the Hidalgo began to innovate to keep audiences coming. It instituted just one general admission price of twenty-five cents, except for special events such as the production of Gabriel Navarro's *Alma yaqui* on June 27, 1932, at which reserved seats cost fifty cents. The Hidalgo also held boxing and wrestling matches on its stage.

Unable to compete with the economic advantage of talking films, more and more theatre companies took to the road. After having had so many steady bookings for so many years in Los Angeles, when the Hidalgo closed, these companies began announcing tours of California cities or northern Mexico, or they simply declared that they were ready to return to the homeland. This was the period at the Hidalgo when more and more benefit performances were held to honor departing playwrights and actors who were now bidding fond farewells to Los Angeles. But the new year, 1933, saw the Hidalgo begin radio broadcasts from its stage and also marked a valiant effort by actors and directors to survive at doing what they loved best. The Gran Compañía Cooperativa was formed in which the artists banded together and divided their reduced pay from the Hidalgo equally. Once again during January and February, some of the major melodramas became part of the Hidalgo program: *La mujer X, La mujer adúltera, María la emparedada, La riqueza de los pobres.* But these were not as depressing as the melodrama being lived by the Mexicans themselves, which was the basis for *Los que vuelven,* Juan Bustillo Oro's play staged on February 27. *La Opinión* on that date highlighted the difficulties in returning to Mexico as depicted in the play: "El tema de la obra es el doloroso tema de la Repatriación. En sus cuadros desfilan los desencantados, los que habiéndose adaptado a un medio de comodidades en el suelo extranjero, se ven ahora viviendo una vida precaria en su propia patria, luchando por readaptarse al nuevo medio."[5]

Once again, from March through August, members of various disbanded companies combined together, under director Pepet, to offer their full repertoire of *zarzuelas,* operettas, *revistas,* one-act comedies, and an occasional full-length drama. If shows were uneven in the early 1920s because of the mixing of genres, they must have been even more uneven now. There was not much variety left in the few remaining actors, singers, dancers, and musicians, and these were constantly coming and going, desperately looking for work, perhaps to raise enough funds to return to Mexico. Nevertheless, here was the last gasp of creativity at the Hidalgo, including everything from Jacinto Benavente's masterpiece *La malquerida* to the Argentine farce *En un burro tres baturros.* Most of these works were featured on "jueves sociales" (social Thursdays), designated for special shows at reduced prices (reserved seats at forty cents). And when these artists were not doing "jueves sociales" at the Hidalgo, they were off performing in Pomona, San Diego, and as far south as the Teatro Zaragoza in Tijuana. The composer and musical director at the Hidalgo, maestro Ernesto González Jiménez, besides performing and touring was also stabilizing his income by operating a music academy in Los Angeles at this time.

The last full company documented as having a run at the Hidalgo was the Pirríns, beginning August 8, 1934. On September 10 the Hidalgo celebrated its twenty-third anniversary with a performance of *El puñao de rosas,* the *zarzuela* performed on its first opening night; the performance was dedicated to the comic Miguel de Lara, who was a member of the 1911 and the 1934 casts. Almost as a symbol of the moribund theatre and the Mexican artists who had brought their life's work to Los Angeles, on October 15, 1934, the Hidalgo sponsored a benefit performance to raise funds for a gravestone for the beloved actor who had many years before come to reside in Los Angeles in the Virginia Fábregas company: Agustín Molinari. His children, Raquel, Juan, and Agustín Jr., all acted that night in *La cuerda floja* in honor of their father. It is somewhat fitting that the November 1 performance by the Pirríns of *Don Juan Tenorio,* in which that great dramatic figure confronts death, is also the last dramatic performance at the Hidalgo reported in the pages of *La Opinión.*

A few months earlier, *La Opinión* on August 19, 1934, had announced that the Hidalgo had been sold by Carlos Emmanuel to Frank Fouce (d. 1962), a Spanish Jew who had become a naturalized American citizen and had been creating a chain of Spanish-language cinemas that also featured variety shows. Its destiny as primarily a movie house was sealed.

Los Teatros México

In the history of the Los Angeles stage, there were two houses that bore the name of the Mexican homeland. The first, baptized originally as Lyceum Hall and then later as the Walker Theatre, built in 1887 and bearer of at least five other names, was short-lived. As early as 1918, Mayo and Company, owners of the Teatro Hidalgo, had been booking companies like Virginia Fábregas's into Lyceum Hall. There is a possibility that Mayo may have been the proprietor of the Lyceum as well. For Mrs. Fábregas's 1918 tour, Mayo charged a dollar fifty for box seats, sixty cents for general admission, and forty cents for the balcony, as well as subscriptions for six performances at seven dollars and four dollars and fifty cents—all hefty sums for the times. All of the above leads us to believe that the Lyceum must have been a grand house, certainly one for proper families and for the first lady of the Mexican stage.

It is not until 1921, however, that, now as the Walker Theatre, we begin to see steady Hispanic use of this theatre, which was situated on Spring Street. The Walker went into full swing on January 30 of that year, following the closing of the Teatro Novel (*El Heraldo de México*, January 30, 1921). The Gran Compañía Hispano-Mexicana de Drama y Alta Comedia, directed by Amparito Guillot, with Ernesto González Jiménez as the musical director, opened with a complete program of dramas and *zarzuelas*. Its run was successful enough and the audiences promising enough so that by March 3 the Walker had officially been rebaptized the Teatro México. Nevertheless, after a couple more companies had been booked, the Teatro México was no more. After the data regarding the December 6 performance of *Malditas sean las mujeres* by a company directed by Arturo Chacel, there is no more news of the Teatro México in the Los Angeles Spanish-language newspapers. It too had succumbed to the same fate as the Teatro Novel. The defunct Teatro México was to have become the best of the Hispanic theatres, as Gabriel Navarro explained in *La Opinión* on July 1, 1932. It had the best stage and the most seats (which were elegantly upholstered), and it was centrally located in the heart of the "barrio latino" right in front of all the trolley car lines.

It is Ernesto González Jiménez, this time joined by that all-important figure, Romualdo Tirado, who revived the name of the Teatro México.[6] The September 10, 1927, edition of *El Heraldo de México* reported on the sale of the Grand Theatre to the pair, who would continue to perform, besides functioning as impresarios. And, indeed, Tirado and González Jiménez formed a stock company which performed dramas and *zarzuelas,* including works by local playwrights, from September 15 to November 24, when the company was then reinforced by portions of an Argentine troupe. Tirado and González Jiménez were getting a quick initiation into the problems of theatre management when, in order to get part of the Compañía Argentina passed through customs at the border, the Teatro México had to leave a hefty deposit. And because they were not successful in getting the whole troupe into the United States, only part of the Argentine's repertoire could be staged. After that contretemps, the Teatro México company performed by itself from December 7, 1927, until June 4, 1928, staging *zarzuelas, revistas*, full-length dramas, and the more successful of the locally written plays. There was hardly a month when plays by Adalberto Elías González were not featured by the company: *Los amores de Ramona, Flor del fandango, El enemigo de las mujeres, La mal pagada, La conquista de California.* Finally, like the Teatro Hidalgo, the Teatro México also began sponsoring play-writing contests in 1928 and selling out its fifteen hundred seats.

It seems that the hunger for new plays was so great and the publicity so intense that even Tirado turned to playwriting in 1930. Amid much publicity, Tirado and Antonieta Díaz Mercado adapted for the stage Mariano Azuela's masterpiece of the Mexican Revolution, *Los de abajo*. Even the great philosopher and writer José Vasconcelos, who was residing in Los Angeles, attended the debut on February 7, 1930. On February 9, the play was panned by the *Heraldo de México* critic and it was never again staged at the Teatro México. In functioning as an integral part of the community and as a protector of Hispanic culture, the Teatro México became the site of occasional community events and fundraisers, even of a political nature. For instance, the December 16, 1927, performance of *La madre* was a benefit sponsored by the Sociedad de Madres Mexicanas to raise funds for the defense of a "prisionero mexicano" (Mexican prisoner). On January 28, 1928, the Teatro México lent its stage to the amateur dramatic company Cuadro Junípero Serra, directed by local playwright Brígido Caro, for the staging of his trilogy *La gloria de la raza*.

In July 1928, the Teatro México hosted the Compañía Andrés Chávez and a full complement of full-length dramas and comedies, only to resume its program of mixed genres by the stock company from July to November. On September 11, the Teatro México competed directly with Virginia Fábregas at the Teatro Capitol by offering the same play, *La mujer X*. Ironically, the Compañía Virginia Fábregas was next booked at the Teatro México for November and December, with a solid slate of heavy European dramas and an occasional Mexican play, such as *Pancho Villa* and *Cuauhtémoc*. Just at the time Mrs. Fábregas was booked, however, more administrative or human relations problems were experienced by the México, with its stock company quitting and, in the process, stealing librettos, including the most popular one, González's *Los amores de Ramona*. Thus, upon the departure of the Fábregas company for New Mexico, Chicago, and points north, Tirado had to form a new company and hire the Compañía de Zarzuela y Operetas L. Mendoza López for the next two months. The popular success of the maestro Méndoza López with his own operettas fortunately carried the México for a while. Mendoza López, who had previously been booked at the Hidalgo, which was too shabby and too working class for his operettas, felt quite at home at the México, whose audience was of a higher category. After the composer's troupe left, Tirado hired La Joyita (Isabel Reina) y Su Cuadro when it finished its run at the Teatro Principal (March 8, 1929) and later numerous other reinforcements. Traveling acts, like comic Pepín Pastor, actress Reina Vélez, magician Justiniani, and others, were hired through 1930 and 1931 as the Teatro México continued its mix of variety, *zarzuela,* drama, and *revista.*

From April 19 to June 2 the México presented Los Pirríns with don Catarino and his *revistas,* followed by the Compañía Landeros and a mixed bag of genres to September 9, then mostly drama by the Compañía Novel, until the house company took over again from October 12 to June 26, 1931. But the Novel's successful presentation of melodramas in a climate dominated by variety acts and *revistas* prompted Gabriel Navarro in *La Opinión* (September 21, 1930), to issue a plea for more of the same and even more serious drama.

In 1930 and 1931, the Teatro México began investing more money in advertising Spanish-language talkies, improving the screen and the sound system, and scheduling appearances of the film stars at their screenings. Romualdo Tirado's own movies were often announced on the México marquee. A number of variety shows at this time consisted of merely presenting a prologue to the film that was showing. By May 5, 1932, a critic in *La Opinión* challenged the México's insistence on film and variety shows (the Pirríns) when, he stated, dramas would draw the public back, even during the Depression. As evidence he cited the money that was made on the last play featured, *La fotografía.* But the film industry was also used as an ally in the effort to attract audiences. One of the greatest attractions of the time was in having live performances by film stars such as Rodolfo de Hoyos, who acted in Gabriel Navarro's play *El sacrificio* on January 7, 1931. Many other film stars, like Rosita Moreno and María Calvó, were advertised as performing at the México.

But by the end of the month all efforts were fruitless. *La Opinión* carried word on January 30 and 31 and February 1 of the signing of a new partnership contract with an American burlesque company. The México reopened on January 31, featuring a chorus line of forty *"bellísimas* [gorgeous] girls," all Americans except for Blanca Calvete and Irene López. The theatre no longer drew Mexican audiences; this was not family theatre anymore, nor was the Spanish language used.

In part as a reaction to the conversion of the Teatro México to American burlesque, the Los Angeles Hispanic artists resolved to form their own cooperative and lease a theatre themselves "para presentar espectáculos en español para la colonia de nuestra raza."[7] On February 7, *La Opinión* reported that the play-writing contest was still on, with nine works submitted, and that a theatre, not the

Teatro México, would be used for the productions. No more was heard until August and September, when the México opened its doors again to Hispanic variety and Spanish-language films. But on September 29 the theatre closed down again because of financial problems. Following this gloomy news, the cooperative Artistas Unidos rose to the occasion and offered five months of *zarzuelas* and a few dramas at the México. But despite lower prices, on October 21 *La Opinión* was reporting poor response from the public and citing the lack of preparation of the artists, who did not make up a complete company. At the same time the México was getting direct and active competition from the Teatro Hidalgo.

From November 7, 1932, to January 24, 1933, there is no record of performances at the Teatro México; however, the theatre must have reopened in July 1933. On July 1, 1933, Gabriel Navarro announced the reopening of the Teatro México and its rededication to Hispanic theatre. He censured the almost pornographic burlesque performances that had recently occupied the theatre, which had reclaimed its earlier name of the Grand, and eulogized the Teatro México and its importance as the center of cultural life for the Mexican community:

> Ahora el antiguo nombre de las seis letras que son casi sagradas, vuelve a brillar en caracteres incandescentes sobre la puerta del "Grand." Otra vez los calendarios aztecas adornan su vestíbulo, y en sus corrillos se oyen las suaves y musicales inflexiones de nuestro idioma. Ya pronto, no quedará en su escenario sino el recuerdo de los bailes lúbricos, del balanceo de caderas y la estridente música de "Jazz," sustituidos ahora por las lánguidas canciones mexicanas, por el espectáculo que es poder y arte, por la cultura hispana que sobrevive a pesar de todo, en este rincón de los Estados Unidos.[8]

By July 24, 1933, newspaper accounts indicate that the México was featuring English-language films and debuting an unnamed Hispanic company, directed by Eduardo Arozamena, the same artist who had gone from Mexico's Teatro Principal to the New York Hispanic stage and had now made the Southwest his destiny. The company, which had just finished a run at the Teatro Hidalgo, staged all the favorite *zarzuelas* and a few *revistas* by local playwrights. The company's performances were complemented at least once (March 30) by a professional wrestling match on stage. In April, Nelly Fernández's troupe reinforced the company, while other artists like Eloísa Valdealde continued to take leave to return to Mexico. Some time after April 1933, the Teatro México was closed down again. On October 18, it was reopened, newly remodeled by the new owner, Carlos Emmanuel, and featuring the reorganized company of Rodolfo de Hoyos, specializing in operettas. The de Hoyos troupe, which featured as orchestra director the former Teatro México impresario Ernesto González Jiménez, announced that it would continue to play the México as long as there were audiences. Prices were kept attractive at fifteen cents for balcony, twenty-five cents general admission, thirty-five cents reserved seating, and ten cents for children. On Sundays prices were even further reduced, according to *La Opinión* (October 29), so that families residing outside of town could come in to see the show. Rodolfo de Hoyos y su Compañía closed at the México on November 7 to begin a tour of the Pacific states of Mexico. On November 8, the México reopened in the hands of Carlos Emmanuel strictly as a movie house for the Spanish-speaking community.

Teatro Zendejas

The Teatro Zendejas (later Novel and then Capitol), which seated nine hundred, was opened by P. Zendejas, the successful developer of a medical elixir. He opened his theatre on October 5, 1919, with the Cuadro Novel, starring the Moor, Félix Medel, and, because of Medel's religion, remained closed on Fridays, the Moslem Sabbath, during that initial run. By December 18, 1919, Zendejas had sold the theatre to the Cuadro Novel to be managed by L. P. Rivas. The Cuadro Novel, with a heavy emphasis on Mexican plays and *revistas,* like *Chucho el Roto, Heroicidad de un mexicano o todo por la patria,* and *En la hacienda,* became the stock company. Medel, a great and popular comic, had many *revistas* created to highlight his virtuosity. On March 26, 1920, it was announced that the Cuadro Novel was going on tour to the Teatro Nacional in San Antonio. In its place it left variety acts and films until April 20, when Romualdo Tirado's Compañía de Operetas y Zarzuelas Arte Nuevo was contracted. Arte Nuevo performed until December 17, 1920, offering early shows for working people who could not stay out late. Some of the *revistas* that were featured at this time were topical in theme and also related directly to working-class audiences: *Do You Speak English?* and *El dinero y el trabajo o lo que vale la honra del obrero.* While Tirado's troupe was on tour, the family of Mexico's greatest circus clown, the deceased Ricardo Bell, La Gran Compañía de Atracciones la Familia Bell, debuted in Los Angeles at the Novel on December 18, 1920, only to see the theatre close on January 2, 1921. According to *El Heraldo de México* (February 10, 1921), Tirado's Arte Nuevo company returned to Los Angeles without a place in which to perform; thus it was rumored that Tirado would buy or lease the Teatro Novel. Tirado and his partner, Ernesto González Jiménez, did eventually buy the theatre and rebaptize it the Teatro Capitol, but not until 1924.

On July 26, 1924, Romualdo Tirado and Ernesto González Jiménez became impresarios of the Teatro Capitol and established their troupe, Arte Nuevo, as the stock company. Now as the Teatro Capitol company, the troupe began performing the standard fare of *zarzuelas* and dramas and also started introducing numerous works by local playwrights, like Adalberto Elías González and Daniel Venegas. Tirado and González Jiménez themselves innovated a number of musical reviews, comic *revistas,* and sketches, like *De México a Los Angeles o aventuras de Romualdo Tirado, Aventuras de Romualdo Tirado, de Los Angeles a Alaska, Tirado bolshevique,* and *El mundo de las pelonas* (by Raúl Castell and Ernesto González Jiménez).

On February 27, 1925, the Capitol was sold to Meyer Trallis, the Jewish-American businessman who, according to playwright Rafael Trujillo Herrera, held a number of anti-Mexican sentiments.[9] According to Trujillo, Trallis said quite often that he dirtied up the theatres so that the Mexicans would feel at home. By April 1, Trallis had also acquired the Principal and Hidalgo theatres, both of which began to place a heavy emphasis on variety acts alternating with films. On May 8, 1925, critic don Basilio expressed his disenchantment at the Capitol's insistence on variety:

En el Teatro Capitol se está convenciendo de que nuestro público no quiere ni dramas, ni operetas, ni zarzuelas. Que quiere revistas. . . . Es que nuestro público se ha frivolizado. Quiere vivir la época. Y esas obras de capa y espada; esos dramones de lacrimeos y gritos desarticulados; esas zarzuelas que nos las sabemos de memoria por viejas y trilladas, ya de eso no quiere ver nuestro público. Quiere reír. Gozar. Ver la fiesta de la luz. Del color. De la canción. . . . La gente quiere reír. Quiere variedades. Sensaciones tras sensaciones. Policromía.[10]

And color, song, and laughter were what the Capitol audiences got in the next few months with the Compañía Pablo Garza, the Compañía Guz Aguila, and the Cuadro México-Perú, all of which specialized in *revistas* and variety.

But the matters of cleanliness and safety were not yet resolved for Trallis and the Mexican theatres. In June 1925, the Los Angeles Fire Department threatened to close down the Hidalgo, Principal, and Estela and demanded that only a limited number of artists be allowed to occupy the tiny stages of these theatres, according to *El Heraldo de México* (June 9 and 23), because of overcrowding, poor hygienic conditions, and insufficient fire escapes. Only six vaudevillians were then allowed to be on stage at one time, until improvements were made, thus making impossible the production of *zarzuelas*, operettas, and *revistas*. *El Heraldo de México* of June 9, as the community conscience, was in complete agreement with the fire department and it also launched into an attack on the "pornographic" costuming and content as well as the poor scenery and esthetic conditions. The attacks continued in *El Heraldo de México* well into August and September, often pointing out that the owners and impresarios of these theatres were not Hispanics (i.e., Trallis) and thus called for Hispanic businessmen to step forward and improve the situation, for there was no other place for the "gente bien" (respectable people) of the community to attend.

In 1925, signs that things were taking a turn for the worst began to appear. In August, Trallis contracted an Italian company specializing in operettas: Compagnia di Varietá Italiana Cittá di Firenze. Then in September he contracted an American vaudeville company from New York. It was not until a year later that the Capitol resumed Spanish-language shows: August 10, 1926, with the Compañía Tirado-Uranga-Iris and a general admission price of seventy-five cents, balcony and gallery fifty cents.

Finally in April of the following year, Meyer Trallis remodeled the theatre and corrected many of the problems censured by the critics and the authorities. He contracted the Compañía Virginia Fábregas for the new opening on April 30. On September 4, 1927, the Familia Ricardo Bell bought the Capitol from Trallis.

The Bell Family installed its company, reinforced by Los Hermanos Areu and Beatriz ("La Chata") Noloesca, as the house company and continued to present variety acts until September 1, 1928, when it contracted Virginia Fábregas once again. After the February 16, 1929, debut of the Compañía Ligia de Golconda, no further word of the Capitol appears in the Spanish-language newspapers until August 8, 1933, when Gabriel Navarro, writing in *La Opinión*, mentioned that it had been razed and replaced by a parking lot.

Teatro California

The Teatro California opened on February 2, 1927, with the Compañía Virginia Fábregas and its repertoire of European and Mexican plays that served as settings for the dramatic virtuosity of its leading lady. According to *El Heraldo de México* (February 19, 1927), the seating capacity was three thousand. In the next few years, it hosted numerous companies that performed *zarzuelas*, variety shows, and drama, but most notably in 1930 Mexico's great musical comedy actress and recording star, María Conesa, who had made Los Angeles her home base.

Some time after Conesa's appearances at the California, it closed down. In 1931 and 1932 it functioned primarily as a cinema, showing films in Spanish and Yiddish. For our study the California Theatre gains importance in its second life, for its stage was reactivated by the cooperative of out-of-work theatre artists, Artistas Unidos, on November 26, 1932, just after this company had left the Teatro México. Under the directorship of Jesús Topete the cooperative began staging mostly *zarzuelas* on Wednesdays, Saturdays, and Sundays, and by the following months the Teatro California and the Artistas Unidos were becoming involved in radio drama, first with the Ernesto González Jiménez Orchestra broadcasting directly from the California on KFVD and then with the broadcasting of the police/detective series, "Aventuras de Máximo Caballero," written by Gloria de la Cruz. During 1933 and 1934 the company and the theatre were also involved in various charity performances to raise funds for the radio program "La hora católica" for the Nuestra Señora de Talpa Church, the Club Atlético México, and many other causes. In June and July 1934, the California began contracting companies like Los Pirríns. On August 18 and 19, Gabriel Navarro's "Revista de Radio 1934" was staged and broadcast and on August 20, 1934, three radio dramas by local playwright Rafael Trujillo were staged and broadcast in a benefit for the radio station "El eco de México." His original plays were "Pancho Villa," "La serenata de Los Angeles," and "Doña Clarines en Jaligú" (Mrs. Clarines in Hollywood).

The Teatro California continued contracting variety shows to complement movies throughout the Depression and well into the forties. Owned and managed since September 1933 by Frank Fouce, the California became one of a small chain of cinemas that regularly and quite systematically integrated Hispanic variety shows and *revistas*. One of the companies quite often contracted during the late thirties and early forties was the Compañía de Revistas y Variedades el Niño Fidencio, directed by Francisco Vega and co-starring Rosalinda Meléndez. The modest Niño Fidencio company, which also performed in the Los Angeles parks under the WPA as well as in outlying towns like Azuza, Cucamonga, Corona, and Santa Monica in tent shows, built its *revistas* around a folk healer who had become famous as a child in northern Mexico, El Niño Fidencio, but who had been discredited and popularly seen as somewhat of a buffoon. The heart of these *revistas* consisted of El Niño Fidencio wearing clownlike make-up, red long johns, suspenders, and a tan hat and poking fun at the establishment, conning people into all kinds of things.[11]

As for Fouce, both Rosalinda Melendéz's son, William Lanceford, and Leonardo García Astol agree that he was a despot and a shrewd businessman.[12] Besides the California, Fouce owned and managed the Roosevelt, the Mason, the Arrow, and, since 1934, the Hidalgo and Electric theatres in Los Angeles and regularly formed variety companies to tour some of these facilities. In 1949 Fouce also acquired the Million Dollar Theatre, in which he instituted the caravan of stars performances by known recording stars (*Los Angeles Times*, October 4, 1971). Leonardo García Astol recounts how Fouce formed a variety company for him with the Padilla Sisters and the Trío Durango to open up at the Arrow Theatre in 1940. After making a hit with the *revista musical* that Astol wrote, Fouce moved the troupe to his most important house, the California. Astol also recalls that actors had to keep an ear out for neighborhood rumors, scandals, and other topics that they could incorporate into the comic sketches.

How long Fouce, who Astol says was also a minor movie producer, continued to book variety acts at the Teatro California and his other movie houses is unknown. The Teatro California is still standing today, dedicated mainly to showing soft pornography and martial arts films to Spanish-speaking immigrant workers.

Teatro Principal

The Teatro Principal, another of the theatres owned at one time by Meyer Trallis, was smaller than the others and, on occasion (as in the debut of the Compañía Tirado-Uranga-Iris, which had just come over from the Capitol), had to turn people away, despite their having lined up at the doors at an early hour (*El Eco de México*, May 10, 1925). The Principal served as a Spanish-language theatre from 1921 until 1929, hosting such companies as Tirado's Arte Nuevo (1921), the Compañía de Operetas, Dramas, Zarzuelas y Revistas Mexicanas, directed by Gabriel Navarro (1922), the Compañía de Revistas Elena Landeros (1928), the Compañía de Atracciones Mexicanas Don Chema (1928), and Dorita Ceprano and Los Hermanos Areu (1924). It was at the Areus' October 1924 performances that Beatriz ("La Chata") Noloesca began to ascend as a musical comedy star and overshadow the Areu brothers. At this time, according to a playbill in the Belia Areu private collection, Willard Wyatt was the owner of the Principal and the Areu brothers were the impresarios. Judging from the same playbill of November 21, 1924, which announces the *revistas El asombro de Celaya* and *Los éxitos del jazz,* the Principal cultivated a working-class audience. The bill employs workers' dialect and satire, much as *revistas* did, proclaiming the Principal as "el teatro de las tres garantías: de chile, de dulce y de manteca" (the theatre of three guarantees: piquant, sweet, and fat), with the best costumes that Goodwill could provide and a newly remodeled auditorium in which the electric fans were replaced by rat holes (meaning the holes were left open in the ceiling after the fans were removed). The Areus are identified as fieldhands (*pizcadores*).

On September 22, 1928, there is news that the new manager of the Teatro Principal was Dionisio Acosta. Following a run at the Principal by don Chema on February 2, 1929, Lee Brothers became the new impresario of the Principal, and on February 16 it was announced that Trallis had just bought the Principal (again?). After this we lose track of the theatre.

Other Theatres

Of the numerous other theatres in Los Angeles that housed Hispanic shows, the Teatro Princesa is notable because of the picture that actress María Teresa Montoya paints of it in her autobiography. Montoya inaugurated the theatre on January 29, 1922, with her Gran Compañía Cómico Dramático María Teresa Montoya, only to experience such a poor reception that her company had to declare bankruptcy, resulting in the dispersal of its members, including actor-playwright Eduardo Carrillo, who stayed on in Los Angeles for at least a decade. Her ill fortune at the Princesa seems to have completely soured her opinion of Hispanic theatre audiences in Los Angeles. She fixes the blame for her misfortunes on Mexicans in the United States becoming Americanized: "La temporada bien, aunque el público no me satisfizo; nuestros compatriotas no son ni mexicanos ya, ni americanos . . . y naturalmente con esa clase de público . . . El género cómico y sobre todo que haya música y bailes, es lo que tiene más éxito; lo comprenden mejor."[13] Following Montoya in March was the Cuadro de Variedades Carmen de Granada, which debuted two new revistas, *Los Angeles al día* and *Tres piedras,* to a great deal of success. Also, major *zarzuelas* and operas were staged, but by April 29 *El Heraldo de México* was reporting on the Princesa's financial problems, despite its featuring one of Mexico's top comedians, Leopoldo Beristáin. On May 11, the Princesa closed. On May 18 it reopened with an American burlesque company, but it is unknown how much longer it was able to survive. On August 8, 1933, Gabriel Navarro mentioned in *La Opinión* that the Princesa used to be situated where the main entrance to city hall was now located.

In 1931 Romualdo Tirado bought the Orange Grove Theatre, hoping to stage everything from dramas to *revistas* with a new company he was forming. The theatre, managed by Juan N. Chavarrí, did not keep its doors open longer than a month. Despite Tirado's assemblage of some of the most talented and favored artists, such as Daniel Ferreiro Rea and Luz Segovia, and the production of some of the most popular plays, including *La enemiga, Esos hombres, Malvaloca, El rey que rabió,* and the most popular *zarzuelas* and operettas, like *El soldado de chocolate* and *El conde de Luxemburgo,* the December 18 function was suspended and no more was heard from the Orange Grove in the Hispanic community.

The California International Theatre on October 19, 1931, began housing productions by a cooperative of out-of-work professionals who idealistically called themselves the Compañía Lírico–Teatral Renacimiento. On October 20 *La Opinión* explained that they were not performing for monetary gain; instead these 100 percent Mexican artists were "entusiastas de la conservación de la cultura hispana que ellos adquirieron, y unidos ahora por la necesidad de contrarrestar la influencia del teatro extraño a nuestras costumbres."[14] The article further explained that most of the artists were donating their labor, that the receipts would go to the costs of orchestra and scenery, and that only with an extraordinarily high attendance would they break even. But they were trying to awaken the taste for "lo nuestro" (what is ours). On October 22, the theatre registered a full house for Camprodón and Arrieta's *Marina.* The Renacimiento went on to do a number of successful shows of *Molinos de viento, El eterno Don Juan, En las redes de la araña,* and *La tía de Carlos* at this theatre, as well as in the Wilshire Ebell Theatre. Nevertheless, the California International closed, with the newspapers only offering one explanation: the Depression.

The Figueroa Playhouse also began scheduling Spanish-language dramas and *zarzuelas* with screen actors in 1931 but without much success, despite the critics' pleas. On July 28, 1931, *La Opinión* decried the lack of box office receipts for *Fata Morgana* by Ernest Vajda, with movie stars Elvira Morla and Carlos Villaríos: "la colonia hispana . . . tiene también el deber de patrocinar manifestaciones por amor de nuestra cultura agonizante."[15] And again on September 10, 1932, sounding an even more nationalistic tone, *La*

Opinión stated, "Necesitamos teatro . . . siquiera sea para contra-rrestar la influencia de letras, costumbres y tendencias sajonas que nos envuelven por momentos."[16] By September 2, 1932, the Figueroa had become the Teatro Major, and it still housed an occasional Hispanic play until 1934, but then it slipped from sight in the Spanish-language newspapers.

As the effects of the Depression increased and movies continued to displace live theatre, many of those artists that did not return to Mexico placed themselves and their art at the service of various church and community charities by raising funds through productions, at times alongside amateurs, in neighborhood churches and mutualist societies. In such Los Angeles Catholic churches as Nuestra Señora de Guadalupe, Nuestra Señora de Talpa, Santa Isabel, Purísima Concepción, María Auxiliadora, San José, and Blanchard Hall could be found performing the likes of Romualdo Tirado, Brígido Caro, the Camacho Vega brothers, and, of course, Daniel Ferreiro Rea in *El anillo de hierro, Alma yaqui, Marina,* and almost any other play that used to be a regular part of their popular repertoires. Community organizations looked continuously to the professional artists to support the needy during the Depression. The Unión de Damas Católicas in 1930 leased the Wilshire Ebell Theatre and produced *Un americano en Madrid* by Navarro y Torrente, with professional actors and director Ernesto Vilches, to raise money for poor children at Christmas. The Mexican consul organized a benefit at Philharmonic Hall for destitute Mexicans with Virginia Fábregas in one of her most famous plays, *Ha entrado una mujer* by Suárez Deza on February 8, 1931. At the same time, Brígido Caro directed the Cuadro Artístico Amado Nervo in numerous benefits for the Sociedad de Madres Mexicanas and the Logia Bella Unión No. 53 de la Alianza Hispano Americana in 1930 and 1931. Also, more and more neighborhood stages began to be used by amateur groups who took on the role of providing wholesome entertainment in Spanish to fill the gap left by the moribund theatre industry and the return of most of the artists to Mexico. Groups like Cuadro Nacionalista Mexicano and the Club Cultural Benito Juárez, directed by Antonio Magaña, began performing plays like Tamayo y Baus's *Hija y madre* and *Arturo o amor de madre* in the auditorium of Purísima Concepción and Santa Isabel churches. In 1933, the Cuadro de Nuestra Señora de Talpa began staging such works as Gregorio Martínez Sierra's *Mamá,* Darío Nicodemo's *La enemiga,* and Benito Pérez Galdós's *Marianela,* under director Jesús María del Campo, at a commercial establishment, the Unique Theatre.

Drama critic Gabriel Navarro encouraged the formation of these amateur groups, arguing in the August 26, 1934, edition of *La Opinión* that the theatre arts should not be allowed to die completely now that the professional stage had become bankrupt. He pleaded with parents to put aside the fears of immorality in their girls' involvement in theatre and frivolity in their boys dedicating time to something that did not bring home cash. He reiterated the argument of exercising the Spanish-language and Hispanic culture through theatre and that through the theatre and art the young people could enter into wholesome association with each other that could lead to marriage. It could also be the beginning of a career in the movies.

The Spanish-language stage had been dealt a triple death blow: Depression, Repatriation, cinema. The Hispanic theatre industry continued to writhe and agonize from 1930 to the middle of the decade, when a few hardy troupes acquiesced to entertaining briefly between films, donated their art to charity, made the transition to radio, toured outlying regions in tents, or performed in the parks and some threatres under the auspices of the WPA. The first unmitigated force that brought the theatre movement to its knees was the Depression. Besides emptying the pockets of theatregoers, it also produced a reaction from the welfare authorities who started to repatriate unemployed Mexicans. Numerous other Mexicans returned home quite independently from the welfare authorities. The Mexican community and, naturally, the audiences began to dwindle in size:

> El ambiente mexicano e hispanoamericano, no ha sido, desde que se inició la repatriación, muy favorable que digamos para los artistas de los diversos géneros. En primer lugar, sólo hay un teatro para la colonia, y ni éste se ve lleno en funciones preparadas con la anticipación debida, y presentando como figuras centrales a las que en otros tiempos han constituido un atractivo real. Luego, las condiciones por las que atraviesa, son difíciles, no sólo en nuestro medio, sino también en el medio americano. Una prueba de ello es que los templos del Cinema, bien acondicionados y presentándose estrenos de películas, han tenido que bajar sus precios al ínfimo nivel, y aún así no registran los llenos de otras épocas.[17]

Again on August 8, 1934, in *La Opinión* Fidel Murillo continued his litany of reasons for the death of the theatre:

> Estremece pensar en la verdad. Lo que falta es público. Hace unos cuantos años, bastaba cualquier incentivo minúsculo para

arrastrar a las multitudes a los salones de espectáculos. Tres
llenos, en sábado, domingo y lunes, eran de cajón. Los demás
días, cuando se les reforzaba con alguna attracción, o un estreno
cualquiera, se defendían decorosamente. Ahora, ni con grandes
atracciones—a no ser que se trate de José Mojica, de Dolores del
Río o de Lupe Vélez—se puede llenar el teatro. Las excusas que
se dan son las del calor, la mala situación económica de la colonia, etc. La verdad desnuda, desagradable como todas las verdades
que hieren, es la asentada antes: que ya no hay público para
nuestros teatros.

Y es que desde hace algún tiempo, han estado saliendo de re-
torno a México, grandes corrientes de repatriados, oficial o pri-
vadamente. Quedan en Los Angeles las familias que no han
podido abandonar la ciudad o las que no han querido hacerlo.
Aquéllas, piensan más en resolver el problema del momento, que
en divertirse. Estas, prefieren francamente el espectáculo
americano.

Los viejos son pocos. Los jóvenes han aprendido inglés, y se
encuentran con que un teatro de primera les ofrece variedades de
primera también, más película, orquesta, etc., por una cantidad
ínfima, algo que no puede hacer nuestros teatros, que no cuentan
con más patrocinio que el de la colonia de habla española local.[18]

As early as 1930 the Hispanic artistic community had become
devastated. Under the headlines of "ES TERRIBLE LA SITUACIÓN DE
LOS ARTISTAS EN LOS ANGELES," on December 13 of that year Gabriel
Navarro informed the public of the hunger and destitution being experienced by the theatrical artists. Without revealing their names,
he alluded to artists receiving food from the county, others dispos-
sessed of their homes, others who spent their nights in all-night res-
taurants with a cup of coffee. And the few that did find work in the
one theatre (Hidalgo) that was still employing artists some three
times a week were getting paid no more than two dollars a day. As
far as the "adventures" touring to nearby towns, they only resulted
in a few pennies apiece for the artists. The times when an artist
could make eight to ten dollars per show—not per day—were gone
forever.

Many were the economic factors working against live theatre in
Los Angeles for the Hispanic community. But they also translated
into the economic feasibility of showing films over risking the considerable investments in theatre companies and orchestras to support them. As noted above by Fidel Murillo, cinema ticket prices
plunged to keep audiences coming. There was no way during the De-

pression to support all the talent and technical personnel involved in live performances of dramas, *zarzuelas,* and *revistas.* Even the famous Compañía de Revistas Roberto Soto, featuring the celebrated comedienne Delia Magaña, had to turn back from the border on its tour from Mexico City in 1934 because no theatre in Los Angeles would risk booking it. Frank Fouce and Carlos Emmanuel may be criticized for their role in promoting the cinema over theatre, but they were also able to sustain small variety shows at their cinemas for a number of years and even, at times, as Fouce did in late 1934 at the California, book in such large companies as Los Pirríns for two weeks with a heavy publicity campaign. Periodically *La Opinión* informed its readers of the fortune of the stars that used to dominate the Los Angeles stages. As of October 6, 1933, don Chema was triumphing at the Politeama in Mexico City; Margarita Carbajal had gotten fat and retired in Madrid; Virginia Fábregas had finally retired in Mexico City; her son, Manuel Sánchez Navarro, was working in films without great success; Elisa Berumes was working in tent theatres in Mexico City neighborhoods; Adelina Iris was trouping through South America; Eduardo Arozamena was working in Baja California with a company of young actors (later he would relocate to Tampa); Carlos Vives was occasionally seen working in comedies and *zarzuelas* in Ciudad Juárez. Romualdo Tirado had become a permanent resident of Los Angeles and was still winning applause on the local stages; during the 1940s he also performed in New York City at the Teatro Hispano. As far as the Areu brothers and Dorita Ceprano, it seemed as if the earth had swallowed them. Little did this chronicler know that Beatriz ("La Chata") Noloesca, formerly of the Areus, was on her way to a second life on the Hispanic stages of New York.

The Los Angeles Playwrights

While it is true that in the Southwest, as in Mexico, Spanish drama and *zarzuela* dominated the stage up to the early twenties, the clamor for plays written by Mexican writers had increased to such an extent that by 1923 Los Angeles had become a center for Mexican play writing unparalleled in the history of Hispanic communities in the United States. While continuing to consume plays by peninsular authors such as Jacinto Benavente, José Echegaray, Gregorio Martínez-Sierra, Manuel Linares Rivas, and the Alvarez Quintero brothers, the theatres and community encouraged local writing by offering cash prizes in contests, lucrative contracts, and lavish productions.

Probably the first Hispanic theatre in Los Angeles to call for local plays was the Teatro Principal, inspired by Romualdo Tirado in 1921. On November 12, 1921, *El Heraldo de México* published an announcement for the Principal inviting local playwrights to submit works in prose or verse of any genre. Works chosen by Tirado to be produced would gain royalties and at the end of the year a contest would be held in which one hundred dollars and fifty dollars would be offered as first and second prizes, respectively. The plays would be judged by a panel and/or by popular acclamation. As mentioned earlier in this chapter, various impresarios of the Spanish-language theatres maintained this tradition throughout the decade, offering at times as much as two hundred dollars in prize money to the winners of the play-writing contests.

It was often reported in the newspapers that the Hispanic theatres drew their largest crowds every time they featured plays by local writers. For instance, Gabriel Navarro wrote in *La Opinión* on April 12, 1930, that the largest profits of 1929 were made at the Teatro México from local plays. Nevertheless, as popular as these plays may have been, business interests at times worked against their production and against the playwrights reaping the benefits of their craft. According to Esteban V. Escalante, writing in *La Opinión* on April 20, 1930, the writer's 25 percent share of the opening-day box office, which often amounted to $100 to $150, led impresarios jealously to limit the author's payment to a flat fee of twenty or thirty dollars or simply to eliminate local plays and produce instead well-worn *obras* in the public domain for which they did not have to pay a dime.

The period from 1922 to 1933 saw the emergence and box-office success of a group of playwrights in Los Angeles composed mainly of Mexican theatrical expatriates and newspapermen. At the center of the group were four playwrights whose works not only filled the theatres on Los Angeles' Main Street but were also contracted throughout the Southwest and Mexico: Eduardo Carrillo, an actor; Adalberto Elías González, a novelist; Esteban V. Escalante, a newspaperman and theatrical director; and Gabriel Navarro, poet, novelist, composer, orchestra director, columnist for *La Opinión*, and editor of *La Revista de Los Angeles*. Writers like Escalante were also important for popularizing on the stage in Mexico the life of Mexicans in the United States, for once they had returned to their homeland they continued to compose works based on their experiences in California.[19]

The serious, full-length plays created by these authors addressed the situation of Mexicans in California on a broader, more epic scale, often in plays based on the history of the Mexican-Anglo struggle in California. Brígido Caro's *Joaquín Murrieta*, the tale of the California bandit during the gold rush days, not only achieved success on the professional stage but was also adopted by the community for political and cultural fund-raising activities. Such groups as the Cuadro de Aficionados Junípero Serra performed this play to raise funds for groups like the Alianza Hispano-Americana, according to *El Heraldo de México* (December 27, 1927). Eduardo Carrillo's *El proceso de Aurelio Pompa* dealt with the unjust trial and sentencing of a Mexican immigrant and also was performed for fund-raising purposes in the community.[20] Esteban V. Escalante's pieces, however, were more sentimental and Gabriel Navarro's more satirical and humoristic. But Navarro's full-length dramas, *Los emigrados* and *El sacrificio*, again dealt with the epic of Mexicans in California, the latter play with a setting in 1846.

By far the most prolific and respected of the Los Angeles playwrights was Adalberto Elías González, some of whose works were not only performed locally but throughout the Southwest and Mexico, made into movies, and translated into English.[21] His works that were produced in Los Angeles ran the gamut from historical drama to dime-novel sensationalism. The most famous of his plays, *Los amores de Ramona*, a stage adaptation of Helen Hunt Jackson's California novel *Ramona: A Story*, broke all box-office records when it was seen by more than fifteen thousand people after only eight performances (*El Heraldo de México*, June 9, 1927) and soon became a regular item in many repertoires in the Southwest, having also been acquired by Virginia Fábregas for performance on her tours. So popular was *Ramona* that composer L. Mendoza López offered to buy the rights and tour it throughout Mexico as a *zarzuela* with music that he would write for it (ibid., January 1, 1929). Two of González's other plays dealt with the life and culture of Mexicans in California: *Los misioneros* (formerly titled *La conquista de California*) and *Los expatriados*. Probably his second most successful work was the sensationalist *La asesino del martillo o la mujer tigresa*, based on news stories in 1922 and 1923 (ibid., October 14, 1923). Another suspense thriller was his *La casa del misterio*. On a more sentimental note are his *El sátiro, Sangre yaqui o la mujer de los dos, La mal pagada, La desgracia del pobre, La flor del fango* (based on a novel by Vargas Vila), *Nido de cuervos*, and *El enemigo de las mujeres*.[22] Two other plays are related to the Mexican Revolution: *La muerte de Francisco Villa* and *El fantasma de la revolución*. Another play, *Los hijos de Pasquino*, seen in Mexico City but written in Los Angeles and copyrighted in the United States in 1941, is a three-act "tragi-comedia mexicana," a copy of which is on deposit at the Sociedad de Escritores in Mexico; the copy includes no production information. All the other plays by González are lost.

As far as the life of Adalberto Elías González is concerned, it was generally known in the newspapers of Los Angeles that he was from Sonora and that he had military experience there and, partly on this experience, he based his play *Sangre yaqui*. In fact, González was born in Altar, the state of Sonora.[23] He moved to Los Angeles in 1920 to further his studies after having graduated from the Escuela Normal in Hermosillo. We must assume that he remained in Los Angeles at least until 1941, the copyright date of his last known play. Most of the other data about his life are related to his career as a writer. He occasionally wrote for the Los Angeles newspapers, including a serialized "Historia de Francisco Villa" for *El Heraldo de México*, out of which developed his play on the same subject in 1923. González also published a novelized version of *El sátiro* (Los Angeles: Linotipografía Hispano Americana) in 1923 and a history book, *México a través de su historia; resumen histórico de México hasta 1937* (Los Angeles: Ediciones para Farmacia Hidalgo), in 1937.

In 1924 González began working steadily for *El Heraldo de México* as a movie critic. In 1924 the Hidalgo debuted four of his plays, his having come to the forefront in the various play-writing contests. It is as a playwright that González is most important. So great was his fame by 1928 that not only were the theatres in Los Angeles producing his plays but in that year alone they were being staged as well in Hermosillo, Mexicali, El Paso, and Nogales, Arizona, as a number of companies whose tours started from Los Angeles had picked up his works. Guz Aguila contracted to produce González's material in Mexico City, and Maestro Luis Mendoza López contracted to write music for his *Ramona* and convert it into a *zarzuela*. Whether any of these agreements were ever fulfilled is not known.

One curious fact about González is that he seems to have been working in 1933 in Los Angeles, collecting information for the Mexican government on its detractors and enemies.[24] In addition, he was charged with rectifying any false information about Mexico through his work on the newspaper. As such, he was designated a reserve confidential agent of the president of Mexico.

Among Adalberto Elías González's most interesting plays is *Sangre yaqui*, which received its debut at the Teatro Hidalgo on April 24, 1924. The three-act play is a melodrama whose plot development is reminiscent of many of the Spanish and Mexican plays that nurtured California audiences at the turn of the century. Set on an hacienda in Yaqui territory in Sonora, the action involves two brothers who fall in love with the same woman, Lydia. The younger of the two, Lázaro, perversely seduces Lydia and then abandons her and goes to study in the city. José Manuel, the older brother, develops a romantic relationship with Lydia, who keeps her prior relationship with the younger brother a secret until her wedding day. On that same day Lázaro appears, determined to regain Lydia. José Manuel finds out after the wedding what has occurred and also that Lydia and Lázaro have renewed their relationship, which leads José Manuel to reap vengeance by having his brother killed. In the end it is revealed that Lázaro was not really José Manuel's brother; he was Lydia's. This leads Lydia to commit suicide in the last scene of the play, and José Manuel, his love triumphing over jealousy, pardons her.

Another melodrama that won a permanent place for González's plays on the stages of Los Angeles in the 1920s was *La flor del fango*, which debuted on January 19, 1928, at the Teatro México. According to the *Heraldo de México* critic on January 21, 1928, *La flor del fango* was one of the best plays he had ever seen and, despite its having been inspired by Vargas Vilas's novel *Ibis*, was truly original. It is the story of Dolores, a poor self-sacrificing servant and governess who gets involved in the marital politics of an aristocratic family. Rafael, who is promised to another, falls in love with Dolores, who in turn is promised to Ricardo. Luisa, Rafael's fiancée, surprises Rafael with Dolores and, in turn, Rafael digs up a relationship that Luisa is having; their wedding, naturally, is cancelled. Things become even more complicated and all the blame falls on the tragic Dolores, who becomes destitute and ostracized in local society until the last scene, when she is vindicated.

The three-act drama *Nido de cuervos*, which opened at the Teatro Capitol on September 30, 1926, was, according to *El Heraldo de México* (October 2, 1928), a typical slice of middle-class Mexican family life. A suffering mother sacrifices herself to give everything to her children, who abuse her maternal love and commit atrocious acts. In 1928 the work was again produced at the Capitol, this time by none other than the Virginia Fábregas company, with, of course, Virginia Fábregas performing the role of the mother with virtuosity.

In March 1928, González opened to mixed reviews with his romantic drama *El enemigo de las mujeres*, the story of a boxer whose love for a woman stops him from winning the championship belt. In its debut production, Romualdo Tirado played to great effect the humorous role of don Tomás, the promoter and manager of a stable of boxers. The play had other high points as well, such as its well-structured plot. But on March 3, 1928, the *Heraldo de México* critic, Rafael Ybarra, was not convinced that boxers were enemies of women. The debut performance was not only attended by Hispanic boxers Bert Colima, Paulino Uzcudún, and others, but boxer Caballero Huarache also had a role in the play.

Romualdo Tirado again became important in González's career with *La casa de misterio* by bidding the highest for this detective drama to be staged at the Teatro México. In addition, the theatre offered a cash prize to any member of the audience who could guess the outcome of the play by the end of the second act. The work itself dealt supposedly with one of the many adventures of the real-life Mexican detective Valente Quintana. Besides dealing with a hair-raising crime, the work also incorporated a romantic subplot and alternated serious scenes with comic ones. Of course the ending of the play consisted of a complete surprise.

As noted above, not all of González's plays were typical commodity theatre fare: sentimental melodramas, sensational crimes, boxers and ladies, the aristocracy, detective stories. González also explored California Mexican history, the Mexican Revolution, and the real-life drama of the Mexican expatriate community in Los Angeles. His 1926 play *La desgracia del pobre,* while still cut in the melodramatic pattern, was a timely piece set in Los Angeles in the Mexican exile community. On April 28, 1926, he debuted another work, *Los expatriados;* whether this was a new play or a newer version of *La desgracia del pobre* is not known. What is clear, however, is that Adalberto Elías González was the most adept playwright in the Hispanic community, knowing full well what moved his audiences, especially to tears and admiration.

Unlike González, Eduardo A. Carrillo, a native of Veracruz, came to Los Angeles as an actor in 1922 in the company of María Teresa Montoya. In the early twenties he made Los Angeles his base and took on many of the serious leading men roles that were available, but he also at times formed his own companies, not only to work in Los Angeles but also to tour the Southwest. It was even reported by *El Heraldo de México* on September 8, 1925, that he was operating a small vaudeville circuit in Arizona. Despite his active career as an actor and company director, Carrillo was a prolific playwright, one of the main luminaries of the Los Angeles stage. What characterizes his work is his persistence in developing Mexican national and expatriate themes: in *Los hombres desnudos* (1922), in which he explored machismo; in the tale of the Mexican Robin Hood, *Heraclio Bernal o el rayo de Sinaloa* (1923); in *El zarco,* a drama based on the novel of the Mexican Revolution by the same title (1924); in *El proceso de Aurelio Pompa* (1924); and in *Patria y honor* (1924). In addition, Carrillo also wrote plays dealing with modern social problems:

the four-act comedy *Un crimen más* (1938)[25] and *Ley—Escena de la vida real* in one act (1938).[26]

By far Carrillo's most important contribution to the serious dramatic literature of the Southwest was his *El proceso de Aurelio Pompa*, the emotive docudrama of the arrest, trial, and execution by hanging of a Mexican laborer. The play won itself a permanent place in the repertoire of many of the Los Angeles companies and was even taken up by amateur groups conscious of prejudice against Mexicans. The play itself bridged the gap from art to reality as it was used in numerous fundraisers, first for the defense of Pompa himself and later to raise money for his widow. So popular had the play become with audiences and impresarios that one theatre critic pleaded with the impresarios to let the dead rest (*El Heraldo de México*, December 12, 1925).

Despite this protest, of course, *El proceso de Aurelio Pompa* saw numerous productions throughout the late 1920s and early 1930s. The play itself was organized in a prologue, "La ilusión del dólar," and three acts, "La realidad," "La ley," "En capilla." These titles seem to indicate that the play must have developed the typical theme of immigration by a laborer in search of the almighty dollar and the streets paved in gold, only to become disillusioned ("La realidad"). Added to this, of course, were the problems of discrimination and persecution, as had occurred in the real life of Aurelio Pompa.[27]

Carrillo also wrote in a lighter vein, creating *zarzuelas* and *revistas*, often in collaboration with Gabriel Navarro. His 1922 *revista*, *Los Angeles al día*, with Gabriel Navarro, lived on to see numerous performances throughout the decade. Other popular musical comedy one-acts were *Malditos sean los hombres* (1924), a parody of the popular play *Malditas sean las mujeres; Su majestad, la carne* (1924), with Gabriel Navarro; *Eva triunfadora* (1925) and *En las puertas del infierno* (1925). In Mexico he deposited two *revistas* with the Sociedad de Escritores in 1938: *Del mecapal a la cámara*, dated 1937, and *Fotos de actualidad* (no date).[28] In the latter *revista* there are some passages indicative of Los Angeles local color and the comic dialogue that stereotyped Mexican workers in the United States as well as Mexican Americans. The title seems to indicate that the *revista* is made up of daily scenes and, therefore, the inclusion of Los Angeles landmarks and dialect seems to indicate that the piece was actually written in Los Angeles and performed there. *Fotos de actualidad* is, in fact, as many *revistas* were, a loosely tied together series of dialogue, local color scenes, and music and dance. Carrillo also composed the music for his *revistas* as well as for his *zarzuelas*.

Gabriel Navarro, originally from Guadalajara, came to Los Angeles as an actor and musician in 1922 in the Compañía México Nuevo. Like many of the other playwrights, he was also a journalist. In the latter, parallel career, Navarro worked for newspapers in Los Angeles and San Diego, mainly as a theatre critic and, during the Depression and demise of the theatre industry, as a movie critic. In 1923 he launched a magazine, *La Revista de Los Angeles*, but it is not known how long this periodical lasted. While in San Diego in 1925 it is most probable that he was associated with the newspaper *El Hispano Americano*, which also printed his novel, *La Señorita Estela*, in that same year.[29] A play by that same title was debuted by him on December 9, 1925, in San Diego.

As a playwright and composer, Navarro experimented with all the popular dramatic forms from drama to *revista*. His known works include the following: *Los Angeles al día* (1922), a *revista* created with Eduardo A. Carrillo; *La cuidad de los extras*, a *revista* he wrote and staged at the Teatro Principal in 1922 as the director of his own Compañía de Operetas, Dramas, Zarzuelas y Revistas Mexicanas; *Su excelencia el amor* (1922), a *revista*; *El gran visir* (1923), a *revista*; *La venganza* (1924), a drama; *Su majestad, la carne* (1924), a *revista* written in collaboration with Eduardo Carrillo; *La maldita guerra* (1924), a *zarzuela*; *La señorita Estela* (1925); *México quiere paz* (1926), described as an *apropósito cómico-lírico* (musical comedy theme piece); *La ciudad de irás y no volverás* (1927), a *revista*; *Los emigrados* (1928), a drama; *La sentencia*, a drama; *El sacrificio* (1931), a drama; *Loco amor* (1932), which took California for its setting; *Alma yaqui* (1932), a drama; *Cuando entraron los dorados* (1932), his only play that did not open in one of the major Hispanic theatre houses but in the María Auxiliadora Hall; *Las luces de Los Angeles* (1933), a *revista*; *El precio de Hollywood* (1933), a *revista*; *Los Angeles en pijamas* (1934), a *revista*; *Revista de radio 1934*; and *La canción de Sonora* (1934), a *revista*.

As can be appreciated from the above, Navarro's favorite genre was the *revista*. It allowed him to put to use both his talents as a composer and writer, in addition to the technical knowledge that he had accrued as an actor and director. In the *revista* Navarro was the celebrant of Hollywood night life and the culture of the Roaring Twenties. One of his most successful works in this genre, *La ciudad de irás y no volverás*, had an elaborate production for its debut at the Teatro Hidalgo on November 13, 1927. Included in the work were fourteen musical numbers, including one for an Arabian scene, another one in which the chorus line represented the Los Angeles Spanish-language newspapers, accompanied by couplets of piquant political satire, a series of fox-trots that were sung and danced, as well as some *bataclán,* or scantily dressed choral numbers. The work itself was divided into five scenes: Mexico, a Hollywood hotel, a movie studio, an apartment room in Los Angeles, and Mexico City. The plot follows a dreamer who comes to Hollywood in search of a career in films. While in Mexico he had become rich and famous; in Hollywood he never gets beyond anonymity. As he becomes more and more disillusioned, he encounters a series of common Hollywood types: a star-struck aspiring actress, an infatuated extra, Mexicans who have forgotten their Spanish before even learning English, those who deny their Mexican identity and call themselves "Spanish," and many others. Again it can be seen that, as in Carrillo and others, even so light a piece as *La ciudad de los extras* took on the heavy task of satirizing Mexicans assimilating Anglo-American culture. Amid all the glitter and music of the *revista,* the social function of reinforcing the nationality and the culture was forefronted.

Gabriel Navarro's serious works draw upon his experiences growing up in Guadalajara and his twelve years in the Mexican army in Veracruz and Sonora during the Mexican Revolution. Both *La sentencia* and *Alma yaqui* directly reflect military campaigns in which he participated. It must be assumed that *La maldita guerra* and *Cuando entraron los dorados* are also based on the Revolution, as well. *La venganza,* set in the Valley of Mexico, also takes the Mexican Revolution for its background. Under circumstances similar to those in Pedro Calderón de la Barca's Golden Age play *El alcalde de Zalamea,* a dashing young military captain and his troops are billeted on the hacienda of a paralytic old man and his beautiful young wife. As in Calderón's play, the relationship that develops between the young woman and the captain ends in tragedy.

Navarro's plays *El sacrificio* and *Los emigrados* take California as a setting in 1846 and in the 1920s, respectively. The latter play uses as a background the expatriate status of Mexicans in the Los Angeles community to show the breakdown of family and culture, with intermarriage and divorce ending in a bloody tragedy. A young Mexican abandoned by his wife, Mary, finds another to love. Mary refuses to give him a divorce and complications ensue, with Mary's drunken brother killing her while trying to shoot the young protagonist. In the end, of course, the young man is free to marry his beloved and reestablish harmony. On March 16, 1928, *El Heraldo de México* criticized the play for its poor structure and its use of coarse language and poor taste.

Esteban V. Escalante was another of the playwright-journalists who on occasion directed his own theatrical companies. His works include *La pura verdad* (1926), *La muerte* (1926) in one act, *Un beso en las tinieblas, La cómica,* the *revista Tres piedras, La vida de amor de Rodolfo Valentino, La que lo amó locamente* (1928), *Al fin solos* (1928), *Las mariposas de Hollywood* (1928), *La agonía de un sueño* (1930), *Almas trágicas* (1932), *Las incomprensibles* (1933), *La cuerda floja* (1933), and *Sangre de tigre* (1933) in one act. Most of his works seem to have been three-act plays. When Escalante returned to Mexico, *La Opinión* stated on April 2, 1933, that he had resided in Los Angeles for almost fifteen years.

One playwright who fared extremely well on the Los Angeles stages was the Salvadoran Gustavo Solano, who went by the pen name of el Conde Gris. In 1927 he was under contract to the Teatro Principal and later to the Teatro Hidalgo to write plays for production. The noted Romualdo Tirado himself produced and acted in Solano's works. Of all of the journalist-playwrights, Solano had the greatest number of works published and the most adventurous life. In his book of poems, *Composiciones escogidas* (Hermosillo: Talleres Artes Gráficas Cruz Gálvez, 1923) Solano lists the following works as having been published: *Verso, Fulguraciones, Trinidad de arte (poesía), Nadie es profeta en su tierra* (a play in two acts of verse), *Apóstoles y judas* (an allegory of the Mexican Revolution; Laredo: Laredo Publishing Company, 1915), and *La sangre, crímenes de Estrada Cabrera (cuatro actos-verso).* In his book, *Uno más— Prosa y verso,* published in Los Angeles in 1929, he added the following to the list: *México glorioso y trágico (Revolución Mexicana en escena—Prosa y verso), Con las alas abiertas (prosa).* Here he also mentioned the following works about to be published: *Prosas dispersas, Prosas rítmicas, Verbo de combate—Política,* and *Comedias y revistas—Teatro.* In his *Volumen de una vida* (Ambers, Belgium: Ratinckx Frères, 1932) are included four of the works that were staged in Los Angeles: *El homenaje lírico a la raza, La casa de Birján, Las falsas apariencias,* and *Tras de cornudo, apaleado.*[30] There also exists a *suelta* edition of *La sangre,* the tragedy that deals with the Guatemalan dictator Manuel Estrada Cabrera.[31]

Gustavo Solano's involvement with Mexico and its politics translated into his writing of two brief allegorical pieces for the stage which were meant for production during patriotic celebrations: *Apóstoles y judas,* a declamatory allegory of the Mexican Revolution, and *El homenaje lírico a la raza,* an allegory which illustrates the birth in Spanish America of mestizo culture, with Spain, Latin America, Columbus, Cuauhtémoc, Time, and the Twentieth-Century Indian as characters. Both pieces were performed in Los Angeles on various occasions. Another play, *La sangre,* is a four-act tragedy that vividly depicts the crimes and finally the overthrow of the Guatemalan Manuel Estrada Cabrera and is probably the motive for the annotation in Solano's file at the Secretaría de Relaciones Exteriores (Ministry of Foreign Relations) in Mexico City as to his having insulted Guatemala. There is no record of the play having been performed in Los Angeles, although the play *Sangre humana* by an unnamed local author and supposedly dealing with the Mexican Revolution was staged at the Principal in 1926. Could this have been Solano's adaptation of *Sangre* to the circumstances of the Mexican Revolution? *Las falsas apariencias,* a twenty-page *juguete cómico,* was performed numerous times in Los Angeles. It is a raucous and perfectly crafted farce about newlyweds who cheat on each other, with the wife's lover disguised as the maid. In the end, the two cuckolded lovers joyfully accept the outlandishly complicated lie fabricated by Aurora, the wife. *Tras de cornudo, apaleado* is another broad farce which deals with infidelity. The twenty-two-page *sainete* develops a comic plot of cuckoldry of the ignorant, old husband by his young wife and his nephew, who is a novitiate entering the priesthood. The plot situation thus allows for numerous *double entendres* and puns based on religious language and the Bible. *La casa de Birján* is a tragedy in three acts and a prologue which openly acknowledges the influence of Jacinto Benavente's *Los intereses creados.* The plot weaves a moralistic tale of deceit with the allegorical figure Birján, who represents the love of money, freely interacting with the realistic characters to bring about their downfall. For some unknown reason, *El Heraldo de México* on August 8, 1926, classified the drama as having socialist tendencies. What it does do is criticize business and government leaders in the name of Humanity, another allegorical character in the play.

In addition to his extensive record of creative writing, Gustavo Solano led a very fruitful career as a journalist, beginning in his native El Salvador but first assuming some prominence in New Orleans, where he was the managing editor of the *Pan American Review* and the founder and editor of the bilingual weekly *La Opinión* from 1911 to 1912 while he was serving in the port city as a consul for El Salvador. In 1912 he moved to Laredo to become editor of *El Progreso,* then later to Saltillo, Coahuila, Mexico, as founder and editor of the daily *La Reforma.* During the period of the late teens he was involved as a soldier in the Mexican Revolution, also doing a stretch in the penitentiary in Mexico City for his political activities. In 1920 his long-standing relationship with Los Angeles' *El Heraldo de México* began with his assignment as an editorial writer. In 1922–23 he was in Hermosillo, where he was editor of the *Revista Sonora* and the *Diario Sonora*. In 1927 he founded *Baja California Ilustrada* with editorial offices in Tijuana, but it was actually published in San Diego.[32] In 1929 he left Los Angeles.

As a creative writer, his first play, *Nadie es profeta en su tierra*, was written and produced in El Salvador at a young age. He later began publishing his books of poetry in New Orleans. In many of the newspaper accounts of his activities he is called a poet and philosopher. In the files of the Ministry of Foreign Relations in Mexico City he appears as a Salvadoran national imprisoned in a penitentiary in Mexico City (1916), a journalist who has insulted the government of Guatemala (1918), and a gunrunner (1924).[33] Add to this additional travels to Cuba, Puerto Rico, and points in the United States and we have one of the most interesting and colorful of the Los Angeles playwrights.

Another playwright who led a politically involved life which was translated onto the stage was Brígido Caro (1858–1940). The native of Alamos, Sonora, was a journalist who also began writing plays. He had to leave his home when his play *Heraclio Bernal* caused him problems with the Durango authorities.[34] He resettled in Zacatecas, where he became editor of *El Amigo de la Verdad*. He later moved to Guadalajara, where he was imprisoned for his journalistic activities. In 1888 he returned to Sonora to work in the government bureaucracy and to edit *El Sonorense*, a newspaper which supported dictator Porfirio Díaz but in which Caro attacked foreigners exploiting Mexican labor. In the following years he held other government posts and served as editor of *El Eco de Sonora* and *Evolución*. He became a strident opponent of Madero, and on November 20, 1911, participants in a popular uprising dragged him out of his house in Alamos and placed him on the train to the border. He later received amnesty and returned to Sonora to publish *El Mutualista*. In 1914 he was again expelled. In Nogales, Arizona, he published *El Día*, a political tabloid, and in 1920 he became part of the staff of *El Heraldo de México* in Los Angeles, later rising to become editor of the newspaper, which he often used as a platform from which to attack Mexican president Plutarco Elías Calles. Twenty years after coming to Los Angeles, he died.

Caro's *Heraclio Bernal o el rey de los bandidos* may have been one of the various plays with the same or similar title that were produced on the stages of Los Angeles and the Southwest. His obvious sympathy for his Robin Hood–type social bandit and his use of the play as a forum for political and social criticism foreshadowed the creation of his two plays that were written and produced in Los Angeles: *México y Estados Unidos* (1927) and *Joaquín Murrieta* (1926).

In 1928 Caro also wrote and staged *El Niño Fidencio*, a *revista* based on the discredited folk healer of northern Mexico. *México y Estados Unidos* was inspired by certain anti-Mexican sentiments expressed by Calvin Coolidge at the American Press Association banquet on April 25, 1927. *El Heraldo de México* on April 29, 1927, assured its readers that Caro's allegory was strictly patriotic and historical and did not deal with political and religious questions, although it must be assumed that at least an indirect defense of Mexico must have been part of the play, especially since Caro was currently serving as president of the Liga Protectora Latina.

In *Joaquín Murrieta* Caro relates the tragic tale of the honorable Murrieta, who becomes a bandit to avenge injustices at the hands of Anglos during gold rush days. Following the time-proven pattern of social banditry, Caro once again, as in *Heraclio Bernal*, was able to relate historical matter and folklore to the current sentiments of the Los Angeles Hispanic community. In the prologue and three acts, Caro vividly protrays the savage attack on Murrieta and his family which leads him to demonstrate generosity and altruism among his own kind and to punish "los 'outlaws' de raza sajona" (Anglo-Saxon outlaws). Such was the success of the now lost play that amateur and community companies staged it numerous times for benefits and charities. For its December 27, 1927, production at the Teatro México, a special appeal was made to the members of the Liga Protectora Latina, the Alianza Hispano Americana, the Foresters of America, and Los Leñadores del Pacífico to attend.

It seems that Brígido Caro either spent part of the early years of the Depression in Tucson, Arizona, or toured there frequently, for in 1929, 1930, and 1931, *El Tucsonense* reported on the staging of three patriotic allegories by him for the local Alianza Hispano Americana: *La gloria de la raza, La virtud y la ciencia,* and *La bandera de la alianza* (October 22, 1929; July 31, 1930; October 10, 1931; January 1, 1931; November 3 and 11, 1931).

Another playwright whose political activity brought him as an exile to Los Angeles was Antonio Helú, who was born in San Luis Potosí on July 17, 1902. As a law student he became a member of José Vasconcelos's entourage and had to leave the country when his mentor went into exile.[35] In Los Angeles he wrote for *El Heraldo de México* as a journalist and for magazines in Mexico as a short-story writer. As a playwright he had two plays produced on the stages of Mexico City: *Un crimen en el jurado* and *El visionario.* He also worked in Mexico City and Los Angeles writing movie scripts based on theatrical works, including *Malditas sean las mujeres* and *Nostradamus.* Monterde (1970: 180) also registers two one-act pieces by

Helú: *Introducción a una comedia de Pirandello* (1927) and *La comedia termina* (1928). In Los Angeles he wrote and saw two of his comedies staged: *El gangster* (1932) and *El hombre que todo lo arreglaba* (1932). He also wrote a *revista* and a sketch, *Esta noche me emborracho* and *La coartada*, which were staged at the Teatro México, and another *revista*, *La ciudad de los temblores* for the Teatro Hidalgo in 1933, shortly before his return to Mexico. Another *revista* produced that year, *Los cuatro náufragos*, was used to raise funds for striking Mexican agricultural workers. But one of his most interesting works for the purpose of our study must have been *Los mexicanos se van*, a one-act play produced at the Teatro Hidalgo in 1932. According to *La Opinión* (June 20, 1932), the play documents how Mexicans were being forced by the authorities to leave the contry during the Repatriation. These last two plays illustrate once again the intimate relationship that at times surfaced between the Hispanic stage in Los Angeles and social and political activities.

A journalist-playwright whose works seem to have nothing to do with politics was José Gou Bourgell, from Cataluña, Spain. A resident in the Los Angeles–Calexico area from 1924 until his death in 1937, Gou was one of the perennial entrants in the play-writing contests, despite the audiences never seeming to appreciate his efforts, according to *El Heraldo de México* (May 1, 1928). In Los Angeles he was a member of the *Heraldo de México* staff in the late twenties and in Calexico he served as the editor of *La Voz* and *El Mundo al Día* during the years 1935 to 1937. He is known to have authored five plays for the Los Angeles stages: *La mancha roja, El crimen de la virtud* (1924), *El parricida* (1926), *El suicida* (1927), and *Virginidades* (1928). The first of these plays failed horribly at its debut at the Teatro Principal, according to *El Heraldo de México* (June 26, 1926). The second play was a dramatic comedy in three acts that depicted Mexican customs and, as *El Heraldo de México* pointed out on October 19, 1924, it pointed the way for other playwrights to create Mexican theatre without relying on *peladitos* and *chinas poblanas*. About *El parricida* nothing is known. *El suicida* is a social drama which shows how the illicit love affair of a father destroys a wholesome relationship between his son, an aspiring playwright, and his beloved. At the very moment of triumph for Jorge as a playwright, his conflict with his father leads him to commit suicide with an overdose of cocaine. While receiving a generally glowing review from *El Heraldo de México*, the play is also said to have had problems with plot articulation and the incorporation of scenes that just functioned to lengthen the play, especially in Act Two. His fifth play, *Virginidades*, was panned outright by *El Heraldo de México* on

May 4, 1928, for its overly complicated plot that even confused the actors in the last two acts.

Numerous other playwrights of varying talents ascended to the stages of Los Angeles. Some, like Agustín Haro y Tamariz, the editor of *La Prensa de Los Angeles*, were able to continue their careers on the stage and in journalism upon returning to Mexico.[36] Another, poet-novelist-playwright Miguel Arce, a minor functionary in the Mexican consular corps in the United States from 1920 to at least 1928,[37] seemed to live from hand to mouth, despite his novels of the Mexican Revolution, *Ladrona!* (1925) and *Solo tú* (1928), having been successfully published by Casa Editorial Lozano in San Antonio and despite the former of the two novels meriting a second edition in 1928 and a dramatic version on the Los Angeles stage. He, too, worked for *La Opinión* in Los Angeles. The names of many more playwrights appear in the theatre chronicles of the newspapers who have one or two titles to their credit and then disappear forever.[38]

An example of a playwright who remained in Los Angeles and continued to produce works for the stage into the 1950s is Rafael Trujillo Herrera. Trujillo, born in Durango in 1897, immigrated to Los Angeles in 1926 and remains there to this date. In the late 1920s and early 1930s he began writing plays for the stage and for radio broadcasts; in 1933 he began directing his own radio show.[39] On August 20, 1934, *La Opinión* reported on three radio dramas written by Trujillo for a benefit for "El Eco de México" radio show: *Pancho Villa, La serenata de Los Angeles,* and *Doña Chiche en Jaligú.* In 1940 Trujillo became associated with the wPA, for which he wrote a play, *El bandido,* which was also later staged in 1940 under the title of *El derecho de la fuerza* by Virginia Fábregas at the Mason Theatre.[40] It was later published under the title *Revolución.* During the 1960s Trujillo published numerous works in various genres in Los Angeles, Mexico, and elsewhere, including a number of these through his own publishing house, Editorial Autores Unidos, in Los Angeles. In all, Trujillo claims to have written some fifty one-act plays, two in four acts, and twelve in three acts. During these years he also directed five or more theatre groups, although most were probably made up of amateurs connected to drama classes that he taught. As the director of the Instituto Norteamericano de Intercambio Cultural, an organization related to the Mexican Instituto Nacional de Bellas Artes, Trujillo had as many as ninety drama students at a time in his classes. The founding of his little theatre house, Teatro Intimo, in 1974 was an outgrowth of this institute. Trujillo's most famous three-act plays, for these are the ones listed in his books, are *Revolución, Estos son mis hijos, La hermana de su mujer, Cuando la vida florece,* and *A la moda vieja.* His two four-act dramas are *Juana Tenorio* and *Una luz en las tinieblas,* the former of which was written for Virginia Fábregas, who became ill before she could stage it.

Of *Revistas,* Comics, and Composers

Revistas were musical reviews that had developed in Mexico under the influence of the Spanish *zarzuela,* French *revue,* and vaudeville but had taken on their own character in Mexico as a format for piquant political commentary and social satire. Also, like the *zarzuela,* which celebrated regional Spanish customs, music, and folklore, the Mexican *revista* also created and highlighted the character, music, dialects, and folklore of the various Mexican regions. During the Mexican Revolution the *revista política* in particular rose to prominence on the Mexico City stages, but later all the *revista* forms degenerated into a loose vehicle for comedy and musical performance in which typical regional and underdog characters, like the *pelado,* often improvised a substantial part of their roles.[41] The Los Angeles stage hosted many of the writers and stars of *revistas* that had been active during the time of formation of the genre in Mexico, including Leopoldo Beristáin and Guz Aguila.

In the theatres of Los Angeles and the Southwest were staged most of the *revistas* that were popular in Mexico and that were of historical importance for the development of the genre. Such works as *El Tenorio maderista, El país de los cartones, La ciudad de los volcanes,* and numerous others were continuously repeated from Los Angeles to Laredo. As has been seen above, Guz Aguila was for a time a perennial attraction at the Los Angeles theatres. Even important composers of scores for the *revistas* like Lauro D. Uranga graced the Los Angeles Hispanic stages.

In Mexico and later in Los Angeles, most of the *revista* writers were also newspapermen who naturally exhibited an interest in politics and current events. Through the works of these playwrights and composers, for the first time on Mexico City stages and before middle- and working-class audiences the lives of *peones, campesinos,* and the urban working class were depicted in such works as the *zarzuela En la hacienda* (1907) by Federico Carlos Kegel, which was important in the evolution of the *revista,* especially in its attack on the system of peonage in Mexico.[42] The most popular *revista* at this early stage of development was *El pájaro azul* (1910) by José Ignacio González and Julio B. Uranga, with music by Luis G. Jordá and Lauro D. Uranga. It attacked the regime of dictator Porfirio Díaz and called for agrarian reform. At its debut at the Teatro Guerrero it starred Leopoldo Beristáin. Numerous actors and *revista* writers were jailed for their political criticism or for their risqué and scandalous *revistas*. Many, like Beristáin, were exiled.

For Armando María y Campos and other critics and historians, the *revista* represented the birth of a truly Mexican national theatre.[43] In the words of Miguel Covarrubias, "These rebellious Mexican *commedias dell'arte* have produced not only a new national theatre, the only one worthy of the name, but a fine corps of actors and comedians whose style and careers have been strongly influenced by the dominant politics of the time."[44]

With their low humor and popular musical scores, the *revistas* in Los Angeles articulated grievances and poked fun at both the U.S. and Mexican governments. The Mexican Revolution was satirically reconsidered over and over again in Los Angeles from the perspective of the expatriates, and Mexican American culture was contrasted with the "purer" Mexican version. This social and political commentary was carried out despite the fact that both audiences and performers were mostly immigrants and thus liable to deportation or repatriation. It must be remembered that the performance language was Spanish, and in-group sentiments could easily be expressed, especially through the protection of satire and humor. Even such a sensitive theme as the Repatriation could be treated in *revistas*. An announcement in *La Opinión* on July 23, 1934, promoted don Catarino's *Los repatriados* as follows: "En esta comedia podrá usted saborear las graciosas tribulaciones de los repatriados."[45] The only sign of hesitancy on behalf of the impresarios was the delay of the opening in 1932 of Antonio Helú's play *Los mexicanos se van*, which realistically depicted the forced repatriation of Mexicans from California, according to *La Opinión* (June 13, 1932). This further substantiates the difference between the play and the *revista* as far as which of the two genres was more open to controversial issues.

The Los Angeles writers and composers were serving a public that was hungry to see itself reflected on stage, an audience whose interest was piqued by *revistas* relating to current events, politics, sensational stories, and, of course, the real-life epic of a people living under the cultural and economic domination of an English-speaking, American society on land that was once part of Mexican patrimony. Of course the *revistas* kept the social and political criticism directed at both the United States and Mexico within the lighter context of music and humor in such pieces as Guz Aguila's *México para los mexicanos* and *Los Angeles vacilador;* Daniel Venegas's *El con-su-lado* and *Maldito jazz;* Gabriel Navarro's *La ciudad de irás y no volverás;* Raúl Castell's *El mundo de las pelonas* and *En el país del shimmy;* and *Los efectos de la crisis, Regreso a mi tierra, Los repatriados, Whiskey, morfina y marihuana,* and *El desterrado,* to mention just a few of the *revistas* of don Catarino, who often played a *pelado* in these works.

It is in the *revistas* that we find a great deal of humor based on the culture shock typically derived from following the misadventures of a naive, recent immigrant from Mexico who has difficulty getting accustomed to life in the big Anglo-American metropolis. A plot summary of Romualdo Tirado's *De México a Los Angeles* published in *El Heraldo de México* on November 28, 1920, gives a good idea of an early example of this immigrant-type comedy:

> Un sastre, establecido en la capital de México, ya entrado en años, ha oído hablar frecuentemente de las grandezas y adelantos de los Estados Unidos, y en especial (porque es lo que a él le interesa) lo referente a su oficio. Entusiasmado por las fabulosas noticias que recibe, y ambicionando aprender y hasta hacerse rico, se viene a los Estados Unidos, sin más compañía que una pequeña libreta en la que alguien apuntó algunas frases en inglés, con lo que él cree estar al cabo de la calle en cuanto a la ignorancia del idioma; pero resulta que desde el mismo momento en que llega, se convence de que el librito de marras no le sirve de nada y después de recibir varias hostiles manifestaciones de parte de unos "primos," un gendarme de quien él hace el panegírico, comparándolo con nuestros polizontes, se lo lleva a rastras y lo mete en un hotel donde sigue pasando la pena negra, por no poder hacerse entender. Por fin llega a un restaurante mexicano(?) donde cree estar a salvo de molestias y resulta que le dan un tremendo golpe con el timo de la "indemnización" que le obligan a pagar a un individuo norteamericano a cuya esposa ha invitado a un modesto "ice cream soda." Va nuestro héroe a Venice, y se encanta; pero a pesar de todo, más impresionado por lo desagradable de sus chascos que por la belleza de la playa, decide regresar a México, sin haber aprendido siquiera un sistema nuevo de ensartar agujas.[46]

Later on in the decade, when the Depression and Repatriation take hold, the theme of culture shock is converted to one of outright cultural conflict. At that point Mexican nationalism becomes more intensified as anti-Mexican sentiments become more openly expressed in the Anglo-American press as a basis for taking Mexicans off the welfare rolls and deporting them.[47] In the *revista,* the Americanized, or *agringado*, and *renegado* become even more satirized and the barbs aimed at American culture become even sharper, especially when the platform for comic monologues and *revistas* was now the tent theatre, or *carpa*, which had become the refuge for many out-of-work theatre artists during the Depression.

The most important figure in the history of the Hispanic stage in Los Angeles is without a doubt the great impresario, director, singer, and actor Romualdo Tirado, who was the author as well of numerous *revista* librettos, including the one cited above, *De México a Los Angeles*. Tirado was a Spaniard who had emigrated to Mexico and developed a career on the stage there during his fifteen years of residence. Since his arrival in Los Angeles in the late teens, Tirado had been a prime mover in the Hispanic theatrical and cinematic industries, and, just as importantly, he was also one of the catalysts that brought about the writing and staging of local plays and *revistas*. Through the various companies that he directed, Tirado was able to stage his own *revista* compositions with musical scores by three of the most important composers in Los Angeles, who were often his business partners: Luis González Jiménez, Lauro D. Uranga, and Francisco Camacho Vega. The following are some of the *revistas* created by Tirado in which he also starred: *Clínica moderna* (1921), *Una noche en Los Angeles* (1921), *Tirado dentista* (1921), *Los pantalones de tirado* (1921), *Aventuras de Daniel después de una noche en la Calle New High* (1921), *De Los Angeles a Alaska* (1924), *Tirado en Paramí* (1924), *Tirado bolshevique* (1924), *Tirado en el polo* (1925), *El valiente cobarde* (1925), *Los chorros de oro* (1927), *El trust de los tenorios* (1927), *El padrón municipal* (1927), *El viejo rabo verde en Long Beach* (1928), *Las mariposas de Hollywood* (1928), *Los pizcadores* (1930). As can be seen from the preceding, like many of the other comics, the comic persona created by Tirado was the *raison d'être* for these compositions. In most of these *revistas* he depicted a *pelado*, the typical Mexican underdog. Tirado, himself a light-skinned, blue-eyed Spaniard, not only was convincing in this role, but in a Mexican nationalist spirit he often admonished the *agringado* and *pocho*.[48] According to Luis Felipe Recinos,[49] Tirado wrote the following song that became very popular among Mexican immigrants in Los Angeles; he would sing it while playing a *peladito* to the music of the Mexican song "Dame un beso":

Andas por hoy luciendo
Gran automóvil.
Me llamas desgraciado
Y muerto de hambre.

Y es que ya no te acuerdas
Cuando en mi rancho
Andabas casi en cueros
Y sin huaraches.
Así pasa a muchos
Que aquí conozco,
Cuando aprenden un poco
De americano
Y se visten catrines
Y van al baile.
Y el que niega a su raza
Ni madre tiene,
Pues no hay nada en el mundo
Tan asqueroso
Como la ruin figura del renegado.
Y aunque lejos de ti,
Patria querida,
Me han echado
Continuas revoluciones.
No reniega jamás
Un buen mexicano
De la patria querida
De sus amores.

Of all of his compositions, *De México a Los Angeles,* summarized above, seems to have been his greatest hit, with as many as one hundred performances at the Teatro Novel in 1920 and 1921. On November 20, 1928, the *Heraldo de México* critic, reviewing this *revista,* praised Tirado's mastery and his acute sense of observation of the local scene, highlighting Tirado's satire of *agringados* and of the horrible treatment of Mexicans in the United States. He also congratulates Tirado on the two "cuadros simbólicos" (allegorical tableaux) which close the *revista* in a patriotic apotheosis with the Mexican national anthem. Once again it is worth noting the Spaniard's deep understanding of his predominantly Mexican working-class audiences.

Romualdo Tirado was also the author, with Antonieta Díaz Mercado, of a full-length play based on a Mexican national theme: the stage adaptation of Mariano Azuela's novel of the Revolution, *Los de abajo.* Unfortunately the play was a complete flop on the night of its debut, February 7, 1930. When the theatrical life fell apart during the Depression, Tirado nevertheless stayed on in California. During the 1940s, however, he was able to obtain some work in Puerto Rico and in New York at the Teatro Hispano, according to New York's *El Anunciador* (March 6, 1943).

Unlike Tirado, who settled in Los Angeles to be a theatre impresario and movie producer, Guz Aguila (Antonio Guzmán Aguilera) established a relationship with *El Heraldo de México* as a journalist but still managed to tour his company as far south as Mexico City and as far west as San Antonio when it was not engaged in Los Angeles. Guzmán Aguilera was born in San Miguel del Mesquital on March 21, 1894, studied in Mexico City until 1913 at the Jesuit Instituto Científico de México, and by 1916 had his first play produced at the Teatro Juan Ruiz de Alarcón, *El amor que vuelve.*[50] After that he began developing his career in journalism in various newspapers and from that perch he flew off to the stage as an author of *revistas* that commented on current events. His first great success in this vein was with his *El diez por ciento,* but it was soon followed by *La huerta de don Adolfo,* the *revista* that would establish him as a political playwright; this same *revista* would be performed for at least two decades from Mexico City to San Francisco. By 1919 Guz Aguila was a favorite of the president of Mexico, Adolfo de la Huerta, and numerous other politicians and members of the intelligentsia. He was even named to posts in de la Huerta's and Obregón's cabinets. But Guz Aguila's total involvement with de la Huerta made him persona non grata when power shifted to Obregón and Calles in Mexico. Obregón ordered Aguila's arrest when he and his theatrical troupe were crossing the border back into Mexico at Nuevo Laredo and, after numerous pleas even from his own nephew, Obregón refused Aguilera's release, stating, "Este es más responsable que los generales que acabo de fusilar, porque también creo que su pluma puede hacer más daño que una espada militar."[51] Guz Aguila was transferred to a prison in Mexicali, but he was released shortly thereafter through some trickery of his friends, and in 1924 the playwright-journalist went into exile in Los Angeles. While in Los Angeles he continued to tour Mexico and the southwestern United States.

Too many are the works of Antonio Guzmán Aguilera to adequately study them in these pages. One biographer suggests the startling figure of five hundred theatrical works for Guz Aguila.[52] None of his theatrical work was ever published, and very few librettos have been saved or registered in archives.[53] It is certain, however, that many of his *revistas* were reworked and renamed to accommodate different current events, locations, and audiences. Manuscript copies at the Sociedad de Escritores in Mexico show these changes fully.[54] Also, on June 12, 1925, the *Heraldo de México* critic accused Guz Aguila of pirating and stitching together scenes and old jokes from various sources in his *Oro, seda, sangre y sol*.

In Los Angeles in 1924 Guz Aguila was given a contract by Meyer Trallis, as reported later by *La Opinión* on August 8, 1933, that consisted of one thousand dollars per month to write for the Teatro Hidalgo. According to an interview in *El Heraldo de México*, on June 7, 1924, the Hidalgo establishment also committed a company of thirty artists to be directed by Guz Aguila, with scenography by Pepet, complete costuming, and, basically, more than Guz Aguila had ever dreamed of: "Hay dinero, obras lindas, mujeres bonitas, buena ropa, decorado y sobre todo mucha, pero mucha voluntad y fe."[55] In the same interview, the playwright revealed that his personal motto was "corrigat riendo mores"; that is, customs are corrected through laughter. And an abundance of laughter, color, patriotic symbolism, and naturalism is what Guz Aguila gave his audiences by pulling out and producing his most famous and time-proven *revistas: Alma tricolor, La huerta de don Adolfo,* and *Exploración presidencial.* At the same time he took the opportunity to present himself as a dramatist with the debut of his play *María del Pilar Moreno o la pequeña vengadora,* based on the story of a young girl recently exonerated for murder in Mexico City. It is a play unknown in the Mexican literature on Guz Aguila, having received its debut in Los Angeles on June 16, 1924. Many of the other *revistas* that followed had made a name for Guz Aguila in Mexico City: *La tierra del sol naciente, El jardín de Obregón* ("Jardín" referring to President Harding), *Sangre en el jaripeo, El príncipe charro, Pierrot mexicano.* But then began to follow the new *revistas,* based on culture and events in Los Angeles: *Los Angeles vacilador, Evite peligro, El eco de México.* In 1927 Guz Aguila returned to the stages of Mexico City but never regained the level of success that he had experienced there earlier. He continued to tour the republic and the southwestern United States in the years that followed.

Eusebio Pirrín decided on his stage name, don Catarino, while in Los Angeles after developing his acts from childhood in his family's tent theatre. Pirrín is also a stage name; the original surname is unknown today (a short mention in San Antonio's *La Prensa* on June 9, 1934, makes it likely that the real family name was Torres), although through Eusebio's mother he was related to the very famous bullfighter, Rodolfo Gaona. His father was a popular clown in the Treviño circus. Born in Guanajuato, Eusebio toured with his family principally in the United States Southwest and somewhat in South

America. He did not appear in Mexico City until the Depression, when he made his debut at the Teatro Principal. Don Catarino was baptized as such by a Los Angeles impresario, who took the name from a comic strip that ran in *El Heraldo de México*.[56] Upon reaching Mexico City, he found that many of his imitators had been exploiting on the stage there the character that he had developed: a tiny old man with a big bushy mustache. Eusebio himself, however, was only a teenager and in his early twenties when portraying don Catarino. Don Catarino was so short and small that women from the chorus line would pick him up like a baby.[57]

The Pirrín family company, directed by and starring don Catarino, was a perennial presence on Los Angeles stages in the late 1920s and the 1930s and somehow managed to even get bookings there during the worst days of the Depression. All of the *revistas*, songs, and dance routines of the Pirríns were original, most of them creations of the enormously innovative don Catarino. Although don Catarino's role was that of a little old *ranchero*, much of the humor, settings, and situations for his work truly represented urban culture through picaresque adventures. His *revistas* are too numerous to list here except for these few: *Catarino madre, Los amores en Tijuana, Catarino en Hollywood, El reloj de pulsera, El niño Fidencio, El barbero de Cucamonga, El doctor don Catarino, Trienta anõs de vicio o la vida de un jugador, La gran vacilada, Los Angeles en pijama, Catarino en el infierno, Los efectos de la crisis, Regreso a mi tierra, Los repatriados, El desterrado,* and *Whiskey, morfina y marihuana.* As can be observed from some of the titles, the real-life dramas of the Depression, exile, and Repatriation were topics that don Catarino did not hesitate to elaborate on in this generally light-hearted, lyric genre.

Another writer who was said to have been favored by working-class audiences was Daniel Venegas, author of a picaresque immigration novel, *Las aventuras de don Chipote o cuando los pericos mamen.*[58] Venegas reveals himself in this novel and in his weekly satirical newspaper, *El Malcriado,* not only to have identified with the working class but also to have been a laborer himself. Whereas most of the other writers studied here came from middle-class and privileged backgrounds, Venegas proudly considered himself to be a Chicano or immigrant Mexican worker. Besides writing and publishing his newspaper and his novel, in which he often used Chicano dialect, Venegas also directed a theatrical company, the Compañía de Revistas Daniel Venegas, for which he created such works as *El maldito jazz* (1930), *Revista astronómica* (1930), the satirical *El con-su-lado* (1932), and *El establo de Arizmendi,* about the popular boxer, Baby Arizmendi. Venegas was also a frequent entrant in the play-writing contests with such works as the *zarzuela ¿Quién es el culpable?* (1924), and the plays *Nuestro egoísmo* (1926) and *Esclavos* (1930). All of these plays reappeared on the Los Angeles stages through productions by the companies of Romualdo Tirado and even Virginia Fábregas. *Nuestro egoísmo* was reportedly dedicated to Mexican women, to their honor and defense. If *Esclavos* was anything like his novel and the stories that he published in *El Malcriado*, then it most surely must have dealt with the conditions of slavery which Mexican laborers confronted on the railroads and elsewhere. *¿Quién es el culpable?*, with music by Ernesto González Jiménez and the great baritone Rodolfo de Hoyos in the lead in its 1933 production, is a drama of middle-class family life in Jalisco. Julio, an orphaned landowner, returns to claim his land and future bride, a childhood sweetheart, after finishing his schooling in Guadalajara. His love is not returned and, as his intended bride is escaping with her seducer, she is killed by him; however, Julio is the one arrested and imprisoned. As the tragedy was precipitated by Julio's actions but the girl was killed by her seducer, the *zarzuela* ends with the ponderous question of "Who is the guilty one?" The August 31, 1924, review of the *zarzuela* praised the libretto but lavished far more praise on the score by González Jiménez.

There were many other writers and composers of *revistas* that brightened the Los Angeles stages. One of the first to really fix the form and popularize it in the City of the Angels was Félix Medel of the Teatro Novel, who, like many others in Mexico at that time, used the form as a framing device for his comic antics. Whether his *revistas* carried titles like *Revista estomacal alimenticia* or simply *Revista Medel no. 3*, the picaresque view of life and the Moorish actor's satire of the authorities was sure to delight working-class audiences. Another to continue the convention of the comic framed by a *revista* was Hilario Altamirano, or don Chema, whose Compañía de Atracciones Mexicanas don Chema toured extensively in the Southwest and performed for a season at Los Angeles' Teatro Principal with such *revistas* as *Jazz Chema, Chema policeman, Luna Park, Cabaret de amor, Chema candidato, Chema periodista, Los viejos verdes,* and *Chema peluquero.* The great Mexican comics and *revista* writers Leopoldo Beristáin and Roberto Soto ("El Panzón") were visitors to the stages of Los Angeles and the Southwest who brought their immortal genius and further inspired the writers who produced works here on a more permanent basis.[59] Various actors like Raúl Castell, a comic tenor in Tirado's troupe, tried their hands at the *revista;* he had more success than most with his *El mundo de las pelonas, La pocha y el charro, El Tenorio en California,* and *La señorita 1925,* all composed and staged in 1925. In all of their years on the stage in Los Angeles, we only have news of one *revista* each by Arturo Chacel (*Se solicita un marido,* 1922) and Ramón Méndez del Río (*Los repatriados,* 1933).

The Los Angeles Hispanic community was also fortunate to have a number of outstanding Mexican composers in residence: Ernesto González Jiménez, Lauro D. Uranga, Luis Mendoza López, Francisco Camacho Vega, and the father-and-son team of José and Ernán Sandozequi. Besides directing the orchestras for *zarzuela, revista,* and musical comedy productions, all of these maestros composed the scores (and sometimes the librettos) of *zarzuelas,* operettas, and *revistas.*

Of course the most important of them all was Ernesto González Jiménez, who, since his arrival in Los Angeles in 1915, had become a prime mover in the theatrical community, forming a long-lasting entrepreneurial partnership with Romualdo Tirado, directing the house orchestras at the Capitol and México theatres, and composing the scores to numerous *revistas,* including the most important: *De México a Los Angeles* (1920), *El alma de México* (1923), *Las luces de Los Angeles* (1923), and *El mundo de las pelonas* (1924). González Jiménez also took companies on tour in the Southwest and operated his own music academy. In a February 18, 1925, interview in *El Heraldo de México* by Salvador Gonzalo Becerra, his theatrical labors were praised for fomenting a truly national theatre. Prior to coming to Los Angeles, González Jiménez had begun directing an orchestra at the tender age of nineteen and had already toured throughout the Mexican republic.

Probably one of the most able and respected composers and conductors to find refuge in Los Angeles during the years of the Revolution was Luis Mendoza López, the composer of numerous operettas. Because of the anticlerical aspects of the Revolution, he left his native Guadalajara with his family and theatrical company to tour up the west coast of Mexico, into El Paso, and over to Los Angeles, where he remained for a little more than four years.[60] After the Cristero War in Mexico had ended, Mendoza López returned to Mexico in 1930 carrying a sound film, *La jaula de los leones,* that he had made with Romualdo Tirado; it was only the second Spanish-language talkie ever made and he promoted it all the way back through the Southwest and Mexico. While in Los Angeles the Mendoza López company continued to perform, most notably at the Teatro México, where he directed the house orchestra. The maestro continued to compose operettas and operas, some of which he debuted at the Teatro México with his own Compañía de Zarzuelas y Operetas Mendoza López. Included in his works performed in 1928 at the Teatro México were *Jugando al amor* (operetta in three acts), *La fiera del mar, La gallina ciega, El héroe de la guerra* (operetta in two acts), *Ninón, La destrucción de Roma* (operetta in five scenes), *Un drama en el Japón* (operetta in three acts), and others. He also performed his *zarzuela Zepelín Zepelón* and various of his *revistas* such as *El angel de la libertad.* On March 3, 1930, *La Opinión* announced that Maestro Mendoza López was forming a company made up of Los Angeles artists to tour the west coast of Mexico but not to perform in Los Angeles because no theatres were available. The article further stated that he owned a complete selection of costumes and scenery, besides his extensive collection of his own works. With that, one of the classiest of the Mexican theatre people returned to his homeland, armed with a new performing arts technology.

Another composer to spend a number of years in Los Angeles was the versatile Lauro D. Uranga. A native of the state of Hidalgo, Mexico, born ca. 1890, Uranga came to Los Angeles as a member of the Trío Iris, which became incorporated into Romualdo Tirado's various theatrical companies. The trio, made up of Uranga and Adelina and Angelina Iris, was a song-and-dance act that had toured throughout the Hispanic world, including Spain. Uranga, considered by *El Heraldo de México* on March 24, 1925, as a virtuoso on the piano and violin, was a composer who wrote the score for many of the *revista* librettists, such as Tirado and Castell. *El Heraldo de México* also stated that Uranga had debuted some twenty-five of his own works on the stages of Los Angeles, including operettas like *Santita,* which was based on Federico Gamboa's famous novel, *Santa.* Other operettas by Uranga were *El príncipe de Sevilla, Guillermo el conquistador* (libretto by A. Grisel), and *El sueño de Caín.* Uranga also composed the music and wrote the libretto for the following *revistas: Studio Iris, Alma peregrina, La influencia española,* and *México tal cual es.*

One fine father-son writing team had Los Angeles as a base and graced the stages of all of the Hispanic theatres there: José and Ernán Sandozequi. At the head of their Compañía de Arte Frívolo in 1932 and later leading their Compañía de Arte Moderno in 1934, their names often appeared linked to original *revistas* like *El libro de oro de Hollywood, Cuentos de navidad, Llama un taxi, Espíritus de alquimia, Los sueños de Nerón, La aventura de María Elena,* and *Los Angeles en el infierno.*

To summarize briefly, the following points have been substantiated and should become a basis for future study: (1) the Hispanic stage flourished in the Southwest during the 1920s and 1930s; (2) Los Angeles was the most important center of Spanish-language writing and production for the stage in the history of the United States—the Los Angeles plays, besides representing commodity theatre, also reflected the life, culture, and politics of Mexicans in California and the United States; (3) the *revista* genre that was so popular throughout the Southwest and Mexico was the most important vehicle in reflecting the language, culture, and political sentiments of Mexicans; (4) the theatre declined as a result of various forces coming to bear at the same time: the Great Depression, voluntary and forced repatriation of Mexicans, the rapid expansion of the talking film industry, which could offer inexpensive shows during those economically difficult times.

It should be emphasized that the lights of the professional Hispanic stage were not snuffed out all at once but that they were dimmed over a period of five to ten years, beginning with the advent of the economic cataclysm of 1929, during which time impresarios and artists struggled to keep the stage alive, even to the extent of forming cooperatives. Furthermore, after the Hispanic professional stage finally died, many of the professional artists put their theatre at the service of a wide array of community activities, including raising funds for local religious charities and celebrating patriotic and religious holidays. These artists simply continued to perform the most popular plays from their secular repertoires and only occasionally did they stage plays with religious themes. A few of the artists were able to extend their careers in the United States by performing solely as vaudevillians between film showings at movie houses; by moving to New York, where Spanish-language vaudeville survived until the early 1960s; by working in local Spanish-language radio broadcasting; or by working for a very brief period for the WPA. Very few, like Rafael Trujillo Herrera, were able to maintain a life solely in the theatre.

3. San Antonio

Before the mass of refugees from the Mexican Revolution began arriving in San Antonio around 1910, it was Laredo, not San Antonio, that was developing as an important center of Mexican theatrical activity. This judgment may be based, however, on the fact that more newspaper accounts from the 1890s and early 1900s have survived from Laredo than from San Antonio. In the two decades in question, 1890 to 1910, there are more reports of Mexican troupes touring to Laredo than San Antonio, and there is even a record of earlier theatre construction and earlier establishment of resident theatrical companies in Laredo than in San Antonio. The Mexican stage in Laredo will be studied in detail in chapter 6.

What word does come to us of theatrical activity in San Antonio before 1910 regards itinerant troupes that performed more or less regularly in Laredo and occasionally toured up to San Antonio: the Compañía Dramática Solsona and the Compañía Solórzano (*El Correo de Laredo*, March 31, 1892). Another itinerant troupe which later took up residence in San Antonio was the Concepción Hernández-Villalongín company, which performed at the opening of the new opera house in 1900 (Brokaw 1975: 24). There is also word of

another company which performed in San Antonio before the outbreak of the Mexican Revolution: the Compañía de Variedades Carlos Landeros, which surfaced again in later years (*El Regidor*, September 28, 1905). All of these itinerant companies were like the
companies that had earlier begun performing in California: they
were built around family nuclei; they presented programs of three to
four hours with mostly Spanish melodramas and lighter, briefer entertainments such as afterpieces and song and dance; they performed
on Sunday evenings; they at times worked by subscription; and all of
them toured northern Mexico and began extending themselves
northward into the United States.

The Solsona company had been performing in San Antonio since
at least 1891, according to *El Correo de Laredo* (March 31, 1892). By
1898 the Compañía Dramática Solsona was performing every Sunday at the Salón San Fernando (*La Fe Católica*, May 7, 1898) and was
still around in 1904, using the hall at the San Antonio marketplace
and the Salón de Benevolencia (*El Regidor*, August 25, September 9,
1904). Like the earlier California companies, the Solsona repertoire
ran the very short gamut from the melodramatic to the historical: *El
esclavo de su culpa, El angel conciliador, L'hereu, Hija y madre,
Paula o la nueva adúltera,* and *Los mártires de Tacubaya.* Two
newer, more contemporary works were also included: *Malditas
sean las mujeres* and *Me conviene esta mujer.*[1] San Antonio's newspaper *El Regidor* on August 25, 1904, noted the upcoming performance of three Mexican plays by the Solsona company on Sunday,
August 28: *Expiación* by Prágedis García, *Aprietos estudiantiles* by
A. López Manzano, and *Torrijiano* by Rafael Téllez Girón. Also noting that the authors would all be present at the performance, the
newspaper wished them new laurels and monetary rewards. These
must have been local playwrights who were considered professionals by the newspaper. *El Regidor*'s review of the Solsona performance of the tragedy *Torrijiano* on September 9, 1904, seems to indicate again that the author of the play, Téllez Girón, was a resident
of San Antonio.[2]

The review also mentions that the audience was so moved by the
tragedy that it stood up various times and was even brought to tears.
The play itself is compared to the Greek classics and Shakespeare's
tragedies: "Drama de vida en que los personajes adquieren propor-
ciones shakesperianas y apocalípticas, y en que el horror, un horror
tormentoso, sacude al público estupefacto, como el huracán a una
palmera. En el océano trágico se libra un duelo colosal de pasiones
infinitamente humanas."[3] This would have been quite an accom-
plishment for the modest performance halls of those times. During

these two decades the only theatres housing the Mexican players seem to have been halls: the San Fernando Cathedral hall (which continued to be used into the 1930s), the hall at the marketplace (as in Laredo), the Salón de Benevolencia, and the Salón de la Unión, which *El Regidor* on September 28, 1905, states the Landeros company was using in 1905.

Despite what was seemingly an auspicious beginning of the century, with original works by local playwrights produced by what may have been a resident company, the evolution of the Mexican/ Hispanic stage in San Antonio did not produce a body of dramatic literature comparable to that of the Hispanic playwrights of Los Angeles. Nor did the theatrical activity expand and flourish as much as it did in Los Angeles, the city that drew the greatest number of refugees from the Revolution. While the story of Los Angeles' Hispanic theatre is one of proliferation of the Spanish-language theatre houses, companies, and playwrights, the story of San Antonio is one that illustrates the persistence of resident companies, actors, and directors who kept Hispanic drama alive in community and church halls after being dislodged by vaudeville and the movies from the professional theatre houses. San Antonio's is also the story of the rise of a number of vaudevillians to national and international prominence. Finally, San Antonio also became a center for another type of theatre, one that served an exclusively working-class audience: tent theatre.

The Theatres

The two most important professional theatre houses serving San Antonio's Mexican community were the Teatro Zaragoza and the Teatro Nacional. Numerous other halls, cinemas, auditoriums, and theatres accommodated Spanish-language performances on a more irregular basis than at these two houses. During the teens and early twenties the following establishments housed shows in downtown San Antonio by professional companies: Teatro Aurora, Teatro Juárez, Teatro Hidalgo, México (primarily a movie house), San Fernando Cathedral hall, Beethoven Hall, Union Hall, the Palace, the Majestic, the Aztec, the three Princess movie houses, Casino Hall, and Beneficencia Mexicana, the latter hosting the Solsona company in 1905 but by the early twenties only accommodating amateurs.

Of these theatres, the Teatro Aurora is noteworthy, for its leasing by the Compañía Hernández-Villalongín in 1910 marked that company's decision to reside permanently in San Antonio in order to escape the hostilities of the Mexican Revolution. This simple hall over a print shop on South Santa Rosa Avenue advertised in *El Regidor* on May 12, 1910, a daily change of program and an admission price of five cents. Broadsides from the Villalongín collection at the Benson Latin American Collection at the University of Texas show that the troupe was performing nineteenth-century heroic and melodramatic works in May and September 1911: *El jorobado o Enrique Lagardere, Los dramas de París o las dos huérfanas, Don Juan Tenorio, Chucho el Roto,* and *La abadía de Castro.* But in the case of both of the latter works, three acts of the plays were offered on one night and four on the next. What was new in the company's repertoire, however, was a popular revolutionary piece, *El Tenorio maderista.* Also in 1911 general admission had risen to ten cents, five cents for children.

The San Fernando Cathedral hall remained active, accommodating performances by various companies, including the Gran Compañía Lírico Dramática de Carlos Villalongín in 1915, with such works as *Los hijos del Pirata Rojo, María la emparedada* (see broadside in Villalongín collection), *Tierra baja,* and *La huérfana de Bruselas* (*La Prensa,* October 17, 1915) and again in 1918 with such patriotic plays as *El grito de Dolores o el cura Hidalgo, El Cinco de Mayo,* and *Maximiliano I, o el cerro de las campanas.* The San Fernando hall continued to house professional companies touring from other cities and shifting over from other theatres in San Antonio, like the Hermanos Rosete y Aranda Puppet Company, coming from Union Hall in 1916, according to *La Prensa* (April 8, 1915), and the Compañía F. Díaz de León, that came to the San Fernando after having performed at the Teatro Nacional and the Aztec, according to *La Prensa* (October 28, 1915).

The Teatro-Salón de la Unión was operated by the Sociedad de la Unión, an association of San Antonio mutual aid societies that included the following Woodmen of the World camps: México, Libertad, Bosque de Chapultepec, Violeta, and others. The Unión used the theatrical facilities to raise funds for its various activities. Teatro-Salón de la Unión had been housing Mexican theatrical performances since at least 1905 and continued to do so until the society decided to build a new theatre. One of the last companies hosted at the old Unión before moving to the new theater was Carlos Villalongín's in March, when *La Prensa* on March 9, 1919, reported its performance of *La mujer adúltera* by José Pérez Escrich. By the end of the year a new theatre, seating two thousand, had been built, financed in part by sales of bonds to the community by the Sociedad de la Unión.

The society itself had invested $30,000 of its own funds, obtained a bank loan for $50,000, and floated bonds for the remaining $20,000, each bond selling for $2.00, according to *La Prensa* (July 20, 1919). It was calculated, based on a survey of the other San Antonio Mexican theatres, that the theatre would be able to make from $1,500 to $2,400 in profits per month, arriving at an annual $24,840 in yearly profits, including the rental of offices on its second floor. *La Prensa* on June 1, 1915, stated that the express purpose of constructing this new theatre was to "levantar el concepto que nuestra raza tiene en el extranjero," or, in other words, create a higher (class) impression of Mexicans in Texas. In fact, the August 30 edition of *La Prensa* promised that only the best Mexican companies would be selected to perform here and only when there were no companies available would movies be shown at the Teatro Unión, but then only those films that were moral, educational, and healthy entertainment.[4] The new theatre housed some of the same performing groups as the commercial Teatro Nacional across town, such as the Cuadro México de Zarzuela, directed by a señor Pajares in February 1921, and such vaudevillians as Paco Escalera, Emma Duval, and Sara Villegas, who appeared in the Nacional and other San Antonio theatres,[5] according to *La Prensa* (October 28, 1921).

Beethoven Hall was much favored by the Mexican community and hosted, among other functions, Virginia Fábregas's company in 1917; community benefits with performances of plays in 1918; the Compañía Mexicana de Opera, directed by Héctor Gorjoux in 1920; Mexican boxing matches in 1921; Los Hermanos Llera, musical concerts by Mexican singers from the Chautauqua vaudeville circuit in 1925; community theatre by Adriana Fuille's company in 1926; La Familia Bell in 1926; and a ceremony honoring the publisher of *La Prensa*, Ignacio E. Lozano, in 1927, at which the *zarzuela Juan José* was performed by professionals. Beethoven Hall was viewed as the proper setting for fine arts by the Mexican community; it was a hall appropriate for more exclusive and higher-class affairs, like opera, concerts, and performances by Mexico's leading lady, Virginia Fábregas. Although the pugilistic art was in greater esteem then than it is today, it still seems difficult to associate it with the high caliber of the other artistic affairs staged there.

By far the most important of these secondary theatre houses was the Teatro Juárez, which opened in 1914. According to *La Prensa* (April 26, 1916), the Juárez offered dramas and comedies on Sundays, Mondays, and Thursdays and smaller, lighter works (*género chico*) and variety acts the rest of the week. *La Prensa* on June 3, 1915, reported that the Juárez was featuring variety acts by Lucina Joya and Manuel Sánchez de Lara, and in 1916 the two hundred–seat theatre hosted the all-important company of María del Carmen Martínez from March until May 23, when the company headed for El Paso's Teatro Estrella. According to *La Prensa* (April 5, 1916), Martínez was not able to use her sets because the stage was too small and lacked wings. Nevertheless, from March 25 to 30, she was able to perform a good selection of Spanish dramas from her repertoire: *Vida y dulzura* by Santiago Rusiñol; *Caridad* by José Echegaray; *La doncella de mi mujer; Pecadora; Amores y amoríos* and *Doña Clarines*, both by the Alvarez Quintero brothers; and the *zarzuela Quién fuera libre*. In April the company performed the following *zarzuelas: Chin chun chan, Quién fuera libre, El bateo, Niños llorones, Pobre Balbuena*, and others, according to *La Prensa* (April 20, 1916). Before leaving for El Paso in May, the company performed the following for a by now dwindled audience, *La venganza de la gleba*, by Federico Gamboa, *El estigma* by José Echegaray, and the *zarzuela El vencedor de cien batallas*, which was supposedly written and composed by members of the company. For the *La Prensa* critic, attendance at the company's performances at the Teatro Juárez was a patriotic duty, and any particular function was "un espectáculo verdaderamente artístico, culto y moralizador. Por otra parte puede considerarse como una obra patriótica y de solidaridad de raza, el concurrir a las veladas artísticas del Teatro Juárez donde un modesto grupo de actores mexicanos luchan por la vida en suelo extraño, haciéndonos conocer las más preciadas joyas del teatro contemporáneo en nuestra lengua materna o sea el dulcísimo y sonoro idioma de Cervantes."[6]

The same critic was crestfallen when the community did not attend the performance of one of the few Mexican plays in the Martínez repertory: *La venganza de la gleba* by Federico Gamboa.[7] The critic called Gamboa a victim of the Revolution, like the majority of the Mexican community in San Antonio; he further stated that this nationalistic play was written by an author "que es espíritu nacional, que es tinte azteca; que es águila de Tenoch."[8] After these patriotic pleas, the next word we have of the Juárez is its hosting of the Compañía Hermanos González vaudeville troupe from December into February; it was reported by *La Prensa* on February 13, 1917, that this company had such success there that its contract was renewed and it had decided to buy a house and settle permanently in San Antonio, only occasionally to tour to Eagle Pass, Del Rio, and Piedras Negras, Coahuila. The last word of the Teatro Juárez was that Sam Lucchese had purchased its land to construct there in 1917 what would become the most important theatre in San Antonio history: the Teatro Nacional. But before we study the Nacional, let us briefly review its predecessor, also owned by Sam Lucchese: the Teatro Zaragoza.

Teatro Zaragoza

Sam Lucchese arrived in San Antonio from Sicily with his brother Joseph in 1882. Beginning in the early 1900s, in association with his cousin Ben Racugna, manager of the Dixie Theatre, Lucchese began to build a theatrical empire in San Antonio and Laredo that was unrivaled. At one time or another, he, with his brother Frank and his son Gaetano, owned and operated the following theatres: Teatro Hidalgo (1913–1914), Teatro Zaragoza, Teatro Nacional, Teatro Guadalupe, Teatro Progreso, Teatro Progreso No. 2, Follies, and Teatro Alameda.[9] The Teatro Zaragoza, which opened in 1912 with the Juan B. Padilla and Carlos Villalongín companies, was bought by Lucchese and his cousin Racugna about 1915, when the lease on the Dixie Theatre ran out. Sam later remodeled and enlarged the 200-seat theatre to hold 850 seats. During the 1920s and 1930s it was his son Gaetano, however, who took over the administration of this empire.

Unlike what seems to have been the practice in Los Angeles during the teens, the Zaragoza, and probably the other theatres as well, closed periodically, establishing three clearly demarcated seasons: Christmas to Easter, May to August or September, and September or October to Christmas. This also was a practice in Mexico and Spain, but that changed about this time to year-round programming, as in Los Angeles.

The first company reported by *La Prensa* as performing at the Zaragoza was the Compañía Dramática de Pajujo, directed by Arturo García Pajujo, a comic actor known as "el chato Pajujo" (the flat-nosed Pajujo) on the stages of Mexico City as late as 1911 (Mañon 1932: 345). He is remembered in Pablo Prida's memoirs as "un magnífico actor de comedia y zarzuela" who by 1924 had retired in Monterrey.[10] In March his company was performing such works as Sebastián Alonso Gómez and F. Luis Manzano's *Benito Juárez o el indio guelatao* but by October had been reinforced by the Ricardo de la Vega company, which integrated into the repertoire such works as the operetta *El Húsar* and the *zarzuelas Postales mexicanas* and *Otelo*. An important member of the de la Vega company, Daniel Ferreiro Rea, would later play a leading role in the Los Angeles theatre movement. On January 1, 1915, *La Prensa* noted that the Zaragoza was now owned by Sam Lucchese and that the Pajujo company had become transformed into a *compañía de zarzuela–empresa Sam Lucchese,* the stock *zarzuela* and dramatic company.

During this time Lucchese continuously hired touring artists to reinforce and expand the Pajujo offerings. Included among these acts was a member of the owner's family, María Lucchese, an opera singer. In 1916, among the acts that took to the Zaragoza stage were figures that would become important in the destiny of the San Antonio Mexican stage: the Hermanos Areu and Bernardo Fougá. By August 1917 the Lucchese family had made a far more important investment; Sam's son Gaetano Lucchese was constructing the new Teatro Nacional on Commerce and Santa Rosa streets. The Zaragoza was thus destined to become overshadowed by the newer, more modern house and would primarily show movies and variety acts during the next two decades.

During the 1920s the Zaragoza, charging twenty cents admission (as compared to the Nacional's fifty-five cents), almost exclusively hosted vaudeville companies to perform between movie showings. Besides employing its own house artists (Sara Villegas, Catalina Rojas Vertiz, Jesús Navarrete, and Roberto Escalera in 1923, for example), the Zaragoza hired the following vaudeville companies: Compañía Nelly Fernández "México Auténtico," Hermanos Justiniani and Higares-Novelty, and the Cuadro de Variedades Iris in 1923. Besides doing variety acts, its house company also performed *zarzuelas* and *operetas de género chico* in summarized and reduced versions, according to *La Prensa* (October 28, 1924). The year 1924 brought Guz Aguila's company to the Zaragoza and 1925 the Hermanos Areu, the Cuadro José Escalera, the Cuadro México Típico, and El Cuadro México Alegre, directed by Juan Suárez, in which Sarita Villegas, Chelo and Manuel Tiesta, and others performed.

On February 5, 1927, P. Viola published an article, "Las Enseñanzas del Teatro," in his satiric newspaper *El Fandango,* which satirized the Zaragoza and the Cuadro México Alegre as a school for good customs.[11] In this article, which takes the form of a fanciful story, a father is content to let his daughters go daily to the Zaragoza since he cannot afford the first-rate theatres. The two daughters are joined by their boyfriends, who snuggle and smooch with them during the movies and whose eyes pop out at La Carcachas (María Luisa García), Sara Villegas, and Chelo Tiesta in their song-and-dance routines. But for the girls, "se les cae la baba al ver a Juanito Suárez y Manuelito Tiesta, y sobre todo al primero cuando sale vestido de charro poblano y se arranca por todo lo alto con alguna canción mexicana."[12] The girls discuss the physical attributes and relative attractiveness of the actors in a combination working-class and teenage dialect. The narrator goes on to show the effects on the two couples of Juanito Suárez and La Carcachas overacting scenes of the melodrama *La plegaria de los náufragos,* and he satirizes in particular her movements: "La Carcachas pone los ojos en blanco, da tres paraditas en el suelo, se lleva una mano al corazón y con la otra se levanta las faldas hasta la rodilla porque se le están empolvando y contesta con acento apasionado: 'Aquí lo guardaré toda mi vida.'"[13] The couples leave the theatre, arm in arm, knowing a thousand times more than what is supposedly learned in the theatre. This account was more than just a criticism of the acting and social mores, it was a direct response to all the established rationale in the Mexican community that considered the theatre to be a school of morality, that the theatre taught young people in particular the language, culture, and traditions of their homeland, Mexico. It was Viola's charge, as writer and publisher of this chronicle, to satirize the shortcomings of the community, and in "Las Enseñanzas del Teatro" he was aiming his pen both at the ignorance of the common folk and the pretensions of the elite while also satirizing the artlessness of the actors and the physical conditions (dirty stage) of the Zaragoza as a second-class theatre.

In 1928 the parade of *compañías de variedades* continued at the Zaragosa. But noteworthy among them was a run by Los Pirríns, who were on tour from their home base in Los Angeles, with all of their original *revistas,* and a run by the Compañía de Variedades don Chema, also very well known. In August the Cuadro de Variedades México Auténtico performed. It included La Bella Netty, who did song, dance, and comic dialogues with her husband, Jesús Rodríguez. The Texas-based couple was important for its durability on the stages of Texas and, during the Depression, New York and for its comic dialogues, which often satirized *pochos* and *agringados,* those who assimilated "gringo" customs and whose Spanish was influenced by and peppered with English.[14]

In 1929, the Zaragoza continued to book vaudeville companies and individual acts, even a physical culturist, El Herculés Alemán. The Cuadro de Variedades Multiforme and Los Pirríns had return engagements, and Jesús and Netty Rodríguez returned with a company now named Cuadro de Variedades México Bello. In August, the Cuadro de Variedades América appeared, and *La Prensa* on August 12, 1929, made the left-handed remark that "no es numeroso el cuadro, ni recurre al tan gastado recurso de 'mucha pierna y chistes cálidos,' y precisamente por esto triunfó,"[15] probably referring to the popularization in the late teens of *bataclán* and *rataplán;* that is, song and dance by chorus girls in scanty costumes interspersed with risqué comic monologues by a *pelado* or other comic type. For the next few years there was more of the same and, as the Depression deepened, more and more emphasis was placed on talking motion pictures and less on the variety acts. Los Pirríns continued to be booked almost yearly into 1934, when we lose track of the Zaragoza in *La Prensa.*

Teatro Nacional

On August 19, 1917, *La Prensa* announced that the event that everyone was awaiting, the opening of the new temple of Hispanic culture, the Teatro Nacional, was near at hand. The María del Carmen Martínez company would inaugurate the new *coliseo* with a Mexican play (as opposed to Spanish) and during her run she would perform various other works by Mexican playwrights. The only problem was that the intended opening for September 16, Mexican Independence Day, had to be postponed until October 1 because the construction was not finished in time. And, as it turned out, María del Carmen Martínez did not arrive until November 3 and she opened her run with *Malvaloca,* the drama by the Spanish writing team of the Alvarez Quintero brothers. But these changes did not discourage the San Antonio audience, which came in such numbers to the inauguration of this 1,200-seat first-class theatre that numerous people were turned away at the doors. For her run at the Nacional, Martínez performed her usual repertoire, which was heavy in Spanish melodrama. The Martínez company played the Nacional into March, with the last two weeks of its stay dedicated to repeat performances of its most popular plays at reduced prices.

On February 19, 1918, it was announced in *La Prensa* that the Teatro Nacional would now open its doors at 10:00 A.M. in order to show movies of the best quality. By May, Lucchese was already booking in such variety acts as the Justiniani brothers, hypnotists, and illusionists to perform between movie showings. Gaetano Lucchese also had his other daughter, Josephine, sing opera between play acts. Later that year she made her debut at the Metropolitan Opera in New York.

After Holy Week, the Compañía Ricardo de la Vega opened at the Nacional with a full fare of *zarzuelas* and operettas for the summer season and was followed by the Compañía Dramática Juan B. Padilla, reinforced by the Villalongín company, opening the fall season. At this point it seems that the Padilla company became the stock company for the Teatro Nacional. By April 13, *La Prensa* was calling the Padilla company the Compañía Dramática del Teatro Nacional. In November the Compañía Rosa Arriaga followed with drama and variety acts. The Juan B. Padilla company returned with drama and *zarzuela* in February 1919 but without the Villalongíns. Then in March and April, respectively, two really important companies occupied the house: Compañía Virginia Fábregas and Compañía de Zarzuela María Conesa. La Fábregas was always a favorite in her virtuoso female roles of European plays. But this was the first time that the stage and recording star María Conesa and her enormous company and entourage had come to San Antonio, a trip now made possible because of the fine new facilities of the Nacional. The newspapers interviewed her and featured advertisements for her Columbia and Victor records of *couplets* and selections from operettas and *zarzuelas*. Unfortunately, Conesa did not draw audiences as expected, which was lamented by *La Prensa* on April 16 and 19. On April 19, 20, and thereafter, however, audiences began to grow, perhaps as a response to Conesa and various other actresses and chorus girls parading around downtown San Antonio in full costume, with mantillas and *mantones* (large flowery shawls) from the *zarzuelas*. Conesa also had photo and autograph sessions at the Fox Company Department Store by a display of her records. At the end of the spring season things quieted down when María Conesa left for a short run in Laredo on her way back to Mexico.

As popular and glamorous as was María Conesa, she did not elicit the admiration in the somewhat elitist *La Prensa* that was lavished on the leading lady of the troupe which played the Nacional that summer of 1919: Carmen Cassaude of the Compañía de Operetas Vienesas Carmen Cassaude de León, directed by Angel de León. In the middle of her run there she was regaled with an original poem in her honor written by Oswaldo Sánchez of San Antonio. The six-stanza poem, published in *La Prensa* on July 18, 1919, not only praised the crystalline voice of the Spanish singer but made her a symbol of solidarity of the Hispanic people (*La Prensa*, April 20, 1919).

The Carmen Cassaude company was made up mostly of Spanish talent and had performed on the Mexico City stages until 1914, when it began touring the republic. The company was seen as bringing the most up-to-date operettas from Mexico City, ones that had not been seen before by San Antonio audiences. The only problem at the outset, however, was that the Teatro Nacional (three-piece) band was not up to Cassaude's standards and, to the embarrassment of the community, had to be reinforced, according to *La Prensa* (May 21 and June 23, 1919).

The fall 1919 season was dominated by variety shows until the arrival in December of the Compañía María del Carmen Martínez, which played until March 1920. This was followed by a drama and *zarzuela* troupe, Compañía María Caballé, and then the Los Angeles–based Cuadro Novel, with more of the same. After the Easter break, the Nacional opened up again with the Los Angeles–based Compañía de Revistas Lauro D. Uranga, directed by actor-playwright Eduardo Carrillo, which offered a selection of political *revistas* from Mexico. In May at his benefit performance, Uranga debuted a *revista* he wrote for San Antonio, *San Antonio en verano*. In June the Uranga company was reinforced by the Hermanos Areu. In August the Martínez company returned again to great success, so much so that people were turned away at the door to the theatre. At this time leading actor Manuel Cotera was still a member of Martínez's company. But the leading man, who was destined to become the backbone of the San Antonio Mexican stage, resurfaced at the Nacional shortly thereafter, in January 1921, at the head of his own company, the Compañía Lírico Dramática Manuel Cotera. At this inaugural run at the Nacional, much of the Martínez repertoire of Spanish drama also resurfaced in the Cotera offerings. Cotera had made San Antonio his home, although he continued to tour throughout central Texas and the Rio Grande Valley for two more decades. Following Cotera were the company of Carmen Máiquez, who was known for her *couplets flamencos*, and the Compañía de Revistas Mexicanas César Chávez, which staged a number of the most famous *revistas* by Ortega, Prida, and Castro, the fathers of the Mexican *revista*.

The year 1922 brought a plethora of vaudeville companies to the Nacional, interrupted only by two runs of the Manuel Cotera company, which was now steadily performing *zarzuelas* as well as dramas, and the Cuadro de Variedades Francisco Díaz de León, which presented a diverse bag of dramas, comedies, operettas, and *zarzuelas*. The Díaz de León company featured a *pelado* among its variety acts, one that brought down one of the most scathing attacks to date by the critics of this character type so beloved of the working classes: "el 'peladito' descamisado y calamburero, que de nuevo torna a presentarse en el escenario del Nacional como avanzada de la tan decantada 'producción artística nacional' que no se entiende si no viene el 'mecapalero', el 'corredor de loterías' o el tenorio de barrio de largos bigotes y mechón rebelde que hace de su léxico una letanía de insulseces y de su presentación un descrédito para el que no conoce México."[16]

It would seem from this impassioned reaction that San Antonio audiences and critics were somewhat more conservative and elite than the Los Angeles ones and/or the working-class Mexicans in San Antonio did not have as much power over the theatre world, the media, and popular culture as in Los Angeles, where even a Spaniard like Tirado had success with his *peladito* and where *revistas* enjoyed many more reviews and greater respectability. It is true that the Los Angeles critics also censured the *pelado,* but it seems never so acrimoniously or so consistently. On the other hand, Leonardo García Astol always insisted that his don Lalo character, which he developed in San Antonio and which he even performed in the tent theatres, or *carpas,* was a "comic hobo" and never ever the lowly *peladito.*[17] Despite Astol's protestations, however, such *peladitos* as don Fito of San Antonio's Carpa García were endemic to the Texas tent shows that served working-class and rural audiences.[18]

The same writer that criticized the *peladito* also began complaining in November that serious plays at the Nacional were poorly attended. On the other hand, the Hispanic vaudeville companies, like those featuring the regional character types and the *peladito,* never lacked audiences. This cry came at a time when the Cotera company had been alternating heavy dramas with *zarzuelas* and the Nacional was charging fifty-five cents general admission, a higher price than the Zaragoza next door was charging for vaudeville, not to mention the more modest admission fees at the other secondary houses.

To the pleasure and relief of *La Prensa*'s theatre critic, Virginia Fábregas had a two-week run of dramas at the end of March 1923. She was followed by the beautiful singer and dancer Nelly Fernández and her vaudeville company. And this critic made a point of applauding her on May 30 for not using a *pelado.* Nevertheless, on June 7, the critic once again unleashed his fury on Raúl Castell—our Los Angeles actor-playwright—for his *pelado* characterization and his improper language, stating that the spectacle was more suited to *jacalones* (low-class theatres); the critic insisted that Mexican shows must be ennobled, not lowered.

Despite the elite tastes of *La Prensa*'s critic, during the remainder of 1923 one vaudeville company after another occupied the stage at the Teatro Nacional, with the exception of a seven-week run from September 28 to November 21 of the Compañía Cómico Dramática Amparo de la Garza, which presented a complete slate of dramas with occasional lighter *entremeses, sainetes,* and *revistas.* Working as a prompter and playwright for the company was Leonardo García, Leonardo García Astol's father. It was he who adapted Vicente Blasco Ibáñez's novel *Sangre y arena* to the stage for the company and he who also wrote such *revistas* as *De México a Texas o efectos de la Revolución*, which included a dialogue with the *La Prensa* newspaper itself.[19]

The new year at the Nacional began with Guz Aguila's company, which at this time included Dorita Ceprano and the Hermanos Areu. The series of Guz Aguila *revistas* was followed by mostly *zarzuelas* and *revistas* performed by the Alejo Pérez Rodilla company, presentations by the stock company, and then a run by the México Bello company, which was directed by the famous *revista* librettist Pablo Prida Santacilia himself of the famous team of Carlos Ortega, Pablo Prida, and Manuel Castro. Following his return to Mexico from exile in New York, Prida and his two partners organized a company to tour to Tampico, Laredo, and San Antonio, with many sets and costumes but not enough money for food for the large company.[20] In San Antonio, besides performing from the repertoire of Prida's own *revistas*, the company also did selections of the same between movie showings at the Palace movie house that Lucchese had arranged in exchange for an agent's fee. According to *La Prensa* on June 13, the troupe also performed at Alamo Plaza, probably publicizing its work at the Nacional. At the Nacional, Prida revealed in a January 8 interview with *La Prensa*, the trio of writers was not going to stage its political *revistas* because it preferred "to wash dirty laundry at home," and these works would be of very little interest outside of Mexico, besides representing a lack of patriotism by showing Mexican political sores and social problems on foreign stages. Nevertheless, México Bello did perform *La elección de Calles* in San Antonio. It also performed a *revista* that was probably written for the tour north to Texas, *Going Up*. After the run in San Antonio, México Bello returned to Mexico City, performing on the way in Piedras Negras, Coahuila, and Monterrey, Nuevo León.

The next full company that we hear from in 1925 at the Nacional is Amparo de la Garza's again in August, this time promising to stage a Mexican (again as opposed to Spanish) play every Thursday. The only dramatic company following de la Garza's is Cotera's, the following year from September to December. Cotera's company at that point included a number of artists that would remain San Antonio residents and become the backbone of survival of Hispanic theatre in San Antonio during the Depression and into the 1950s: Carlos and María Villalongín, Sara and Ignacio Contla, Leonardo García Astol (Lalo Astol) and his playwright-prompter-actor father, Leonardo F. García, and the irrepressible Bernardo Fougá. In 1926 a number of vaudeville *revista* companies took to the stage, including Dorita Ceprano and the Hermanos Areu. Dorita was at the apex of her popularity now and was filling the theatre to standing room only. An additional attraction was her dancing the Charleston and judging a Charleston contest among audience members for a five-dollar prize.

During the summer of 1926 the Nacional was closed for remodeling. The building was enlarged, as was the general admission section to accommodate 1,200 seats. On November 1, the remodeled theatre opened its doors once again; on November 20 Virginia Fábregas's company graced its stage, starting a three-week run. The year ended with a *revista* and operetta company that was followed in January 1927 by the San Antonio leg of the historic tour of the Compañía María Guerrero y Francisco Díaz de León that was discussed in the previous chapter. Following María Guerrero was a series of vaudeville companies, with only the Manuel Cotera and don Chema companies offering a few months of drama. On September 6, 1927, *La Prensa* announced that the Teatro Nacional would henceforth be showing Mexican and European silent movies with dialogue in Spanish. The film industry had just taken a giant step into the Teatro Nacional's main programming.

The year 1928 offered much of the same, except for Virginia Fábregas's annual visit and a run by the Villanova Argentine company, which performed plays from Argentina and Uruguay during July and August. In June the company of the great comic Leopoldo Beristáin performed *revistas* at the Nacional. It was also in June that the Nacional started trying to develop new audiences by offering discounts to high school Spanish-language teachers and students.

The year 1929 was historic in the evolution of Hispanic theatre in San Antonio; it was the year when the Teatro Nacional began showing talking motion pictures. In late May of that year, the Nacional began screening them on Wednesdays and Thursdays. Aside from this novelty, all was the same. Vaudeville and *revista* companies dominated the boards, with the exception of the Fábregas annual visit, which this year featured Adalberto Elías González's play *Ramona.*

During the next few years Mexican/Hispanic vaudeville continued to be featured at the Nacional, along with talking pictures in a more prominent role. As the Depression and the film industry gradually displaced live performances from the San Antonio stages, there came a point when *La Prensa* on April 24, 1932, decried that the Nacional was the only San Antonio theatre offering vaudeville, but because of this it was still attracting large audiences. The only slot now for *drama, zarzuela,* or operetta at the Nacional was at an occasional midnight showing, where it would not interfere with the regular receipts. Presumably, the troupes of local artists organized by Manuel Cotera and Bernardo Fougá were just performing for a percentage of the box office receipts, but in no other way were contracted by the theatre. Lucchese's other theatre, El Progreso, was also holding these midnight functions by Cotera at this time. And thus, in 1932 Gaetano Lucchese and the Teatro Nacional brought the curtain down on the splendid show of live Mexican drama in the professional theatre houses of San Antonio. But the show did not stop here; the next act would be set in community and church halls, in a manner somewhat similar to the beginnings of the theatre movement three decades earlier.

Community Theatres and Church Halls

The valiant response of the resident theatrical artists of San Antonio to their displacement from the professional theatre houses was to take their art directly to the people. Manuel Cotera, Bernardo Fougá, and Carlos Villalongín—all of whom were once united with María Villalongín, Lalo Astol, and Leonardo F. García in Cotera's 1925–26 company—continued to direct and manage companies that now toured the neighborhood halls in San Antonio and also traveled to Austin, Dallas, Houston, Laredo, and small cities during the 1930s. In most cases in San Antonio, theatrical arts were placed at the service of the community and the church during those hard times of the Depression. Most of the performances by the San Antonio artists were for raising funds for one charity and worthy cause or another. Just what percentage of the proceeds of these fundraisers went to keep the artists' life and limb together is not certain today. What is certain is that many of the same secular plays that were formerly performed by professional artists had now found their way into the churches, community auditoriums, and even parks.

The community not only responded by attending and supporting these functions by their now well-known artist-neighbors, but amateur groups and performances began to proliferate in the void left by the absence of professional theatre on a daily or weekly basis. The Cuadro Artístico Granito de Oro, for instance, performed the comedy *Al fin solos* by Mexican authors Lázaro and Carlos Lozano García and the *sainete Un matrimonio modernista* by Carlos Bueno at the Sidney Lanier High School in June 1932. La Asociación de Señoritas Esclavas de la Virgen performed the secular one-act comedy *Levantar muertos* by Eusebio Blasco and Ramos Carrión and the *juguete cómico Los apuros de un fotógrafo* at the Nuestra Señora de Dolores Church hall in January 1930. The Círculo Fraternal Victoria performed the one-act drama *Justicia humana* and the comedy *Los demonios en el cuerpo* in March 1932 at Christopher Columbus Hall. This was followed that month at the same hall by the comedy *Las solteronas* and *El muerto que habla,* a *sainete,* sponsored by the Mexican Orthodox Church. Santa Teresita Church also had an amateur theatre group, which performed in its auditorium in 1932.

But the more serious artistic efforts were in the hands of the three consecrated San Antonio directors—Cotera, Fougá, and Villalongín—in church and community auditoriums that were somewhat better equipped for professional productions. The first and most important of these was the San Fernando Cathedral auditorium. Used since the turn of the century for professional, amateur, and charity performances, the San Fernando had built a long and intimate relationship with the Mexican community. In fact, San Fernando Cathedral had developed out of one of San Antonio's original missions and probably had an unbroken history of religious theatre, *pastorelas,* and pageants. In 1929, a lay organization associated with the cathedral emerged as favoring theatrical arts: Hijas de María (Daughters of the Virgin Mary). This lay society began sponsoring plays by San Antonio's professional actors to raise funds for the church. For the most part, most of the performances sponsored were of secular drama, except during feast days, Easter week, and special occasions. For Mother's Day on May 13, 1929, the society sponsored Netty Rodríguez, Delfino Rangel, and other professionals in *Bendita seas* by A. Nervión. Among other performances sponsored by the organization were Manuel Cotera and his company in *Caridad* by José Echegaray in 1931; it probably sponsored the Cotera troupe numerous times, but the newspapers do not list the sponsoring organization. Other sponsoring lay and community organizations for professional theatre at the San Fernando were Club Mexicano de Bellas Artes, Club de Jóvenes Católicos de San Fernando, Juventud Católica Mexicana, Asociación de la Iglesia San Alfonso, Campamento Cuauhtémoc de los Leñadores del Mundo, Salesianos, Sociedad de Damas Profesionales en Obstétrica (a benefit for the Committee in Defense of the School of Del Rio, Texas), Madres Adoratrices, Sociedad Vasallos de Cristo Rey, and the Club Recreativo México.

The following were plays directed by Cotera at the San Fernando: *La enemiga* by Darío Nicodemi (1930); *La raza* by Manuel Linares Rivas and *La hija de Juana,* a *sainete* by the Alvarez Quintero brothers (1930); *Romeo y Julieta* by Shakespeare and *A la luz de la luna,* an *entremés* by the Alvarez Quintero brothers (1930); *La misión de San Fernando,* a local play written to celebrate the bicentennial of the San Antonio missions (1931); *Caridad* by José Echegaray (1931); *El amor que pasa,* a comedy in two acts by the Alvarez Quintero brothers and *Alma de Dios,* an afterpiece (1931); a *pastorela* for the Christmas celebration (1931); *Buena gente* by Santiago Rusiñol (1931); *Lo que no muere* (1931); *El herrero* by Federico Ohnet (1931); *La condesa María* by Juan Ignacio Luca de Tena (1931); *El rey pacífico* by Father Manuel Sancho for Easter (1932); *La doncella de mi mujer* by Francisco Raparaz (1932); *La madre* by Santiago Rusiñol for Mother's Day (1932); *Manos largas* by Vital Aza (1932); *El beso* by the Alvarez Quintero brothers (1932); *Santa Casilda o la princesa Mora* (1932); *Lo que tú quieras* by the Alvarez Quintero brothers (1932); *El anillo de hierro* (1932); *El reino de Dios* by Gregorio Martínez Sierra (1933); *La media naranja,* a *juguete cómico* by the Alvarez Quintero brothers and *Los apuros de don Polo,* a *juguete cómico* (1933); *El señor cura* (1933); *La dama de las camelias,* a benefit performance for Manuel Cotera (1933); *Las dos madres* (1933); *La vida que vuelve,* a comedy by the Alvarez Quintero brothers (1933); two stage adaptations by writer-actor Leonardo F. García, *¿Cuándo te suicidas?* and *La cenicienta* (1933); *El drama del Calvario* for Easter (1934); *Bendita seas* for Mother's Day (1934); *La casa de Socorro* by Santiago Rusiñol (1934); *El sueño dorado* (1934); *El soldado de San Marcial* by Félix G. de Llana; *La tía de Carlos* (1935); *El cuarto mandamiento* by Martin Scheroff and *Los hombres,* a sainete (1935).

Bernardo Fougá's Cuadro Artístico Alpha performed *Malditas sean las mujeres* and vaudeville, and *La casa de salud* by Joaquín Dicentá and Antonio Paso, both in 1931 at the San Fernando. Carlos Villalongín directed *La jaula de la leona* by Manuel Linares Rivas (1931) and the comedy *De potencia a potencia* and the *zarzuela Torear por lo fino* (1934). The Cuadro Artístico Dramático y de Revistas Estrellita performed there in 1934. Various amateur groups also presented such works as *La gracia de Dios, El martirio de Santa Bárbara,* and *El día de juicio* during these years. Admission to these performances was usually fifty cents for adults, twenty-five cents for children.

After the San Fernando, the church (school) auditorium that was most used for these functions was that of the Inmaculado Corazón de María, associated most with productions by Bernardo Fougá. At the Sacred Heart of Mary, Fougá directed the group entitled Club Dramático del Inmaculado Corazón de María, but it should not be considered an amateur organization, not with such professional stars as Elodia Calvó, Berta Almaguer, Luis Astudillo, and Gonzalo Gómez. From 1931 to 1934 Fougá performed almost as many plays at this church as Cotera did at San Fernando. The last word we have of the club is about its evenings of banco to raise funds to buy a curtain for the auditorium stage in 1934.

Cotera also performed at the Sacred Heart of Mary and at one point was also teaching drama at the Academia Dramática del Inmaculado Corazón de María, where he occasionally integrated one or two of his best students into these plays. Besides Fougá and Cotera, the Cuadro Artístico Montes-Baldit, the Cuadro Artístico Iris, El Club Artístico y de Variedades, and Leonardo F. Garcia's Cuadro Azteca de Drama y Comedia also performed there during these years. But also at Sacred Heart an actor from one of the early touring family companies, José Solsona, surfaced, directing the historical drama straight out of the company's nineteenth-century repertoire, *Los mártires de Tacubaya* by Aurelio Gallardo on March 27, 1932. Had the Solsonas been residing here in San Antonio all along? Had they become a resident company, perhaps playing in a theatre never covered by *La Prensa*, like the Teatro Obrero, mentioned in Manuel Gamio's 1926 survey?[21]

Other halls and auditoriums used by Manuel Cotera and his Compañía Cómico-Dramática were the Our Lady of Guadalupe Church auditorium, where ticket prices ranged from twenty-five cents for general admission to forty cents for reserved seats and fifteen cents for children, the Nuestra Señora de Dolores Church, whose prices were thirty cents general admission, fifteen cents for children's general seating, fifty cents reserved seating, and twenty cents for children's reserved seats, and the Washington Irving School Auditorium. Bernardo Fougá also utilized the auditorium at San Pedro Park and the Sidney Lanier High School auditorium. Luis G. Astudillo, who formed and directed his own troupe, the Cuadro Artístico Kawama, also used San Pedro Park auditorium and the Nuestra Señora de los Dolores school auditorium. Carlos Villalongín and his family remained active during this period, performing at the Ursuline College Hall and at Our Lady of Guadalupe. These performances were in addition to the others by Villalongín mentioned above.

The comic actor Gonzalo ("Flaco") Gómez also formed his own troupe, the Cuadro Artístico Bohemio, which performed at the Amigos del Pueblo hall in 1932 and 1933. The group also included the following professional troupers: character actor Leonardo F. García, leading man Gustavo Puelma, leading lady Zelma Villalongín, and character actress Ester Suárez.

It is not known how many of these troupes that performed in neighborhood auditoriums were also touring out of town during this time. The most active of them all in this regard was Cotera's com-

pany, which somehow stayed together at least until 1940, performing in the San Antonio neighborhoods and touring to secondary theatres and mutualist and church halls in Houston, Austin, Dallas, and
small towns.[22] It is clear from the titles of plays listed in *La Prensa*,
however, that the repertoire used for these community performances
was drawn directly from the dramatic works that these directors and
actors had performed for the last fifteen years in the professional
theatres of San Antonio.[23] Moreover, a definitive preference for serious dramatic works for these performances is also obvious. Cotera,
who had always kept serious drama on the bill at the Teatro Nacional and the other houses, continued to do so at the church and
mutualist halls. Unlike many a Los Angeles company, his troupe
never really converted to doing primarily *zarzuela, revista,* and
variety acts. The same is true of Villalongín's performances. Oddly
enough, although these troupers were now forced to do community
work for their art to survive, they no longer felt the pressure from
theatre managers and owners for higher box office receipts or the
competition from the movies. Thus, with more control over their
stock and performance spaces (humble as they may have been), they
opted for the repertoire that they loved best and that allowed them
to exhibit their virtuosity as serious actors. This also maintained
high regard for their profession and themselves in their community.
Because of these efforts and those of other San Antonio artists like
them, occasional performances of serious drama in the Mexican
community survived well into the 1950s.

Leading Men, Hoboes, *Peladitos,* and Circus Clowns

While San Antonio did not contribute a body of dramatic literature
to the Hispanic stage as did Los Angeles, it did become the home
base and cultural environment that led to the birth and development
of an important community theatre movement. San Antonio also
nurtured the development of two comic actors, Lalo Astol and La
Chata Noloesca, who became living symbols of the survival of Hispanic theatrical arts in the United States. San Antonio, the well-
known winter quarters of American circuses, was also the center of
the Hispanic circus and tent-theatre industry in the United States.
Circus and theatre had been associated together since colonial days
in the Mexican tradition. That association remained strong in San
Antonio, in Texas, and generally throughout the Southwest, as will
be illustrated below.

Like many of the Hispanic performers of the Southwest, Leonardo

(Lalo) García Astol was born into a family that had been in the theatre for generations.[24] Because of the very nature of their travels and tours, the particular nationality of any one family member could be at times hard to fix. Don Eduardo Astol, Lalo's maternal grandfather, was an Argentine; his maternal grandmother was a Spaniard. His mother, Socorro, an actress of some prominence in Mexico, was born in Chile. His father, Leonardo F. García, was Mexican. Leonardo García Astol was born in Mexico City in 1906. When Astol began his acting career he took his mother's maiden surname as his own stage name. Astol's half-brother by his mother became a famous comic actor in Mexico: Fernando Soto, "Mantequilla."

Astol began touring as a child with his mother in Mexico when the Revolution was raging. He states that despite the hostilities the people filled the theatres, they so much needed relief from the carnage. As soon as he reached early adolescence Astol began performing. He toured with the Compañía Roberto Soto until 1921, when he decided to go to Laredo to join his father, who brought Astol with him into the Compañía Manuel Cotera, which was then performing in different Laredo theatres and touring the small towns in the Rio Grande Valley. During their six-month season in Laredo, Amparo de la Garza reinforced and stayed with the company, which then was contracted to play the Teatro Nacional in San Antonio. The company that eventually debuted on the Nacional stage was very large and included, among others, Astol's father and his brother Paco; Catalina Rojas Vertiz, an actress who spent a great portion of her life on southwestern stages; Elisa López, Leonardo F. Garcia's future wife; the comics Jesús Mena and Roberto Escalera, the latter making a career on the San Antonio stages into the Depression; and many others. At this time the company was prepared to do major dramas and *zarzuelas*. After its run at the Nacional, the company began touring again, and in Kingsville, Astol contracted typhus and remained hospitalized there for six months. He later rejoined the company in Nuevo Laredo for a while but separated from it there to return to Mexico City. In Mexico he acted in various places and also worked hand copying roles. He also took a job in a hardware store for a while but left that to join up with his mother in the Hermanas Gutiérrez company in Veracruz, where he was admitted as an actor.

In 1925 Astol returned to San Antonio to join up with his father, brother, and Cotera at the Teatro Nacional. At that time these very important personalities for the history of the Mexican theatre in San Antonio were also in the company: María Luisa Villalongín, Elena Contla, and Bernardo Fougá. After the season at the Nacional, the company toured the small towns, including Benavides, San Diego, and Corpus Christi, where the company split up. In Laredo, Leonardo F. García formed his Compañía Azteca with his two sons and other former members of the Cotera company. Later Cotera reformed his group, including at this point Paco Astol and Socorro Astol (Leonardo's ex-wife and Astol's mother), and gave competition to the Compañía Azteca in Laredo, resulting in both companies doing poorly by dividing the audiences. Then Azteca left Laredo to go *puebleando*, or touring the small towns like Pharr, Mission, Edinburg, and McAllen. Astol continued to work like this with one company and another for a number of years. After working in Torreón with the Compañía Roberto Soto in 1935, he rejoined his now ailing father in McAllen, where his company was still doing plays, afterpieces, and variety acts. It was his father's intention to work all the small towns on the way to Los Angeles, but his father died in Marfa and Astol took over the company; in Arizona, he decided to return to the Valley. Later in Matamoros, Astol became manager of the Compañía don Chema of Hilario Altamirano and from Brownsville set out in 1937 to tour the small towns. But the movies were too much competition and the company was "mal formada" (badly formed); that is, it did not have the appropriate actors and musicians. It nevertheless traveled all of Texas but finally disbanded in San Antonio in 1938.

Astol now went to work with Lucchese as a vaudevillian at the Nacional and the Zaragoza doing comedy routines and dancing. He was paid twelve dollars a week, with four dollars going for his hotel and five dollars for his meal ticket at the Jalisco restaurant. He became such a hit that Lucchese gave him two hundred dollars a week to form and pay his own variety troupe ("cuadro de variedades"). He recruited Netty and Jesús Rodríguez for song and dance and his brother Fernando Soto ("Mantequilla"), among others. During this time he had fully developed his comic hobo character for the duo don Lalo and don Suave, which also did comic dialogues on the radio. During these last few years Astol also worked in tent theatres and also married his second wife, Susie Mijares, an acrobat from the famous Mijares circus family. She became a dancer in his variety troupe.

In 1940 Astol worked in Los Angeles at the head of a *cuadro* formed for him by Frank Fouce at Fouce's theatres: Mason, Arrow, Electric, and California. Upon returning to San Antonio in 1940, Astol again began working at the Nacional and also working as an emcee for "La Hora Comercial Mexicana" on KMAC while he continued to play the Nacional. In the 1940s he also began broadcasting "La Hora Nacional" from the stage of the Nacional. Over the years radio took over as the variety acts ebbed and disappeared. In 1952 he began doing soap operas in Spanish on KCOR radio; he also acted in a radio dramatic series, "Los Abuelitos," with Carolina Villalongín. During the 1950s he emceed a quiz show, "El Marko." In 1956 Astol made the jump to television, where he wrote, directed, and acted in a live television dramatic series, "El Vampiro." From 1967 until the present he has worked for radio KUKA doing "El Mercado del Aire."

As can be seen from the preceding, Astol's life in the theatre illustrates the course taken by Hispanic theatre arts in the United States Southwest, from serious drama to *zarzuela* to vaudeville and the *carpas* and then on to radio and television. Astol, his wife, and associates, Carolina Villalongín and her daughter Sandra Bojórguez, Belia (daughter of La Chata Noloesca), and Mateo Camargo (d. 1985) throughout the years also kept serious drama alive with occasional performances in community and neighborhood productions, and Lalo and Susie Astol to this date occasionally perform comic sketches for events in the community.

One of the greatest stars to develop in the Southwest was La Chata Noloesca, the comedienne who, like Lalo Astol, experienced firsthand the evolution of Hispanic theatre in the United States. Born in San Antonio on August 20, 1903, Beatriz Escalona was raised by her widowed mother, the proprietor of a boardinghouse facing the Southern Pacific railroad station. The young Beatriz assisted her mother by selling food and coffee to train passengers and, later, at age thirteen, she began working in the box office of the Teatro Zaragoza.[25] At age seventeen she began working as an usherette and in the box office at the Teatro Nacional. It was here that she met her future husband, José Areu, and joined up with his family's troupe, was trained as an actress, dancer, singer, and *tiple cómica* by them, and made her stage debut at the Teatro Colón in El Paso in 1920.

The Areus were one of the most important theatrical families on the southwestern circuits. José, Enrique, and Roberto Areu were brothers who had theatre in their blood, much like Astol. Their father, Manuel Areu, was a Spaniard who had managed the Teatro Albizu in Havana for thirty years. He saw to the voice and acting training of his three boys. José, Beatriz's husband, sang bass and played serious leading men; Roberto, who had studied with Enrico Caruso, was a tenor who took on comic parts; and Enrique, who later married the Italian actress-singer Dorita Ceprano, was a baritone who played dashing young men. Their father initiated them as the Trío Trovatore, a singing act that gradually developed into *ópera bufa*. During the Spanish-American War don Manuel and the trio left Cuba and toured all of Central and South America. In Mexico in

1913 the trio had worked the entire Granat movie circuit, acting behind movie screens as the film was projected in an early version of talkies. In the wake of the Mexican Revolution they were already performing in Arizona by 1917 as a *zarzuela* and variety company, Sexteto Estrella de los Hermanos Areu.[26] By the time the Areus incorporated Beatriz Escalona into their acts, they were seasoned actors of melodrama, comedians, singers, and hoofers.

During the entire 1920s the Areus, including Beatriz Noloesca (she rearranged the letters of Escalona), toured Mexico and the Southwest, spending a great deal of time especially in Los Angeles. At this point, Beatriz was considered beautiful and, in fact, won a contest sponsored by Kaiser Stockings for the most beautiful legs. The Areus were so successful that they became the impresarios of the Teatro Principal in Los Angeles in 1924 while the theatre was owned by Willard Wyatt. Following their association with the Principal, the Areus became members of the Bell company and later the Guz Aguila and Pirrín companies. By 1926 Dorita Ceprano and Enrique went their own way. By 1930 Beatriz, now as La Chata Noloesca, had formed her own company, Atracciones Noloesca, in Los Angeles. When Belia, her daughter, was asked why her mother had decided to become a comedienne, she answered that La Chata had always been so inclined, especially when singing humorous couplets, but that La Chata also had grown fat and could no longer make it as a beautiful chorine. In 1936 her company performed for two years at the Teatro Nacional in San Antonio. After this La Chata selected only San Antonio talent for a new group. She chose four young women from San Antonio: Amparo Cruz, Juanita Puente, Gloria Zea, and her daughter Belia. La Chata, Tito Siller, Pepe Burrón, and the chorus girls hit the road in a trailer in 1938 as the Compañía Mexicana, but this time for points east and north, where other Hispanic populations were still growing and supporting vaudeville. La Chata's novel idea was to bring to the Cubans, the Puerto Ricans, and others Mexican vaudeville, the troupe's particular brand of humor, its regional costumes, and, of course, its distinctive music based on the rich folklore of Mexico. There was one problem that at times led to embarrassment: the girls were raised in San Antonio and some of them did not speak Spanish very well. La Chata was always instructing them, trying to teach them Spanish or transform their Tex-Mex dialect into standard Spanish. Another problem was that they were really Americans trying to represent Mexico in their art. In Cuba a reporter asked one of the girls what part of Mexico she was from, to which she responded, "San Antonio." La Chata told her to be quiet and firmly instructed the company that she, as manager, would be the only one allowed to speak to the press or anyone else about the troupe.

In 1938 the company began its long string of successes in Tampa, Miami, and Cuba. In 1941 the Compañía Mexicana took the last boat out of Cuba before Havana Harbor was closed at the beginning of the war. From there they traveled to Chicago and finally to New York. The company stayed in New York for nine years, during which time it covered the Hispanic circuit in the city: Teatro Hispano, Teatro Puerto Rico, Teatro Triboro (Tri-Borough), the 53rd Street Theatre, radio, and television. La Chata, besides being the favored performer that she was, became an important company manager who was able to introduce other San Antonio and Texas talent to New York, including Pedro González González ("Ramirín"), who later made a career in movie westerns; Sarita Villegas ("La Flaca"); dancers Lauro and Lolita Guerra; and the team of Netty and Jesús Rodríguez. During this time, the Compañía Mexicana would return to San Antonio on occasion to perform three condensed half-hour shows a day after films at the Teatro Nacional. In New York the *tandas* were one hour long.

Beatriz Escalona's comic persona, La Chata, was a street-wise, fast-talking *peladita* in the tradition of the Mexican urban *peladitas* created by such famous *tiples cómicas* as Emilia Trujillo, Delia Magaña, and Lupe Rivas Cacho and *peladitas* like Lupe Inclán and Amelia Wilhemy.[27] Dressed in a costume that, at times, was that of a housemaid and, at other times, was made to look like that of a child (her hair in two pony tails, a print dress with ruffles, oxford shoes and rolled down sox, exaggerated make-up), she developed a picaresque style that allowed her character to survive and ironically get the upper hand at all times.

At one point Lalo Astol and a number of other artists that were not able to make the transition to radio or to the more and more limited opportunities for vaudeville found refuge in the tent theatres, the same tent theatres that had also at times housed companies like the Villalongín and that had produced artists for the stage: don Catarino, Roberto Escalera, Ramirín (Pedro González González). La Chata herself had had experience in the circus theatre and had brought up to New York such well-seasoned *carpa* performers as Ramirín and Netty Rodríguez and Jesús Rodríguez. In her early career she had also been part of the Areus, who had formed a partnership with the famous Mexican circus family, the Familia Bell.

That circus and theatre under a tent should be so well integrated may seem strange to those only familiar with the European circus tradition as transformed by Barnum and Bailey. A brief review of the development of circus theatre and the *carpa* in Mexico and the southwestern United States is in order.

The Mexican American circus experience is one that has benefited from a diverse series of roots and influences. Hernán Cortés's chronicler, Bernal Díaz del Castillo, recognized circus-type diversions at the court of Montezuma, emperor of the Aztecs. From then on the circus activities of the American Indians and those of the Spaniards were blended to give a distinct character to the circus as it developed in Mexico and later in the Southwest. On this early base of *mestizo* circus culture the nineteenth and twentieth centuries added layers of European and Anglo-American influence until after World War II the Mexican American circus ceased to exist and the *mexicanos* in the United States were assimilated into the large American circus companies or they left the circus life completely.

Well into the nineteenth century, circuses would stage their performances at theatres and at bullrings. In 1833, Carlos E. Green's circus, originating from the northeastern United States, was the first to feature pantomimes such as the one entitled *Don Quijote & Sancho Panza* (María y Campos 1939: 24). Also at this time, the *payaso* or *gracioso* of the Spanish theatrical tradition was featured singing popular songs in the circus. The most famous of these *payasos*, José Soledad Aycardo, appeared in the Mexican circus in 1852 to dominate it for the next five decades. El Chole Aycardo's diverse talents included horsemanship, acrobatics, gymnastics, *maroma*,[28] acting, composing, and reciting poetry on topical themes. In fact, his is the most important contribution to the evolution of the Mexican clown as a poet and satirist, a feature that later reappears in the *peladito*. Aycardo organized all of his circus's acts and also directed and acted in operettas, *pastorelas*, and five-act melodramas. Aycardo combined European-type circus with the indigenous *maroma* of pre-Columbian heritage and Spanish theatre.

During the second half of the nineteenth century, the Mexican circus received important influences from Italian, English, and Anglo-American circuses that performed in Mexico. Most noteworthy of all was the introduction of the English-type clown by the Chiarini Circus in 1867 (ibid.: 150). The clown wore baggy pants, a face made up with flour, and a red wig with three lumps of curls on the forehead. Chiarini was also important for having integrated Mexican acts into the show and bringing them back to the United States. In 1869 he introduced to Mexico the Bell Family from England (ibid.: 165). Five-year-old Ricardo Bell was to become the most famous clown in Mexican history and the patriarch of a large and very famous circus family. Although Ricardo Bell was born in England, he grew up in Mexico, he and his children intermarried with Mexicans, and for all intents and purposes he and his family became Mexican. In 1873 Chiarini also introduced the Orrin Family, which originated in England and the northeastern United States (ibid.: 168). The Orrins also founded a circus dynasty in Mexico. The Orrins' popularity virtually drove the more traditional Mexican circuses from the capital. Only when Orrin was on tour did such companies as Ortiz (later to reappear in the United States Southwest), directed by Jesús Ortiz, perform in Mexico City. At this time the Rivas Brothers were also appearing with Chiarini and Bell; after the turn of the century, the Rivas Brothers would also tour their own circus in the Southwest.

In the nineteenth century there existed a more humble, poor man's circus that traveled the poorer neighborhoods of Mexico City and the provinces and set up a small tent, or *carpa,* to house its performances. The term *carpa* is ancient Quechua for an awning made of interwoven branches.[29] In Spanish it signifies canvas cover, tent, and, finally, a type of folksy and down-to-earth circus. During the Mexican Revolution, actors and clowns from the more established theatres and circuses took refuge in the *carpas,* where the pantomimes originated by Ricardo Bell and the satire of Aycardo fermented to bring about the creation of the satirical, often political, review which starred the character that today is recognized as the Mexican national clown: the *pelado,* or naked one, penniless one, underdog. Somewhat reminiscent of Charles Chaplin and best exemplified by Cantinflas, the *peladito* improvises a dialogue which brings to the scene "el humor fino del pueblo, su espíritu crítico, sus quejas, sus anhelos y éste, al ver retratada en las tablas, su propia existencia y su personalidad coopera directamente con los cómicos diciendo chistes, dialogando con ellos, planteándoles problemas que acuzan su espíritu inventivo, premiando o castigando, con ruda sinceridad, a los 'buenos' y a los 'malos.'"[30] In the *carpa* is also found some of the same picaresque and critical spirit that we have seen in the *revistas políticas.*

The *carpas* functioned quite often as popular tribunals, repositories of folk wisdom, humor, and music, and were incubators of Mexican comic types and stereotypes. They continued to function in these ways in the Southwest, but especially in San Antonio, which had become, especially after the outbreak of the Mexican Revolution, a home base and wintering ground for many of the *carpas.*

From the 1850s on there is considerable documentation of *maromas* touring throughout the Southwest. The earliest note concerning *maromas* comes from Monterey, California, in 1846.[31] Gipson mentions a Mexican circus of acrobats, clowns, rope walkers, and stock characters of devils and skeletons in Tucson from 1853 to 1854 and attests that by the 1870s the Mexican circus was the most popular and frequent type of entertainment in Tucson (Gipson 1972). In California during the 1850s a Circo de Los Angeles appears with the Spanish clown Nicolás Martínez (*El Clamor Público*, February 6, 1858). Both Chiarini and Orrin made their way to San Francisco in the 1860s, where they were already performing with Hispanic acts. Orrin's California Circus continued to tour the Pacific Coast of the United States and Central and South America from the 1860s to the 1880s, and by the time of George Frederick Orrin's death on May 15, 1884, the Orrin Brothers Circus was firmly established as the great amusement institution in the capitals of Mexico and Cuba.[32] In 1894, the Orrins opened a Circo Teatro building on a plaza in Mexico City (María y Campos 1939: 207).

The earliest reference to the Mexican circus in Texas is the following comment from the San Antonio *Ledger* on November 8, 1852: "The Mexican circus is with us. We knew in our hearts the season for fun and jollity was about to commence." The comment seems to indicate that the San Antonio public was familiar with the Mexican circus, and we can probably assume that these circuses had performed in San Antonio prior to that date. Years later, the Mexican circus seems to have lost some of its appeal; the *Daily Herald* on December 31, 1869, published this reaction to the Great Mexican Havana Circus Company: "For once—the *Herald* and the *Express* agree on the merits of the Mexican circus—that it is humbug." The *Daily Herald* shows this circus performing both in June and December 1869; either San Antonio was becoming a base for the circus or the Mexican Havana was limiting its circuit to Texas and the border regions. On January 17, 1879, the *Herald* reported that the Mexican Havana was "being laid up in San Antonio." From this time until the 1950s, San Antonio seems to have been an important show town for Mexican circuses as well as a home base for some of them.

During the period of the Mexican Revolution many circuses began touring north of the border and chose places like San Antonio and Los Angeles for their home bases. After the hostilities ceased, some returned to Mexico but others remained in the United States, where they had established lucrative circuits. A fruitful avenue for many Mexican circus performers was the Mexican vaudeville circuit in the United States. Some of the performers even made their way into the American and Canadian vaudeville circuits during the 1920s and 1930s. The Bell Family, after relocating in the Southwest, for instance, not only toured the vaudeville circuits but, as noted in chapter 2, also bought the Capitol Theatre in Los Angeles to house its own performances and those of other touring companies. Even the great Escalante Circus at times booked some of its family members into vaudeville houses to raise some extra funds. Members of the Circo Mantecón family, which perennially toured Texas and northern Mexico, at times calling itself Compañía de Vaudeville Mantecón, were often found on the stage of San Antonio's Teatro Nacional and the other local houses. María Mantecón in 1925 had become part of the Teatro Zaragoza stock company. Consuelo García of San Antonio's Carpa García, which was active until 1947, recalls working the vaudeville circuit in San Antonio, going from one theatre to the next for half-hour *tandas* between movies.[33]

A number of the *circo-teatros* that resided in the Southwest were very large, possessing great tents, equipment, vehicles, and a full complement of performers. Probably the largest was the Escalante Family Circus, whose great tent enclosed a proscenium stage. The Escalantes owned their own lots in Los Angeles on which they would erect their tents but continued touring throughout the Southwest from the mid teens until the 1950s. Manuel Mañón (1932: 398), however, places them on the stage of the Teatro Principal for a very brief run in June 1921; they therefore must have continued touring in Mexico as well during this period. Although the Escalantes were originally acrobats, their tents housed a wide variety of acts including melodramas, *zarzuelas,* and *revistas,* and in the early 1930s one of the impresario's daughters, Elodia ("La Chatita"), made quite a reputation for herself at the Teatro México in Los Angeles as a *tiple cómica.* The Escalante patriarch and impresario was Mariano Escalante (1881–1961), and the clowns featured in his shows were Cara Sucia, Tony, and Chamaco. As was typical of all of the circuses, many of their performances helped raise funds for charities and causes. One such performance by the Circo Escalante Hermanos Compañía de Baile y Variedades in Phoenix, Arizona, on March 29, 1927, was to raise money for the defense fund of Alfredo Grijalva, accused of shooting an American sheriff.[34] In 1934, probably affected by the Depression and Repatriation, the company announced that it was going back to Mexico (*La Opinión,* August 10, 1934). It later returned to the United States; *Billboard* brought down final curtains for Yolanda Escalante (b. 1928) in 1950 and for Mariano in 1961.[35] In its day, the Escalante circus was the pride of the community and a motive for Mexican nationalism: "Si usted no ha ido al circo, dispóngase a hacerlo hoy mismo, no olvidando que se trata de un espectáculo mexicano, que en muchos sentidos, como en su arroyo y limpieza de sus actos, es superior a los grandes circos americanos."[36]

But the type of Mexican circus that survived the longest in the United States was the small, family-based *carpa* that performed along the Mexican American border. For the most part the *carpas* survived the Depression, Repatriation, and the other economic and social forces that put Mexican and Hispanic entertainments out of business during the 1930s and 1940s. Some *carpas* continued to perform along the border into the 1960s and even followed the migrant labor stream north. Today there is still an occasional *carpa* that visits the towns of the Rio Grande Valley.

Probably because of their small size, bare-bones style, and organization around a family unit, the *carpas* could manage themselves better than the larger circuses. Furthermore, they were able to cultivate smaller audiences in the most remote areas. The *carpas* became in the Southwest an important Mexican American popular culture institution. Their comic routines became a sounding board for the culture conflict that Mexican Americans felt in language usage, assimilation to American tastes and life-styles, discrimination in the United States, and *pocho* status in Mexico. Out of these types of conflicts in the popular entertainment arose the stereotype of the Pachuco, a typically Mexican American figure. The *carpa* also preserved the format of the Mexican *revista* that in the late sixties would find new life in Chicano theatre. Finally, the *carpas* were a refuge for theatrical and circus people of all types. These artists could ride out the Depression, Repatriation, and World War II with a steady although meager employment, doing something akin to their regular acts. More importantly, these cultural arts were preserved by the *carpas* for the postwar generation that was to forge a new relationship with the larger American culture.

The theatrical entertainments of the *carpas* also followed the same evolution that these arts did in the theatre houses and cinemas, beginning with melodrama at the turn of the century and gradually evolving toward *zarzuela, revista,* and variety acts, until during the Depression the *carpas* became a haven for vaudeville. But, of course, the tent theatres never converted to showing films, although competition from the motion picture industry did erode attendance at the *carpas,* especially after World War II.

In San Antonio, the Carpa Sanabia housed melodrama by at least two companies that we are familiar with: the Villalongín dramatic company and the Compañía de Drama, Opereta y Zarzuela, directed by Ricardo de la Vega. On May 11, 1914, *La Prensa* reported the latter troupe performing *zarzuelas* to full houses in the *carpa.* Unfortunately, on June 18 the city authorities closed down the tent theatre for unknown reasons; the newspaper cited envy of the *carpa's* success by other impresarios. Forced to leave the Carpa Sanabia, the de la Vega troupe moved to the Teatro Aurora and by January 1915 was successfully performing at another theatre in El Paso.

In the next few years, numerous are the announcements of *carpas* in San Antonio. In 1917 and 1918 the Teatro Carpa Independencia, otherwise known as the Carpa Guzmán, played San Antonio with its mixture of acrobats, gymnasts, mimes, and song-and-dance teams. On April 29, 1918, *La Prensa* alluded to the members of the *carpa* having been long-term San Antonio residents. These included María del Carmen and A. Guzmani, María P. de Sampers, Aurelio Díaz, and Amelia Solsona; it is not known if this Solsona was from the Solsona dramatic company that toured Texas at the turn of the century. In 1919 the Carpa Metropolitana, featuring "circo y variedades," made its way into town. In 1923, another San Antonio resident company was noted in *La Prensa* on January 14 as embarking on a tour to the central United States: the Carpa Romana of the Compañía de Variedades Emiliano Ortiz. Known as well by the name of Ortiz Brothers Show, this company was still active in 1936 in Socorro, New Mexico, where it was featuring twelve acts of song and dance, magic, and clowns, as well as debuting a new *corrido* entitled "El Relief" (*El Defensor del Pueblo,* May 29, 1936). From 1920 to 1925 the Circo Mantecón, also known as the Compañía de Vaudeville Mantecón, was documented as performing in San Antonio, Floresville, Beeville, Corpus Christi, and Del Rio. According to Arturo Mantecón, the Circo Mantecón had engagements as far north as Saint Louis, Missouri, during these years, but between 1925 and 1930 toured mostly in northern Mexico.[37] Later there were offshoots of the Mantecón Circus in the form of *redondeles,* shows that were even more modest than *carpas* in that they only stretched a canvas wall around a ring. The Mantecón company included twenty-eight members, many of whom belonged to the immediate family.

Two of the most well known resident *carpas* of San Antonio were the Carpa García and the Carpa Cubana, whose descendants still reside in the Alamo City. Manuel V. García came to settle in San Antonio with his wife and family in 1914. The native of Saltillo, Coahuila, was an acrobat who had performed with the Carpa Progresista in Mexico.[38] Manuel, an orphan who joined the circus at age fifteen, became a trapeze artist, dancer, and everything else that it took to run a small circus. Featured in his Carpa García was the famed *charro* (Mexican-style cowboy) on the tightrope act. One of the comic actors of the Carpa, Pedro González González ("Ramirín"), later had a successful career in Hollywood westerns, as mentioned earlier in this chapter. Other members of the family performed magic, ventriloquism, song and dance, and comedy. The highlight of the show became the *peladito,* don Fito or El Bato Suave. Played by Manuel's son Rodolfo, he became a typical wise guy from the streets of West Side San Antonio, speaking the urban Mexican American dialect, or *caló.* He also satirized the language of Mexicans and Pachucos and often engaged the audiences in repartee.[39] The Carpa García at times also hosted don Lalo (Lalo Astol) and Lydia Mendoza, the famous singer, and her family of singers and dancers. Daughter Esther García, an acrobat, later went on to the center ring of the Barnum and Bailey Circus. Among the dramatic material performed by the García family was the time-proven photographer sketch that has been a staple of vaudeville in numerous languages and traditions.[40] "By 1947 La Carpa García decided to call it quits after a final run-in with the Fire Department about making its tent fireproof."[41]

In Latin American and U.S. circus history, the Abreu name appears frequently at the end of the nineteenth-century and beginning of the twentieth. The Abreu company, directed by Virgilio Abreu, owned and operated the Carpa Cubana—also known as the Cuban Show and the Circo Cubano—that made San Antonio its home base in the 1920s and 1930s. But before that the various members of the family had appeared as acrobats, tumblers, and wire walkers[42] with Orrin (1885–1886), the Lowande and Hoffman Circus (1887), Barnum and Bailey (1910), Sam Brothers Circus (1916), Ringling Brothers (1911), John Robinson (1917), and Sells-Floto (1919). In San Antonio the Cuban circus included trapeze artists, rope walkers, jugglers, clowns, dancers, and its own ten-piece band. According to San Antonio's *La Prensa* (July 16, 1921), the circus was advertising pantomimes on Mexican national themes for its Kingsville and Lyford, Texas, performances. Although based in San Antonio, the company toured as far as California and central Mexico by truck and train, but mostly limited its tours to the Rio Grande Valley in the south and north to Austin during the 1930s.[43] Virgilio Abreu and his wife, Federica, owned a home on the west side of San Antonio but lived in tents with the rest of the company when on the road. The company would tour for four or five months in the spring until summer heat set in and then not leave San Antonio again until the fall, returning home for the Christmas season. The members of the company would also do variety acts in the local San Antonio cinemas.

Various other *teatro-circo* and *carpa* companies performed in the Southwest and probably toured in San Antonio at one time or another during the early twentieth century: the Compañía de Vaudeville Texas Show; the Circo Hidalguense, with the actor-clown

Rodolfo Domínguez ("Pirrimplín"), formerly with Ricardo Bell in Mexico; the Cuadro Artístico Salazar with its own *carpa;* the Maroma Pájaro Azul during the 1920s and 1930s in the Valley; the Esqueda Brothers Show, active in California and Arizona throughout the 1920s; P. Pérez Show Circo y Variedades, Los Angeles; Circo Carnival Iris Show, directed by Juan Soto, which was perhaps related to the Iris Show variety acts on the stages of Los Angeles and San Antonio in the 1920s; Teatro Carpa Hermanos Rosete Aranda in Texas and California during the 1920s; and the Gran Carpa Circo-Teatro Juárez, featuring a nightly show of drama, *zarzuela,* operetta, and *revistas.*

4. New York City

Although the first Spanish-speaking immigrants, made up of expatriate Spanish Sephardim, had arrived in New Amsterdam as early as 1654,[1] it was not until the 1820s that Hispanic cultural life began to develop in New York City. The year 1828 marks the founding of two Spanish-language newspapers, *El Mensajero Semanal* and *El Mercurio de Nueva York*, which provided a lively fare of information as well as poetic and dramatic literature for the mainly Spanish and Cuban residents (still officially Spanish subjects) of Manhattan.[2]

During the second half of the nineteenth century, New York's Hispanic community also supported a nascent Spanish-language publishing industry that issued a number of books of plays. In the early 1840s, a comedy by Orman Tu-Caes (probably a pseudonym), *El hermano hermoso*, was published by the Imprenta de la Granja. For the next forty years, other plays issued by various publishing houses were *El rico y el pobre* by Justo Eleboro in 1864; *El grito de yara* by Luis García Pérez, relating to the Cuban call for independence, published in 1879; *Abufar o la familia árabe* by José María Heredia, in 1854; *La muerte de Plácido* by Diego V. Tejera in 1875; *Después de la lluvia el sol* by Rafael Diez de la Cortina in 1879 and *El indiano,* also by Diez, in 1893; *Hatuey* by Francisco Sellén in 1891; *Polilla regional* by G. Gómez y Arroyo in 1892; *La fuga de Evangelina* by New York resident Desiderio Fajardo Ortiz in 1898, which most probably relates to the escape to the United States of the heroine of the Cuban independence movement, Evangelina Cossío, from a Spanish jail in Cuba; and *La apuesta de Zoleika* by M. M. Hernández in 1901.[3] Unfortunately, there is no documentary evidence showing that these plays were produced or that there was ongoing professional theatrical activity during these years. It is most probable, however, that the publications were the outgrowth of theatrical interest in the community and that the plays and other standard Spanish fare were presented by amateur companies. It is certain, however, as can be seen below, that the plays promoting the Cuban independence movement were performed at political and social gatherings in support of fund raising for the war.

It is during the 1890s in New York that regular amateur and semiprofessional shows begin to be noted in the Spanish-language newspapers. It is also in the 1890s that we witness once again the influence on the evolution of the Hispanic stage exerted by internal conflict in the homeland and immigration to the United States. Of course, the diaspora brought on by the Mexican Revolution (1910) more than any other factor characterized the theatre in the Southwest during the first half of the twentieth century. In the 1890s New York became an organizing and staging center for Cuban, Puerto Rican, and Dominican expatriates seeking the independence of their homelands from Spain. In the 1920s and 1930s the Puerto Rican nationalist movement in pursuit of independence from the United States would also manifest itself on the city's stages, as would the efforts by exiled Spanish Republicans fighting fascism during the Spanish Civil War during the mid-thirties.

From 1892 to 1898, the newspaper *La Patria,* the forum for Cuban revolutionary activities in the United States, occasionally covered theatrical performances in New York which were produced to raise funds for the Cuban wounded and, it must be assumed, to generally sustain the war effort itself. A central figure at this juncture was the actor Luis Baralt, who was reported as having spent thirty successful years on the stage of Havana's Tacón Theatre (*La Patria,* January 1, 1896). As early as 1893 he was known to have operated in Manhattan, with Emilio Agramante, a school of opera and oratory at which plays were produced. The core members of Baralt's company were Blanche de Baralt (his wife?), Leonor Molina, García Cisneros, and artistic director Lincoln D. Zayas, a medical doctor by profession. Another actress who was noted as coming out of retirement especially to play the role of Mariana in Tomás Mendoza's play *De lo vivo a lo pintado* was Adelaida Baralt, according to *La Patria* (January 1, 1896). It is not known if Adelaida was his mother, sister, or wife. It is probable that some four other actors and actresses mentioned were amateurs.

The information provided by *La Patria* is extremely spotty and, therefore, it must be presumed that many more plays than noted were performed during this six-year period, especially if we use the intense activity of December 1895 as an indication. Although *La Patria* begins to mention Baralt's theatrical work in 1893, it is not until December of 1895 that actual plays are mentioned. In this month plays were performed on three occasions at the Berkeley Lyceum for a one-dollar admission charge: the *zarzuelas Niña Pancha, Don Segismundo,* and *Tragarse la píldora;* on December 21 a repeat performance, under the sponsorship of Los Independientes Club; on December 23 *El que con lobos anda* by Isaac Carrillo y O'Farrill and *De lo vivo a lo pintado* by Tomás Mendoza, a playwright who was said to have lost his life at the Battle of Las Tunas in Cuba. Again during 1896 and 1897, Baralt and his theatrical work rarely appeared in *La Patria,* except for occasional reviews of plays in English that Baralt published there. The magazine *Cuba y América* in its December 1, 1897, edition noted performance of *Los dominós blancos* for the Revolution by Baralt's company

In 1898, again there are a number of performances noted, once again in support of the war effort. All of them took place at the Carnegie Lyceum. On February 2, the *juguete La fuga de Evangelina,* directed by Lincoln D. Zayas, was performed at a meeting of the Club las Dos Banderas. On February 5, the Club Lírico Dramático Cubano, whose president was Lincoln D. Zayas but whose artistic director was probably still Baralt, debuted with *La gallina ciega* by J. M. Bermejo and *Robo en despoblado* by Ramos Carrión and Vital Aza. On February 12, *La Patria* published the fundraiser's balance sheet, noting that $136.40 was raised for the revolution after $233 in tickets had been sold, with a discount to members of the sponsoring club, Las Dos Banderas. The Club Lírico Drámatico Cubano had its second performance on March 19, with *Su excelencia* and *Con la música de otra parte,* both by Vital Aza. In April *Juego de prendas* was produced, in which couplets were sung describing the sinking of the battleship *Maine* in Havana harbor. The June 12 issue of *Revista de Cayo Hueso* noted a May 28 performance without specifying the play titles. In June, *Los hugonotes* by José Echegaray was reported by

La Patria, along with some allegorical scenes based on Cuban history. The last performance noted was to take place on a change of venue to the Central Opera House on January 16, 1899; funds were to be raised for the sepulcher of the great Cuban philosopher, poet, and revolutionary, José Martí. The *juguete cómico No lo quiero saber* was performed for an admission fee of thirty-five cents. After this last production there is no further mention of theatrical performances in the newspapers that have survived until the advent of a truly professional Hispanic stage some seventeen years later in 1916.

Unlike the theatrical experience in Los Angeles, San Antonio, and Tampa, in the mid teens of the new century the Hispanic community could not claim any theatres of its own. Rather, a number of impresarios would rent available theatres around town, but mainly those located around the Broadway area, from midtown Manhattan up to the 80s: Bryant Hall (6th Avenue and 41st Street), the Park Theatre at 59th Street and Columbus Circle, the Amsterdam Opera House, the Leslie Theatre (88th and Broadway), Carnegie Hall, the Cort Theatre (48th Street), the Central Opera House, the Forty-Fourth Street Theatre, and the Sixty-Third Street Music Hall. The first impresario to lead companies on this odyssey through New York theatre houses was a Spanish actor-singer of *zarzuelas* who had made his debut in Mexico City at the Teatro Principal in *Chin chun chan* in 1904: Manuel Noriega (Mañón 1932: 264). Noriega became a figure in New York that in many ways was comparable to Romualdo Tirado in Los Angeles. Like Tirado, he was a tireless and enthusiastic motivator of Hispanic theatre and, for a number of years, his was practically the sole responsibility for maintaining Spanish-language theatrical seasons. Like Tirado, he became one of the first impresarios to found a Hispanic motion picture company. And like Tirado, Noriega's genius as a comic actor could always be relied on during difficult financial straits. But Noriega was also an inventor of sorts: he had come to New York, according to Pablo Prida Santicilia (1960: 76), to sell plans for a submarine that he had designed.

Noriega found his way to New York in 1916 via the Havana stage. According to the *Revista Universal* (September 1916), Noriega had been performing at the Amsterdam Theatre with the famous Spanish *coupletista* María Conesa in March. In the same year *Las Novedades* had him at the head of the Compañía Dramática Española at the Teatro Leslie from June 4 through September 3, through October at the Amsterdam Opera House, and at Carnegie Hall in December. In Noriega's repertoire was the typical fare of Spanish comedies, along with *sainetes* and *zarzuelas,* including the works of Vital Aza, Angel Guimará, and the Alvarez Quintero brothers. These first two seasons did not go well, judging from the reviews. For instance, on July 2, 1916, *Las Novedades* criticized the company for being uneven in its production of *Juan José*. And on December 24, 1916, the Unión Benéfica Española had to arrange for a benefit at Carnegie Hall for the poverty-stricken Spanish actors at which Noriega showed films that he had produced starring María Conesa and himself. On May 26, 1917, *La Prensa* chastized the Hispanic community for not supporting the theatre and urged the public to see Noriega's company, which, unlike other companies which had been *mamarrachescos* (messy), was very good and even included an orchestra of twenty musicians.

It was in 1918 at the Amsterdam Opera House, which according to Prida (1960: 79) held about a thousand seats that would sell out for performances, that Noriega's Compañía Dramática began finding some stability, performing each Sunday, with an occasional special performance on Thursdays, charging fifty cents general admission and seventy-five cents for reserved seats at first and then in November raising the prices by twenty-five cents. Noriega, the comic actor, had become the main attraction: "Del Señor Noriega apenas hay que hablar. Es el héroe de la fiesta y por él va al teatro la casi totalidad del público. Hombre culto y artista admirable, le basta aparecer en escena para que el público celebre sus gracias y le aplauda con gran entusiasmo."[4] Such were the success and the growth of his audiences that in November Noriega began matinee showings on Sundays and in December began advertising in *La Prensa* to recruit theatrical artists. As Noriega hired on more actors, mostly Cuban, Spanish, and Mexican, the nature of the company began to change, at times highlighting Galician or Catalonian works, at others Cuban blackface comedy. It was at this time that exiled Mexican librettist, Pablo Prida Santicilia, teamed up with Noriega and began serving as part agent, part artistic director and prompter and in an acting role in *La raza latina* on October 10 (ibid.: 78).

From October through December 1918, the works produced included the following *zarzuelas* and *entremeses*: *El contrabando, Solico en el mundo* by the Alvarez Quintero brothers, *Ya somos tres, Los chorros de oro, El terrible Pérez, La guerra capitana, Los tientos, Los granujas, Fea y con gracia, El puñao de rosas, Eden concert* (revista), *La macarena, Los chicos de la escuela, San Juan de luz, La gatita blanca, El amor asusta, Los guapos, La alegría de la huerta, Tony o la risa del payaso, La reja de Dolores*, and *La borrica*. At the end of 1918 Noriega took on a partner, Julián Benlloch, who doubled as the orchestral and musical director and talent scout. In December, Noriega and Benlloch formed a partnership with a Mr. Fortuny in an attempt to acquire the Forty-Fourth Street Theatre, rename it, and offer *zarzuelas* on a daily basis, but for some reason the deal never got off the ground.

In January 1919, therefore, the Compañía Dramática Española continued at the Amsterdam Opera House with the following: *San Juan de luz, El caperuchito, Películas callejeras, La real gana, Mala hembra, Apaga y vámonos,* and *Las campanadas.* In January, the company also began offering variety acts, comic routines, and *revistas de actualidad,* which featured the Cuban actor Pepe Luis in blackface. Pepe Luis also wrote and starred in the five-act play *La república catalana.* Prida reports that when the company performed *revistas,* despite the world war that was raging, the actors attacked Yankees and their government, feeling quite secure in that everything was done in Spanish; but at one point, a theatre guard, a Texas native who understood Spanish, warned Noriega that they were exposing themselves to trouble (ibid.).

The Noriega company, despite reports of its director's attempt to acquire a theatre of his own, continued to perform at the Amsterdam while also performing at the Cort Theatre, the Central Opera House, and the Park Theatre, which became the Teatro Español. In the meantime, Noriega had reinforced his company with Adelina Vehi, the *primera tiple* who had experienced success in Mexico and the Southwest. At the Amsterdam, from February through September, Noriega staged numerous *zarzuelas* and an occasional melodrama, such as *Don Juan Tenorio.* At the Cort Theatre he staged intermittent performances in June and July and on February 19 Noriega repeated *Don Juan Tenorio* at the Central Opera House. He also performed Jacinto Benavente's *La malquerida* and, it must be assumed, other plays there during that month.

In March 1919, Noriega formed a partnership with Hispanic, Greek, and Anglo-American businessmen to lease the Park Theatre from L. A. Anhalt and make it the premier Hispanic house, rebaptizing it El Teatro Español. The Park had actually been used by the Hispanic community in an unsuccessful run by Mexican playwright Quinito Valverde with a company of fifty Spanish artists in his and José F. Elizondo's *revista La tierra de la alegría,* which was produced with a mixture of Spanish and English in the libretto.[5] Two years later here was Noriega forming a stock company, the Gran Compañía de Opera y Zarzuela, which was to alternate major *zarzuelas* with shorter ones and *revistas* and featured such well-known stars as Pilar Arcos, Eduardo Arozamena (active in Mexico and the Southwest), and Fernando L. Caballé. Noriega also brought in the noted baritone of the Boston Opera Company Ricardo Blanchart to sing the lead in *Maruxa* at the April 19 opening of the theatre. According to *La Prensa* (April 8, 1919), the following were the officers and partners in this new business enterprise: President Andrés P. Segurola, Honorary President Leoncio Mosquera (a Greek), Treasurer Roberto C. Pelkington, Business Manager William Small, and American Press Agent Mary Worswick. Noriega was listed as the director and Caballé as the director of the thirty-five-piece orchestra. A list of some thirty actors and actresses, many contracted directly in Mexico City and Havana, was also published in the article. On March 11, 1919, in a vein similar to the nationalistic pleas given by Mexican theatre critics in the Southwest, Juan del Júcar wrote in *La Prensa* calling for community support of Noriega's patriotic artistic efforts at the Teatro Español, which would have the effect of combating the "Spanish Black Legend" in the United States.

Prida (1960: 81–82) provides an account of the preparations for the opening and how Noriega's naiveté in business affairs brought about the ruin of this venture. When Prida went to Havana to contract artists for the run, Noriega totally destroyed the agreed-upon budget by contracting other actors in New York. Thus when Prida returned from Havana with Adelina Vehi and others and other contracted actors arrived from Mexico, Noriega was faced with a redundancy for various parts, but there were also specific parts that had not yet been filled. Despite a full house on opening night, the budget was far from covered. Because of this Mosquera and his associates abandoned Noriega; the actors were paid part of their salary and some of them returned to Cuba and Mexico.

As Prida reported above, they had started well with decent box office receipts and playbills that included popular *zarzuelas* such as *Maruxa, Marina, Los bohemios,* and *La corte de Faraón.*[6] But on May 2, *La Prensa* announced the breakup of the Noriega company, attributing its failure to poor administration, strained relations between the impresarios and the artists, and under-capitalization. After not having been paid, the artists refused to perform and instead lodged a complaint with the police. The May 7 *La Prensa* announced a benefit performance to raise funds for the penniless Mexican and Cuban artists stranded in New York. The owner of the Park Theatre, L. A. Anhalt, donated the facility for the charitable affair, at which the famous opera stars María Barrientos and José Mardones took roles in Emilio Arrieta's *Marina*. Despite the benefit performance, which sold out at ticket prices of three dollars each, some of the actresses stood in front of the Park for a week collecting donations.

The failure of the Teatro Español reverberated even as far away as San Antonio, where the newspaper *La Prensa* on May 9, 1919, reacted with a story lamenting the closing of the New York theatre. After reviewing all the expectations and preparations and the successful opening night for its readers, *La Prensa* attributed the failure to Noriega's poor choice of works, concluding that the Galician *zarzuela Maruxa* was too regional a work for New York's cosmopolitan audiences and that Quinito Valverde's *La tierra de la alegría* would have been a wiser selection. As can be seen, the news of mismanagement was not generally known in the community.

After the unfortunate ending to such an idealistic artistic venture as the Teatro Español, the Park Theatre was never again used by the Hispanic community. But it seems that impresario Mosquera was a glutton for punishment. According to Prida (1960: 84–85), Mosquera combined with another Greek, a Mr. Coutoucas, and leased the Cort Theatre for Noriega's company. On July 14, 1919, the company opened successfully with the operetta *La viejecita* and the *zarzuela Musas latinas*. During the course of the fall, the company continued with success at the Cort, presenting such lyric works as *Marina* and *Molinos de viento*, but, because of internal problems, it broke up.

Later, Noriega reestablished the company and went on to the Princess Theatre and Leslie Hall during 1920 and 1921, where he presented the same playbill for two and three nights in a row and at matinees on weekends. Again, the most popular *zarzuelas* were featured, along with an occasional play by the Alvarez Quintero brothers or Pedro Muñoz Seca, or by a Cuban playwright such as Gustavo Sánchez de Garralaga. After October 1921 no further word in New York is heard of Manuel Noriega until 1927. He resurfaces at the end of the decade in Los Angeles where, presumably, he had also been developing his career in film. His leading lady, Pilar Arcos, remained in New York throughout the 1920s.

From the late teens through the mid 1920s Pilar Arcos and Eduardo Arozamena, and numerous theatrical companies that toured to or were formed in New York, attempted to establish a resident Hispanic theatre culture by leasing theatre houses for individual shows as well as for short seasons. In his memoirs, Bernardo Vega commented that the Hispanic theatrical artists of the early 1920s made a superhuman effort to establish the Hispanic stage but that conditions, especially economic ones, were not propitious.[7]

Bryant Hall, housing *zarzuelas* and *sainetes* by the company of J. Madariaga as early as 1916, in 1920 housed a series of performances of Spanish plays by Eduardo Arozamena's company, including *Marianela*, *El indiano*, *La zancadilla*, *El trébol*, *El chiquillo*, and *Los monigotes*. The 63rd Street Theatre was leased by the touring Compañía Hispano-Mexicana Fernando Díaz de León, which was quite well known in the Southwest, for performances of such plays as *Basta de suegros, Los pantalones, El sexo débil, Echar la llave, Los demonios en el cuerpo,* and *Malditas sean las mujeres* in November and December 1920, followed in 1921 by the Compañía de Zarzuela Española Arcos-Sardina, directed by Pilar Arcos. The Arcos company presented a series of *zarzuelas, sainetes,* and comedies that diverged somewhat from the usual fare by including more than just the well-worn works; alongside standards like *El terrible Pérez,* Arcos included *La mala sombra* by Serrano; *Tío . . . yo no he sido* by Felipe Pérez y González and Angel Rubio; *El lucero del alba* by Mariano Pina; *Ruido de campanas* by Antonio M. Viergol; and variety acts. After closing at the 63rd Street, the Arcos company had a short run at the end of February at the Leslie Theatre on 83rd Street and Broadway. The Cuban blackface comedian Arquímides Pous also began doing comic numbers with the company here.

Numerous other theatres housed occasional performances in the late teens and the 1920s: the Compañía de Comedia de la Sociedad Artística Española at Palm Garden Hall in 1919; an unnamed company featuring Luisa Bonoris at Yorkville Casino in 1920; the Compañía de Teatro Español, with Miguel de Zárraga as artistic director, with more than twenty-four performances at the Little Theatre and the Belmont Theatre in 1922; Pilar Arcos with the Teatro Lírico Español and the Gran Compañía Española in 1922 and 1923 at Town Hall; Conchita Piquer and vaudeville at the Ambassador Theatre in 1924; the Teatro Lírico Español, directed by José T. Cervera, at Carnegie Hall in 1924; and the Compañía de Zarzuela y Variedades Tempranita Beltri, which had also been active in the Southwest and featured Los Angeles playwright Eduardo Carrillo as a comic at the Park Palace in November 1927. Other theatre houses achieved popularity with Hispanic audiences for one or two years and then faded from the scene.

The Compañía de Teatro Español began leasing what was described as the new and elegant National Theatre on 41st Street and Broadway on October 30, 1921, with a performance of José Zorrilla's *Don Juan Tenorio* and continued alternating dramas and comedies each Sunday through November 1923. The Teatro Español also leased the Longacre Theatre on 48th and Broadway from August to December 1922, for performances of *zarzuelas* and comedies; it also occasionally played at the Lyceum Theatre during 1922 and 1923. The group, which at times included the services of Pilar Arcos, also performed on Saturdays from 1921 to 1923 in Newark, New Jersey. *La Prensa* reported on November 17, 1921, that the backers of El Teatro

Español—Miguel de Zárraga, Jorge Keen, and Fernando de Adelantado—had only been able to make $632.97 in profits by the end of the season and, therefore, that it was obvious that they were more patriotically than commercially oriented. According to the same article, the actors were paid a total of $6,000.

Two other theatres that were frequently engaged during the 1920s by Pilar Arcos and other companies were the 14th Street Theatre and the Lyric Theatre on Broadway in midtown Manhattan. The 14th Street started serving the Hispanic community when Arquímides Pous began recording songs for Columbia Records in New York. He and his wife, Conchita Llauradó, organized a company for Cuban farce, Compañía de Bufos Cubanos, for a short run with daily performances which debuted on July 11, 1921. Pous also took his company to Saengerband Hall in Brooklyn in August. Later in the decade numerous of Pous's original works, such as *Pobre Papá Montero* and *Las mulatas de Bombay*, would find their way back onto the stages of New York. Pous died in Mayagüez, Puerto Rico, in April 1926. The farces, which featured stock character types of *negrito* (blackface), *mulata*, and *gallego* (a Galician), relied heavily on Afro-Cuban song and dance and improvised slapstick comedy, much in the manner of the Mexican *revistas*. Like the *revistas*, the *bufos cubanos* often found inspiration in current events, neighborhood gossip, and even politics. Arquímides Pous was also the creator of more than two hundred *obras bufas cubanas*. Pous, who always played the *negrito*, was famous for his social satire and especially his attacks on racism. The *bufo* genre itself had been influenced in its development during the second half of the nineteenth century by the *buffes parisiennes* and the Cuban circus. Under the Spanish the *bufos* were particularly repressed for being native Cuban, causing many of them to go into exile in Puerto Rico, Santo Domingo, and Mexico.[8]

Up through 1927, the 14th Street was an occasional stop for numerous touring and resident companies such as, in June 1925, the Compañía Española, which was directed by the impresario of the Teatro Italiano, Clemente Gioglio; the Compañía de Zarzuela Española Antonio Trujillo, with Marita Reid and Vicente Cordellat in July 1925, which, besides Spanish *zarzuelas*, also performed Cuban *zarzuelas* such as Pous's *Las mulatas de Bombay*; the Compañía—(Pilar) Arcos–(Fortunato) Bonanova in June and July 1926, with *zarzuelas*; and the Teatro Italiano itself, reinforced by Hispanic artists, performing Spanish *zarzuelas* in Spanish, in July 1927. In 1925 the Olympic Theatre at 143 East 14th Street and the Bramhall Theatre at 138 East 27th Street also housed performances by Trujillo's Spanish *zarzuela* company. At the Olympic Theatre Trujillo's company, which featured leading actress Marita Reid (who still resides in New York today), often performed on a double bill with the Compagnia di Opera Italiana Verdi, which presented such works as *Cavalleria Rusticana* and *Pagliacci.*

On November 1, 1925, New York's Lyric Theatre became a Spanish-language house for a period of three months while it was contracted by Carmen Gaona and Manuel Fernández, the impresarios that brought together Pilar Arcos and Rodolfo de Hoyos, whose career in lyric theatre was important in Mexico and the U.S. Southwest. For a number of years thereafter de Hoyos became a fixture on the New York Hispanic stage. After performing a familiar lineup of *zarzuelas* for one month and a half, the company disbanded and merged with the Pilar Arcos–Fortunato Bonanova company under the new name of Compañías Unidas and lasted at the Lyric until February 25, 1926.

On December 2, 1927, the Palm Garden Theatre became a center for Spanish drama and comedy with a decidedly Galician flavor. The Compañía Cómico-Lírico-Dramático de Narcisín leased the house, which was located on West 52nd Street, through April 7, during which time it staged such works as *Rapaciño,* which was called the odyssey of a Galician immigrant; *El pibe del corralón, Amor de madre, El golfillo o el pilluelo de Madrid* (which was Torres y Vanti's adaptation of *El pilluelo de París*), and numerous *zarzuelas.* In February, the Compañía Narcisín relocated to the Park Palace Theatre on West 110th Street and repeated its repertoire until March 1. It then began alternating runs at the Park Palace with a mixed company of Spanish, Cuban, and Puerto Rican actors, including Pilar Arcos, Juan C. Rivera, Luis Inclán, and Alberto González, through 1929.

The Park Palace Theatre was important in setting a precedent that the famous Teatro Hispano would later follow. Located farther uptown and closer to Spanish Harlem than any of the other Hispanic theatres, it became a meeting ground for the different Hispanic nationality groups. Besides featuring the Galician fare of Narcisín, the Park Palace also housed Cuban and Puerto Rican companies. In fact, it was on the Park Palace stage that the growing Puerto Rican community first began to see its life reflected in drama. As mentioned above, a mixed Hispanic group began alternating runs with Narcisín in March 1928. It began by featuring such Cuban farces as *La bayadera* and *revistas* such as *Del puerto a la gloria.* By August the company had taken the name of the Compañía Hispana de Nueva York and begun offering works featuring the Cuban comedian and playwright Alberto O'Farrill such as *Cubita bella* and *Si papá lo mandó.* On October 10, 1929, the company performed one of the first Puerto

Rican plays written and produced on the United States mainland, Gonzalo O'Neill's *Pabellón de Borinquen o bajo una sola bandera,* which supported the Puerto Rican nationalist movement. On October 24, a newly baptized Compañía Artistas Unidos brought together diverse Hispanic artists, including the Santigosa family, to stage the *zarzuela El hombre de tres mujeres* and the comedy *La casa de los milagros.* On October 31, the United Artists staged the seasonal *Don Juan Tenorio.* A newly formed Compañía Teatral Puertorriqueña performed *Bajo una sola bandera* again on November 2.

In April 1930 the same company, under the direction of a señor García (could this have been *el negrito* Antonio García?), began performing again through May, mostly Spanish works by Dicenta and the Alvarez Quintero brothers, but staged the Puerto Rican *zarzuela, Día de reyes* by Juan Nadal de Santa Coloma on May 10. It is likely that Nadal was a member of the cast at this time. Hispanic theatrical activity at the Park Palace was definitely waning from 1929 to 1931, with news of only an Asociación de Artistas Extranjeros (Sección Hispano-Americana) staging the *revistas Momentos frívolos, El emigrante,* and *La familia de solé* on March 28 and April 4, 1931, and an unnamed company that transferred to the Park Palace from the closed San José Theatre for performances of *La mujer del otro* and *El milagro de la virgen* on August 8 and 9. The Park Palace continued to be leased on a one- or two-night basis occasionally through the 1930s, with the last recorded performances being by the Artistas Hispanos Unidos, directed then by Eduardo Díaz Ochoa and featuring Spanish dancer *cum* playwright-director Paco Perafán, who had moved to New York from Chicago, and Puerto Rican soprano Virginia Ramos in comedies.

Another uptown theatre, located at 7th Avenue and 125th Street, was rebaptized the Teatro Alhambra in 1927 but was short-lived in presenting mainly Spanish *zarzuela* and Cuban musical farce to its diverse Hispanic audiences. Under the name of the Compañía Lírica Española, a group of resident artists, including Mexican baritone Rodolfo de Hoyos, Cuban blackface comedian and playwright Alberto O'Farrill, and Cuban comedian and playwright Juan C. Rivera, who was known for his renditions of the *gallego* in *obras bufas cubanas,* offered such melodramas, *zarzuelas,* and Cuban musical farces as *Tres para una* and *La herencia del amigo,* both written by Juan C. Rivera, from February through May 1927. Another original Cuban farce produced by the company, according to *Gráfico* (February 27, 1927) was *En la Calle 116* by local poet René Borgia; presumably it was replete with local color.

From the late 1920s through the 1930s numerous theatres were rented for one or two performances or for short runs by the Hispanic companies in search of audiences. Many of the performances were by companies that were already contracted by the Apollo Theatre or the San José but who were moonlighting in another part of town. Other theatres were simply rented to accommodate foreign touring companies for their New York runs. Among the houses that accommodated companies on tour were the New Manhattan Opera House in 1926 and the New York Theatre in 1932, which were rented for Spain's Compañía Dramática de María Guerrero y Fernando Díaz de Mendoza; the Forrest Theatre at 49th Street and Broadway for Spain's Compañía Cómico-Dramática de Gregorio Martínez Sierra in 1927; and the Nora Bayes Theatre at 44th Street and Broadway for the 1937 engagement of Argentina's Teatro de Drama y Comedia, directed by Enrique de Rosas, which in between the acts of serious dramatic works by Alejandro Casona, Miguel de Unamuno, and Florencio Sánchez accommodated the local Puerto Rican tastes with poetry recitals by the famous Puerto Rican *declamador* (poetry reciter) Santiago Lavandero. It should be noted that these large companies which produced serious drama were able to rent theatres that were more centrally located in Manhattan and that they probably attracted a higher-class audience to them. According to the April 28, 1927, *La Prensa*, the Gregorio Martínez Sierra company was able to charge $3.00 to $11.00 for tickets for the debut of his newly written play *El camino de la felicidad*. For the other dramas produced by the company and written by Martínez Sierra, Carlos Arniches, and other Spaniards (also featured in this run was a Spanish adaptation of George Bernard Shaw's *Pygmalion*), prices ranged from $2.50 to $5.50 for evening shows and $1.65 to $3.30 for matinees.

Included in the houses used by resident companies in New York from 1926 to 1937 were the Casino Theatre for a benefit performance in honor of Rodolfo de Hoyos in 1926; the Star Casino for the *cuadro de declamación* directed by Mexican actor Rubén Ruiz in presenting *zarzuelas* and *sainetes* in 1927; *obras bufas cubanas* with Fortunato Bonanova, Alberto O'Farrill, and Juan C. Rivera on Thursdays at the Jewell Theatre at 116th Street and Fifth Avenue during 1926 and 1927; Spanish *zarzuela* and *obra bufa cubana* on Saturdays and Sundays during 1927 at the Nation Theatre on 14th Street (actors Cueto, Inclán, Moreno, and Garralaga were also appearing concurrently at the Apollo Theatre uptown); the Gran Compañía de Opera, Opereta y Zarzuela Española de Angel Soto, the Compañía de Operetas y Zarzuelas, and the Compañía de Paquita Santigosa at the Star Casino in 1928; the Compañía Bufo-Cubana, directed by Juan C. Rivera and the Compañía Teatral Puertorriqueña, which featured actor-playwright Erasmo Vando's Puerto Rican *obra bufa De Puerto Rico al Metropolitan o el Caruso Criollo* at Clairmont Hall on 106th Street in 1928; Narcisín's company and the Compañía Llaneza with Pilar Arcos at the Verona Theatre at 2092 Second Avenue in 1928 and Narcisín next door at the Irving Theatre in 1928 (in 1929 Narcisín was also venturing out to Newark); the Roerich Theatre from May to June 1932 for Spanish drama and comedy and for works by Spanish playwright Abelardo Fernández Arias, who was residing in New York, by the Compañía de Drama y Comedia Juan Nadal de Santa Coloma; and in 1935 a *zarzuela* company directed by Spanish baritone Antonio del Val at the 5th Avenue Theatre. From April 12 to May 8, 1937, the Ambassador Theatre at 49th and Broadway was used by the Compañía Argentina de Comedia y Drama Paulina Singerman on the New York leg of its tour of the Hispanic world. For prices ranging from $.55 to $3.30, the Singerman company presented a daily performance of works by contemporary Argentine, Brazilian, and Spanish playwrights.

As in the Southwest, the halls and stages of mutalist societies and clubs were increasingly used by both professional and amateur companies during the Depression. There is no evidence, however, that church halls and religious societies were involved in Hispanic theatre anywhere close to the degree that they were in the Southwest. As can be surmised from the above, the availability of numerous theatres for leasing in New York City meant that the Depression, vaudeville, and cinema did not drive serious drama into the mutualist societies and churches as early as it did in the Southwest. But as the major Hispanic houses to be studied below increasingly dedicated their stages to vaudeville, revues, and *bufos cubanos* and as the principal actors and actresses had to make the conversion to working in these genres, these artists also chose the alternative of keeping serious theatre alive by performing at the societies and clubs and putting their art at the service of community charities and causes. One personality took the energetic lead in preserving Hispanic drama in New York through the late 1930s and 1940s as an actress, director, and playwright: Spanish-English actress Marita Reid. It is in the mutualist societies and in the clubs, furthermore, that political theatre flourished. Although houses like the Park Theatre and the Teatro Hispano did, on occasion, support theatrical functions whose purpose was the raising of funds and providing support for the Puerto Rican nationalist and Spanish Republican causes, it was societies like the Mutualista Obrera Puertorriqueña and the Club Obrero Español that were more appropriate for these activities.

Two mutualist societies regularly sponsored performances on their stages by professional companies that were touring to New York and companies that were resident and/or simultaneously playing the professional stages. Serving since 1919 as a site for amateur productions by the Cuadro de Declamación, in 1926 the Centro Andaluz began sponsoring productions by local professionals such as the librettist-actor Alberto González, the comedians Juan C. Rivera, Alberto O'Farrill, and Juan Olivera and singer-actor Vicente Cordellat. From 1928 through 1931 the Centro Andaluz was periodically leased by two professional companies that were also performing at the Park Palace, the Apollo, the Centro Español in Newark, and elsewhere: the Compañía Narcisín and the Compañía Marita Reid. Both companies specialized in serious Spanish drama by the leading playwrights of the times: Jacinto Benavente, Gregorio Martínez Sierra, and the Alvarez Quintero brothers. By 1931, both Narcisín's company and Marita Reid's ran into hard enough times to have merged under the new name of Artistas Unidos and to continue to perform at the Centro Andaluz in an effort that was very similar to that of the United Artists in Los Angeles and San Antonio.

From September 5, 1923, through February 24, 1924, the Compañía Hispano-Mexicana F. Díaz de León, a perennial Southwest attraction, leased the Unión Benéfica Española as a home base for its mixture of *zarzuelas* and *dramas* but also toured to Newark, Elizabeth Port, Perth Amboy, Philadelphia, and other points in the New York–New Jersey–Pennsylvania metropolitan areas.

Other mutualist societies that occasionally offered performances by both professional and amateur companies during the late 1920s and 1930s were the Sociedad Hispana La Amistad at 149 East 23rd Street, with performances by the Compañía de Comedias y Revistas, directed by Felipe González, in 1924; the Círculo Valenciano (later renamed the Ateneo Hispano) at 24 New Chamber Street that sponsored its own amateur Cuadro de Declamación's productions of dramas and *zarzuelas* in 1929 through 1934 and from then to at least 1941 with professional performances by Marita Reid's companies; the Casa Galicia, with its own Cuadro de Declamación in standard Castilian and Galician comedies and dramas in 1929 and 1930 and from 1933 through 1935 housing professional drama and *zarzuela* companies in elaborate productions; and Hungarian Hall in the Bronx at least once by Mary Reid. In 1936 the amateur Cuadro Unidad Artística offered dramas and variety shows at the Club Pomarrosas. From 1937 through 1938 the Calpe American's Cuadro Artístico del Calpe, directed by Marita Reid, was active. At the Calpe she directed and starred in standard melodramas, *zarzuelas*, and comedies, while at the same time she was directing a group named in *La Prensa* as the Spanish Players at the Heckscher and the 58th Street theatres. By 1938 Mary (name changed) Reid was directing the theatre group at the Centro Libertario; here she produced some of her own compositions, including her *entremés Sor Piedad*.

By 1940–1941, Puerto Rican societies had become firmly established and had also begun to support theatrical productions. Most important of these was the Mutualista Obrera Puertorriqueña (IWO Lodge 4792) on 178 East 105th Street, which sponsored its Cuadro Artístico Caribe that, besides including professionals like Luis Mandret and Edelmiro Borras, also offered training for up-and-coming Puerto Rican amateurs such as María and Adelita S. Barcena. In 1940, the Puerto Rican actor and singer Jaime Estrella was paid homage at the *mutualista* (mutualist society) with a performance of *La Tosca* by an all professional cast that included Mary Reid, Luis Mandret, Edelmiro Borras, Paco Perafán and, of course, Estrella himself. Also, the 1940s saw more and more activity by such itinerant companies as the Compañía Teatral Puertorriqueña, directed by R. Miquelí and R. Mojica Solá, which embarked on an odyssey of performances at halls and mutualist societies. This group was later followed by the Sociedad Cultural Puertorriqueña and the Compañía Teatral Bethancourt in the same manner. Finally, the Puerto Ricans in the 1940s also began using church halls for performances, as in the 1942 production of Enrique Codina's original play *Nobleza boricua*, starring María Barcena and Edelmiro Borras, in celebration of the Virgen de la Providencia, the patron saint of Puerto Rico.

There probably were numerous amateur companies in action during this time, but *La Prensa*, *Gráfico*, and *La Voz* newspapers rarely mentioned them. Except for those mentioned above and Agrupación de Juventudes Españolas performing at the Manhattan Plaza theatre, the others mentioned were involved in political consciousness raising and fundraising during the Depression.

Also, throughout the 1930s various clubs and theatres became the sites of theatrical performances in support of developing socialist organizations in the Hispanic community and to raise funds for the Republican cause in the Spanish Civil War. Even the Casa de Galicia, which had mainly dedicated its stage to Hispanic mainstream commodity theatre, in 1934 began sponsoring the socialist group Cultura Proletaria in such plays as *Carne de esclavitud* and *Guerra*. Cultura Proletaria as a theatrical group was active at least until 1936, when *La Prensa* noted its February 1 performance of *Como palomas sin nido* at the Manhattan Opera House. Perhaps one of the reasons this performance was covered by the press—as opposed to numerous others which were not—was that rising star Xavier Cugat and his Waldorf Astoria Orchestra provided the music. On December 12, 1934, the Galicia sponsored the Comité Pro Víctimas Sociales in its performance of *Esclavitud* as a benefit for prisoners and their families of the Asturias Revolution in Spain. The same committee went on in 1935 to produce the political courtroom drama *El proceso de Ferrer* at the Hunts Point Palace Theatre.

The Club Obrero Español, Branch 4763 of the International Workers of the World, with its headquarters at the Masonic Temple at 71 West 23rd Street, sponsored the Artistas Unidos theatre company during the late 1930s and other companies into the 1940s. From 1935 to 1937, such artists as Alberto O'Farrill and other professionals mentioned above were performing for the club in works that seem to have been of a typical comedic and nonpolitical nature: *Una conquista militar* (*boceto cómico*), *Las tres mujeres de Eduardo*, *El chiquillo*, *El puñao de rosas*. But by May 1937, such works as *Rebeldía* by I. Castilla and L. González were being staged by the club's own itinerant group of players to raise funds for ambulances and medicine for the Spanish Popular Front. Too, the Comité Antifascista del Bronx sponsored the group's performance this same month of *Opera muda* in one act and *Pueblo en armas*. During the early 1940s the club sponsored professional performances by a company directed by Venezuelan actor Luis Mandret that included Cuban Edelmiro Borras and Puerto Ricans Raquel Abella and Nita de Soto.

Two other itinerant theatre companies that were also active in New York in support of the Spanish Republic were the Comité Pro-Democracia Española, with its production of *El pueblo en marcha*, written by the *escritor revolucionario* (revolutionary writer) José Enamorado Cuesta and directed by Julián Benedet at the Manhattan Lyceum in 1937; and the Grupo Representativo de Sociedades Hispanas, affiliated with the Comité de Socorro para la República Española in its performances of *Tierra baja* and *Los mineros* at the Royal Windsor Theatre in 1937. *La Voz* on November 1, 1937, featured photos of two actors from the latter operetta costumed as miners, the male with a pickax and the woman with a hoe; the performance was part of a Gran Festival de Unidad, which was to promote unity among the various Hispanic political and social organizations.

Additionally, Mary Reid was active in political theatre. Among her various political works was her production of Vital Aza's *Las codornices* at the head of the Cuadro Artístico del Ateneo Hispano in a Pro-Presos Sociales de España (On Behalf of Spanish Social Prisoners) at Mt. Carmel church on May 13, 1934, in conjunction with the Italian Compañía Dramática Moderna, directed by Peppino Ca-prero, in the two-act *Dopo.*[9]

One final group, the Cuadro Artístico Proletario (this may be the same Cultura Proletaria cited above) performed at the American La-bor Party Hall on Third Avenue during this period. In an undated newspaper clipping of the time in the Elsa Ortiz Robles archive, the group, which included Edelmiro Borras, was reported as performing the *obra bufa cubana Criada enredadora* and the *palpitante* (pal-pitating) dialogue relating to the tragic situation in Spain, *La despe-dida del miliciano.* The clipping further states that "'El Cuadro Artístico Proletario' está efectuando una positiva labor de arte y propaganda. Tiene en su repertorio varias obras escritas expresa-mente, sobre la palpitante y trágica actualidad española."[10] The Cuadro Artístico Proletario is also documented as having performed *La reconciliación* at the American Labor Party Hall in 1938.

Many of the above theatrical functions were preceded and/or fol-lowed by political speeches and fundraising activities. It was com-mon for prominent Hispanic socialists to take part in these events and support them with speeches and lectures. On May 6, 1933, noted Mexican muralist David Alfaro Siqueiros delivered a speech on "El arte para las masas" (Art for the masses), preceding a performance of *Tierra baja* at the Ateneo Hispano. In addition, Dr. Salvador Men-doza similarly addressed an audience after the performance of An-tonio Mediz Bolio's "intenso drama social mexicano" (intense Mexi-can social drama) *La ola* at Palm Garden Hall on 8th Avenue and 53rd Street in honor of May Day, 1935. Just how many political or agitprop Hispanic theatres were active and how many political fund-raisers took place during these years is difficult to assess. News of them only appears sporadically in the Spanish-language press, which, naturally, was more interested in covering commerical, ad-purchas-ing entertainment. Obviously the press was more reticent about re-lationships with openly political and possibly socialist or commu-nist organizations, given that most of the community, including the owners and workers of the press, was alien. Therefore, we have today only vestiges of what may have been a very important chapter in the history of Hispanic theatre in the United States.

The Major Hispanic Theatres

While all of this activity was taking place on an intermittent basis at a variety of large and small theatres and clubs, beginning in 1922 the Hispanic community was able to lay claim to a number of houses on long-term bases, at times even rebaptizing the theatres with the names of Spanish writers or in honor of the Hispanic community as a whole. During the decade of the 1920s the first two theatres which began to stabilize Hispanic theatre culture in New York were the Dalys and the Apollo theatres. After 1930 the Apollo no longer offered Hispanic fare; the leadership then passed in 1931 to the San José/Variedades, in 1934 to the Campoamor, and finally in 1937 to the most important and longest-lived house in the history of the Hispanic stage in New York: El Teatro Hispano. In briefly monitoring the development of these theatres, we shall see a process of evolution similar to that of the Southwest Hispanic stage, in which melodrama and *zarzuela* gradually gave way to musical revues and vaudeville, while in the 1930s artists of serious drama (Marita Reid, for example), as noted above, were forced to take refuge in the clubs, mutualist societies, or minor houses and to develop audiences for themselves more directly.

The Dalys Theatre

Located between Broadway and Central Park on 63rd Street, the Dalys Theatre served Hispanic audiences on a weekly basis from 1922 through 1927. Throughout this time the Dalys primarily offered the community Spanish *zarzuela* as interpreted by Pilar Arcos, although the important director Manuel Aparicio, who during the Depression would direct the Federal Theatre Project in Tampa, also headed up a dramatic company at the Dalys in 1924.

The record of Hispanic performances at the Dalys begins on Sunday, October 15, 1922, with the production of the comedy *Pipiola,* written by the Alvarez Quintero brothers and performed by the Compañía de Comedia Marita Ríos (it is not known whether this was an early stage name of Marita Reid), which was also repeating the same show at the Longacre Theatre that day. Prices for these Sunday performances at the Dalys ran the range from seventy-five cents to two dollars. No further mention of the Ríos company at the Dalys is made in *La Prensa.* On Sunday, November 5, 1922, Pilar Arcos's Teatro Lírico Español opened and dominated the Dalys stage through March 1924 with matinee and evening performances of a wide variety of the most popular and standard Spanish *zarzuelas* and operettas. Also featured were one- and two-act comedies, again by the Alvarez Quintero brothers, Pedro Muñoz Seca, and the standard Spanish playwrights of the late nineteenth and early twentieth centuries. Periodically, Arcos integrated new actors into the company, such as the Spanish baritone Juan Pulido, the *primera tiple* Carmen

López, leading men P. Coto Fuego and Eduardo Fort, and a blackface Cuban actor whose benefit performance on November 18, 1923, was celebrated with a specially written one-act *revista, Un negrito más en Nueva York*. Besides performing at other New York theatres during these years, the Arcos company would periodically tour to Moose Auditorium in Philadelphia, to Bayonne, New Jersey, and other nearby cities. So popular was Pilar Arcos as a singer and leading lady that letters were sent to *La Prensa* requesting favorite songs for her to sing at the Dalys (*La Prensa*, February 3, 1923) and the newspaper would often publish photos of the star. After closing in March 1924, it was not until December 1925 that Pilar Arcos returned with her new Compañía de Zarzuelas, co-directed by Fortunato Bonanova, to run through October 1926.

Following Pilar Arcos at the Dalys in March 1924, the Compañía Teatro Lírico Español, directed by Manuel Aparicio and managed by V. Simón, opened, featuring leading lady Marita Ríos, who had formerly directed her own company at the Dalys, and Carmen López, who had been appearing with Pilar Arcos. Charging from eighty-five cents to two dollars for tickets, Aparicio presented a varied fare of such comedies as *Lo que tú quieras* by the Alvarez Quintero brothers and *La pasión* by Gregorio Martínez Sierra, melodramas such as Alexander Dumas's *La dama de las camelias* and the obligatory *Don Juan Tenorio*, as well as *zarzuelas*, vaudeville, and variety acts. It is not clear from *La Prensa* notices just how long the Aparicio company remained at the Dalys, but from December 15, 1924, through 1925, *revistas*, vaudeville, and chorus lines of twenty girls are featured at the Dalys, with such artists as E. R. Fort, Juan Pulido, and Conchita Piquer. As noted above, the Compañía de Pilar Arcos returned on December 6, 1925, to stay until October 1926. In 1927 there is only news of a Compañía Dramática Española performing through November 1927, and after that, nothing.

The Apollo Theatre

It was the Apollo Theatre (formerly the Hurtig and Seamon Theatre) that was to fix and systematize what became distinctive of New York Hispanic theatrical culture: balancing the theatre and entertainments of the diverse Hispanic nationalities for working-class audiences. The formula for alternating Spanish, Cuban, and Puerto Rican shows and for integrating lyric theatre with vaudeville and musical revues was one that later the Teatro Hispano would elaborate to perfection. Located at 125th Street, farther north and closer to Harlem than any other theatre housing Hispanic programs, the Apollo began featuring Hispanic comedies, variety, and Cuban musical farces intermittently on Sundays in March 1926.

Regular Hispanic programming, however, was not to begin until March 28, 1928, with the debut of the Compañía Española de Zarzuelas, Comedias y Variedades, directed by Ramón Reynado, in a continuous show that lasted all day Sunday, from 2:30 P.M. until 11:00 P.M. Under the impresarios the J. Miranda Brothers,[11] one-act comedies, *zarzuelas*, and variety acts were featured together each Sunday for ticket prices ranging from fifty to eighty-five cents. Through June the company featured such comedies as *La casa de Quirós* and *La casa de los milagros* and even the comic opera *El diablo en el camposanto* with Rodolfo de Hoyos, but in June the Apollo also began booking the Compañía de Bufos Cubanos, directed by Cristino R. Inclán (who had been quite active in Tampa), along with a Spanish company that produced *zarzuelas*, topical musical revues, and farces such as *Mientras Nueva York duerme*. Juan C. Rivera, playing the *gallego*, and Alberto O'Farrill in blackface also began to stage the farces they had written as members of the Compañía de Bufos Cubanos: Rivera's *Cleopatra, Cosas que pasan, Amor verdadero, El país de los secos o efectos de la Prohibición*, and *El desprestidigitador* and O'Farrill's *Un negro en Andalucía, Un doctor accidental, Kid Chocolate, Los misterios de Changó*, and *Una viuda como no hay dos*. Director Inclán also staged his own original *La reja Tapatía*, with its musical score written and performed by Nilo Meléndez, the successful Afro-Cuban music recording star.

In February 1927, Juan C. Rivera, who had joined the Gran Compañía Lírica Española, was replaced by Fernando Mendoza, the *gallego* from the company of the famed blackface Cuban actor-playwright Arquímides Pous, who seems to have brought along some of Pous's original repertoire such as *Los novios, El muerto vivo*, and *La huelga de hambre*. Of the interminable list of *obras bufas cubanas* performed weekly at the Apollo by Inclán's company from June 1926 to March 1927, the following seem to have been the most topical and related to New York culture (all were announced by *La Prensa* without mention of authorship): in 1926, *Mientras Nueva York duerme, Mosaicos del Apollo, Bronca entre latinos, Terremoto en Harlem, Cuadro en el precinto, El intérprete;* in 1927, *Lo que hace el Black Bottom, Los besos de Rodolfo Valentino, Cosas de policías*. Most of these took as their comic themes Hispanic night life, rumba and jazz, confrontations between Latins and the authorities, and problems with the English language. Others, such as Arquímides Pous's two works *Los dos de negrería* and *El velorio de Papá Montero* and

O'Farrill's *Un negro en Andalucía* and *Los misterios de Changó* explored Afro-Cuban culture, religion, and music and were related to the Afro-Cuban music craze that was soon to greatly influence mainstream music in the United States. O'Farrill's support of Afro-Cuban culture even extended to his writing an *obra bufa*, *Kid Chocolate*, based on the exploits of the popular black boxer from Cuba by the same name. Finally, another frequent theme of the *bufos* was nostalgia for Cuba, often expressed in the evocation of idyllic scenes of rural life, as in *Alegrías y tristezas de Cuba*. While the Spanish *zarzuelas* and Cuban *obras bufas* were the main attractions, the Miranda Brothers also played to Puerto Ricans by featuring singing groups such as the Trío Borinquen, along with such vaudeville standards as impressionist/transformist Edmund de Bries.

In March 1927 the Miranda Brothers impresarios took on a Mr. Audinot as a partner and a new stock company, featuring Pilar Arcos, began performing *zarzuelas* and an occasional comedy. The *bufos cubanos*, featuring Rivera, O'Farrill, and Olivera, continued on through August 1927. The only novelties were the *bufos'* productions of a *zarzuela* supporting *Puerto Rico independiente* and an *obra bufa* by G. Pando, *El negro que tenía el alma blanca*, which elaborated the popular Afro-Cuban folk theme dealing with the equality of races beneath the skin.

From September 1927 through March 1928 a variety of small companies, even duets and trios, of *bufos cubanos* played the Apollo. On November 18, 1927, Manuel Noriega, who had been furthering his cinema enterprises in Los Angeles, came to New York and debuted in the Pilar Arcos–Fortunato Bonanova company, which was featuring old standard *zarzuelas*. How long Noriega remained with the company is uncertain, but his replacement, Angel Soto, the Mexican Caruso, was introduced on February 26, 1928. Shortly thereafter the Arcos-Bonanova company was replaced by the Galician Narcisín company, which reintroduced melodrama on a regular basis to the Apollo on Fridays, Saturdays, Sundays, and occasionally on Wednesdays and Thursdays through January 1929. Along with occasional *zarzuelas*, Narcisín produced standard melodramas and a handful of works evocative of Galicia: *Airiños de Miña Terra*, *El Pibe del corralón*, *La casa de Quirós*. One of the works presented by Narcisín is that rare melodrama first featured in the United States in California during the 1860s and that later reappears in the Hernández-Villalongín repertoire in San Antonio: *El terremoto de la Martinica*. Along with this fare was offered an occasional realistic drama by Benavente, and, surprisingly enough, a January 13, 1929, production of

Puerto Rican playwright Erasmo Vando's *De Puerto Rico al Metro-politan o El Caruso Criollo*, the humorous tale of the rise of Puerto Rican opera star Antonio Paoli and his career at the Metropolitan Opera.

In 1929 the Narcisín company was followed by the Compañía Lla-neza with Rodolfo de Hoyos and by the Arcos-Bonanova company, both featuring comedies and *zarzuelas*. On February 23, 1929, the Apollo Theatre was renamed El Teatro Español. On March 10, the Cuadro Bufo Cubano, featuring O'Farrill and Olivera, opened at the Español and on April 4 Narcisín returned with more dated melo-dramas, even *La cabaña de tío Tom*. From June 16 until January 4 *La Prensa* and *Gráfico* newspapers carry no further news of the Apollo.

On January 5, 1930, the Teatro Español (Apollo) opened with a Spanish *zarzuela*, a Cuban *zarzuela*, and an American vaudeville company all on the same bill: the Gran Compañía de Zarzuela Es-pañola, the Gran Compañía de Zarzuelas Cubanas, and the Scandals Follies. While the Scandals offered scantily clad chorines, the Span-ish company performed the *zarzuela* version of Vicente Blasco Ibá-ñez's *Sangre y arena* and the Cuban group, directed by Ramón Es-pigul, presented Ruperto Fernández's Cuban *zarzuela Un toque en el trigémino (o las curas del Dr. Asuero)*,[12] with the score written by Espigul. The following Sunday the theatre booked in two new com-panies, the Spanish Compañía de Paquita Santigosa and the Com-pañía de Bufos Cubanos, the latter performing *Cuba en el año 2000*. The following Sunday, the two original opening *zarzuela* compa-nies, the Spanish group and Espigul's Cuban group, returned, the latter presenting in the weeks to come Afro-Cuban *obras bufas* such as *El espiritista, El negro que tenía el alma blanca, Los africanistas, Kid Chocolate, La mulata, El tabaquero o un negro en Sevilla*, and *Menéalo que se empelota*, starring Alberto O'Farrill. Paquita Santi-gosa's company offered standard *zarzuelas* featuring Margarita Cueto, Rodolfo de Hoyos, and Pilar Arcos, all of whom were probably per-forming with other companies at other theatres in town. The last noted Hispanic performance at the Apollo was on June 15, 1930. From then until early 1931 the only Hispanic theatrical entertain-ment to be had in town was variety and musical revues at the Teatro San José and plays at the mutualist Círculo Valenciano and the Casa Galicia. *Zarzuela* and drama had reached a nadir at the professional theatre houses; from here on the *bufos cubanos* and musical revues would predominate.

From October 30, 1933, through April 11, 1936, *La Prensa* spo-radically mentioned Hispanic performances at the Teatro Español

(Apollo). In 1933, the Teatro Español offered Spanish *zarzuelas* and an occasional Spanish comedy or drama on Sundays for prices ranging from forty to sixty-five cents. From 1934 to 1936, the theatre was occasionally used by an amateur group, Grupo Artístico Cervantes, for staging its two- and three-act comedies. The last noted production was Grupo Cervantes's *Los gatos* on April 11, 1936, under the new name of the theatre house: the Masters Theatre.

Teatro San José and Teatro Variedades

It is from 1931 to 1933 at the Teatro San José (in 1933 renamed Variedades) that serious artists like Pilar Arcos make the definitive transition to vaudeville and that Puerto Rican culture begins to take center stage. While Hispanic theatre was suffering the effects of the Depression and the increasing attraction of Spanish-language cinema, the social, economic, and ethnic makeup of the Hispanic population of New York was changing. According to Miller (1978: 41), although Cubans represented 40 percent of the New York Hispanic population in 1930, they were fast becoming outnumbered by the Puerto Ricans. Not only was the population becoming more and more Puerto Rican but also more derivative of rural areas of Puerto Rico, which accelerated the evolution of public tastes toward musical variety, slapstick comedy, and cinema.

Whereas the San José opened its doors on September 28, 1931, with two *zarzuela* companies sharing the bill in producing standard *zarzuelas* (with the exception of *Los sin trabajo*, which was billed as a "zarzuela de costumbres cubanas" and assuredly related to the effects of the Depression), by the end of the year Fernando Luis was directing his company in a musical revue ushering in the New Year, *Revista 1932*. And it was musical revues that would dominate the San José stage for the entire year of daily performances, alternating with film showings. In May, Luis was followed by Rodrigo Lila y su Compañía, which featured the Cuban singer Benito Ochart as a *negrito* and the Puerto Rican blues singer Diosa Castrello in such *revistas* as *Marinería, Modernismo, Luces de Nueva York,* and *Bataklán*. In June Pilar Arcos debuted with the company in the timely revues *Depresión y prosperidad* and *Veraneando*. On June 24 followed the Compañía de Revistas Sergio Rojas, with Antonio Rodríguez as its artistic director, Hilda Francés as concertist, Alberto Galo as choreographer, and Luis Mandret and Agustín Llopis among the actors, singers, and dancers. Later in the decade the Venezuelan actor Luis Mandret developed into an important director of Hispanic theatre. Besides presenting the expected musical revue fare such as *Carnaval de amor, La alegría de vivir,* and *Un sueño ideal,* the Sergio Rojas company also produced a social (socialist?) drama *Canto obrero* on June 22 and the often repeated *revista Cuando la vida es sueño,* which in front of a beautifully painted backdrop of the Puerto Rican countryside staged renditions of Puerto Rican composer Rafael Hernandez's songs "Lamento borincano" and "Alma boricua." The revue also nostalgically recreated scenes representing Spain, Cuba, and Mexico for the musical numbers "Jota Aragonesa," "Bella Cuba," and "Ojos Tapatíos."

On October 19, 1932, the San José abruptly closed its doors, announcing remodeling and the future opening of a company directed by Leopoldo González that was currently performing in Havana. It was not until May 12, 1933, that the theatre reopened its doors but under new management and a new name: Teatro Variedades. A large *revista* company, directed by Fernando Luis and Francisco Gómez, opened with *La floración,* featuring Diosa Castrello as *mulata,* Alberto O'Farrill and Benito Ochart as *negritos,* the Estrellas Habaneras sextet, and a chorus line of ten *bonitas jóvenes* (pretty girls). On July 14, the theatre booked Li-Ho-Chang y su Compañía for a week of magic and the *revista El palacio encantado de Pekín.* For the week of July 21, *La fiesta de las naciones,* with words and music by Puerto Rican authors José Limón de Arce, Dios de Lieban Córdoba, and Julián Sánchez, was presented by the Luis company and the Puerto Rican singers of mountain music, Cuarteto Canario. Luis's company had become the stock company of the Variedades and followed with productions relating to Puerto Rico and Cuba: the *revista Aprende usted español* by the Cuban writer Diosdado del Pozo; Puerto Rican actor-director-playwright Juan Nadal de Santa Coloma's *zarzuela puertorriqueña Día de reyes,* under his direction and with music composed and directed by Rafael Hernández; *Verde y rojo,* with Fortunato Ramos, the Dueto Puertorriqueño, and Pilar Arcos; *Melodía en azul* (after Gershwin's *Rhapsody in Blue?*) with Argentine tenor Rodolfo Ducal; *Radiomanía* with el Trío España; and various other innovative programs to please the audiences of diverse Hispanic nationalities. On August 25, 1933, one of the very few revues of a political nature was presented, *Cayó el tirano,* which satirized the recent fall of Cuban dictator Macías. *La Prensa* noted that the *revista* was divided into three scenes—Mexico, Cuba, and New York City—and that the satire of the dictator was biting. *La Prensa* also noted Nadal de Santa Coloma's extreme success in his leading role in the *revista.*

During the summer of 1933 Nadal not only became the leading man but the artistic director of the stock company of the Variedades and was probably responsible for the high quality and innovation of the above series of productions that promoted Cuban and Puerto Rican nationalism.

It is not clear from *La Prensa* whether or not Nadal continued at the Variedades in September 1933, but from September on into 1934 the Variedades staged numerous, sometimes surprising shows relating to Hispanic life in New York, Caribbean negritude, and Puerto Rican nationalism. The first of these was *Harlem arrabalero*, a vaudeville revue that *La Prensa* on September 26, 1933, stated had plenty of dynamite and action. The newspaper summarized the *revista* as follows: "'Harlem Arrabalero' es una descripción de una noche en el 'barrio latino' de Nueva York con su fárrago de marihuana, bolita, trompadas, estocadas, mujeres, hombres, miseria, policía, pito, bolita y sangre. Pocas veces se había recogido y logrado presentar en un espectáculo sólo una más vivida descripción de lo que se supone ser el arrabal de Harlem."[13] Whether the *revista,* starring Alberto O'Farrill, was describing Harlem or Spanish Harlem is not clear from the review, although it is clear that O'Farrill had competition from another *negrito* actor and that the reviewer praised the performance of the cast "this time" ("esta vez"). During the remainder of September and October the Variedades continued to present variety acts by its stock company and contracted from Havana the Compañía Camelia, which presented a series of revues such as *Maracas de Cuba* and *Piernas del aire* and the evocation of Puerto Rican rural life, *El jíbarito*. With support from the stock company, Camelia Bermúdez forefronted her artistry as a rumba dancer.

On November 1, at a special midnight benefit performance for Club Borinquen Atlético, Juan Nadal de Santa Coloma directed and acted in Luis Llorens Torres's intensely nationalistic, two-act dramatic rendition of Puerto Rico's declaration of independence from Spain, *El grito de Lares,* with a prologue by Puerto Rican patriot Luis Muñoz Rivera. The drama by one of Puerto Rico's master poets had its debut performance by an amateur company at San Juan's Teatro Municipal on November 1, 1914. It was not until September 25, 1925, that it was produced by a professional company at San Juan's leading house, the Teatro Tapia,[14] and not until 1927 that the play was first published.[15] *El grito de Lares,* along with Muñoz Rivera's poetic plea for justice and liberty, would be staged again in New York in support of the current independence movement led by Albizu Campos. *La Prensa* does not mention Nadal de Santa Coloma in conjunction with the *revistas* produced in November and December, although *El grito de Lares* was repeated again as part of the regular fare on January 4, 1934. From January 16 through March, Nadal directed his own company at the Teatro Cervantes on 64th Street. In April the Compañía Nadal de Santa Coloma appeared again at the Variedades.

But before Nadal left the Variedades, numerous topical and *negrista* revues were produced in November and December 1933: *Mosaico hispano, Locuras de Nueva York, Una noche en Hawaii, Rapsodia azul, Mamá . . . cómprame un negro* (after the song by the same title), *Navidades, Revista 1934.* In January, Pilar Arcos had a run at the Variedades, starring in the revues *Pompas* and *Adiós, Pilar* and in February and March various others that elaborated Spanish, Cuban, Puerto Rican, and Argentine cultural and muscial themes, and two relating to New York and California: *En la antigua California* and *Ecos de Harlem.*

When Nadal opened with his new company on April 26, 1934, at the Variedades, he not only succeeded in returning melodrama and comedy to the theatre in the form of *Robo en despoblado* and *La leyenda del monje,* but he once again staged an intensely nationalistic Puerto Rican play: Gonzalo O'Neill's *Pabellón de Borinquen o bajo una sola bandera.* Nadal's company remained at the Variedades until the week of June 12, and then nothing more was published in *La Prensa* about the theatre.

Teatro Campoamor, Teatro Cervantes, and Teatro Hispano

As early as July 1932 the Mt. Morris Theatre (inaugurated in 1913) on Fifth Avenue and 116th Street had served the Hispanic community. On that occasion it was leased to the Compañía Fernando Luis for Cuban *revistas* and variety acts that included the Puerto Rican blues singer Diosa Castrello. On August 8, 1934, the Mt. Morris became the Teatro Campoamor, named for Spain's nineteenth-century romantic poet Ramón del Campoamor, and began presenting Hispanic theatrical entertainments exclusively. The newly reconditioned theatre opened with famed tango singer Carlos Gardel and a Cuban company that included actress Alicia Rico (as *negra/mulata*), actors Antonio Valdivia, José Lugo, the *negrito* Antonio García, the *gallego* Guillermo Moreno from the Tampa stage, and Puerto Rican actress Raquel Abella. With the exception of Gardel, these artists became the nucleus of the Campoamor stock company, directed by the Cuban Fernando Luis. Marcial Flores served as the Campoamor's impresario. The company staged *Frivolidades 1934* and *Un toque en el trigémino,* supported by the Alberto Socarrás Orchestra and the Trío Matamoros. For the general admission price of one dollar (seventy-five cents balcony), the audience was also offered a showing of Carlos Gardel's latest movie *Cuesta abajo,* which had been filmed at studios in Long Island. According to *La Prensa* (August 13, 1934), fifteen hundred people packed the house on opening night, while three thousand waited outside for the arrival of Gardel. With the excitement that was more typical of Hollywood cinema openings, the police had to be called in to control the crowd.

From August through December, the company performed the usual variety acts, *revistas,* and *obras bufas cubanas,* which included *Cubanización cocktail, Un viaje a la luna,* which also featured the ballet duet of Sharduskaya and Kudenoff, *El desastre del Morro Castle, El velorio,* the don Juan parody *Don Juan Tenorio, Un viaje a Cuba, La mulata, La negra que tenía el alma blanca,* and so on.

Beginning on January 10, 1935, the Campoamor paid a week-long homage to the famed Puerto Rican composer living in New York, Rafael Hernández, with artists from all of the Hispanic cabarets around town performing in his honor. This was followed the next week with a Professor Armandes recreating on stage nightly the destruction of Nicaragua by earthquake, seconded by a play created by the stock company which now featured Alberto O'Farrill: *La caridad destruida.* Through March the Campoamor offered more variety, *revistas,* and movies, except during the week of March 8, when the house orchestra, Orquesta Alberto Socarrás, was at the Apollo Theatre competing with the Louis Russell Orchestra in what was billed as *Harlem vs. Cuba.* During Socarrás's absence, the Campoamor covered by contracting a Mexican orchestra, Marcos Dávalos y su Orquesta Típica Mexicana, which featured a *peladito,* don Chano. Through October the Campoamor continued with variety and *revistas,* at times booking Puerto Rican orchestras but varying the fare to include the diverse nationalities: *Fantasía borinqueña, Flores de España, Argentinidades, Las maracas de Cuba,* etc.

It is notable that the future impresario of the Teatro Hispano made his debut here at the Campoamor where Fernando Luis had been able to strike a balance of the diverse nationalities. Del Pozo learned the lesson well. His señor del Pozo y su Compañía Mexicana, which included Celia Villa and the Hermanos Hernández, nineteen stars, and twenty-two chorus girls, according to the December 9 *La Prensa,* offered *revistas* such as *México lindo, Aires nacionales,* and *Rapsodia en azul de 1936,* the latter to usher in the New Year.

In January the Del Pozo company was replaced by the Compañía de Zarzuelas Españolas, directed by Julián Benedet and Victoria Martínez, but this only lasted one week. Through June the stock company, reinforced with tango dancers Tanco y Lorca and the comedy team of Netty and Jesús Rodríguez of Texas, produced *revistas*, including *La sinfonía del tap, Ha salido del Sing Sing*, and *La Jibarita o nobleza borincana*. On May 1, 1936, *La Prensa* announced that the Campoamor stock company was going to participate in a benefit at the Star Casino Theatre to raise funds for Puerto Rican nationalist prisioners. The announcement was made openly and without commentary, despite the grave political nature of the event and of the activists who were seeking Puerto Rican independence from the United States.

The Campoamor closed in June and was reopened on August 5, 1936, now as the Teatro Cervantes, with Fernando Luis as the impresario. Whether the management of the earlier Teatro Cervantes that had offered Hispanic theatre at 153 West 64th Street in 1934 had taken over the Campoamor is not certain. It was clear, however, in an August 14 *New York Times* story that the theatre had been redecorated and that its opening performance was for that night. Through February 6, 1937, the Cervantes offered a steady fare of movies and variety acts, with an occasional *revista* such as *Una noche gitana* and *De Puerto Rico a Nueva York*. After February 6, 1937, nothing else is heard from the Teatro Cervantes.

On August 19, 1937, the Mt. Morris was again metamorphosed into another Hispanic house. This time the name would live on into the 1950s: El Teatro Hispano. The same Mexican orchestra leader who had brought his vaudeville company to the Campoamor, señor del Pozo (he never used his first name), resurfaced to organize a board of directors and financial backers and to assume the role that he would hold for more than twenty years: president and general manager. Joining him in the administration were Eduardo Alvarez as assistant manager, G. Díaz Estrada as artistic director, and the Puerto Rican businessman and playwright Gonzalo O'Neill as comptroller (administrator). Del Pozo also reserved for himself the job of directing the house orchestra. As the Teatro Hispano grew, Del Pozo's supporting team was gradually replaced by vice-president and treasurer John Vohs, comptroller Rafael C. Villa (a former Argentine "hoofer"), assistant manager Sunia Samuels, and stage manager Morris Seidelman and was expanded to include other assistants, technicians, and scenographers. Under Del Pozo, besides movies the Teatro Hispano offered three daily stage shows at 2:00, 5:30, and 9:00 P.M., except on Sundays, when four shows were given at 1:30, 4:30, 7:00, and 9:30 P.M. In order to maintain the interest of his working-class audiences, Pozo instituted a weekly schedule that included bonuses and surprises: on Tuesdays and Fridays banco was played at the theatre and prizes were given to the winners, Wednesday audiences participated in talent shows that were broadcast over radio WHOM, on Thursdays gifts and favors were distributed to audiences, and Saturday mornings at 10:30 A.M. there was a special children's program. On Sundays radio WHOM broadcasted live from the Hispano from 4:00 to 5:00 P.M. There were also occasional beauty contests, turkey raffles, and such. Weekly programs changed on Friday evenings and were billed and promoted as debuts. The playbill for the October 21–28 week of 1938 claimed that 500,000 people had attended the Teatro Hispano in the previous season. The first few seasons must have been particularly difficult, however, given the Depression and the history of Hispanic closings of the old Mt. Morris.

Possibly because of its unabashed courting of the working classes through its vaudeville programs and its other promotional strategies, there were members of the Hispanic elite who looked down their noses at Del Pozo and the Teatro Hispano. These certainly did not flock to attend performances.

The Teatro Hispano published eight-page playbills, which opened up to a two-page weekly program in the center folios and included numerous ads, reviews, jokes, poetry, numerous photos, and columns by Del Pozo and other commentators. A 1939 edition of the weekly playbill that coincided with Del Pozo's birthday included a poem writted in honor of Del Pozo by a young girl only identified as Rosita. Not only was Del Pozo adept at keeping his working-class audiences happy with raffles and banco, but he was also capable of using radio and, especially, his playbills to promote the theatre as a family institution and himself as a great paternal and kindly protector of the community, even if at times he had to employ maudlin sentimentality to that end. Assuredly the content of many of the revues was overly sentimental and nostalgic, especially when celebrating Hispanic patriotic holidays and, of course, Mother's Day.

Upon opening in August 1937 Del Pozo immediately began to elaborate the formula of alternating shows relating to the diverse Hispanic nationalities. For one week he played to the Puerto Ricans with the revue *En las playas del Borinquen*, starring Zoilaluz Furnis and singer Johnny Rodríguez. He then followed in September with an Afro-Caribbean revue *Fantasía en blanco y negro*, starring the Venezuelan comic Luis Mandret; then *De México vengo*, with his Orquesta Típica Mexicana and Mexican singer-actress Raquel Saucedo; the Compañía de Comedias Argentinas, directed by Enrique de

Rosas; and by the end of September Del Pozo was again announcing Cuban week featuring the *Cuba bella* revue. Each week a movie was shown to coincide with the country featured in the revue. And so it went.

On September 24 there was a special celebration of El Grito de Lares, the proclamation of Puerto Rican independence, featuring Antonio García, *el negrito*, who had begun his acting career in New York City and who later had great success, according to *La Voz* (September 24, 1937), on the stages of Madrid and Barcelona. Finally, the first week in October was dedicated to Spaniards and their popular *zarzuela La gatita blanca*, starring Mexican comic soprano María Luisa Crespo, Puerto Rican comic tenor Jaime Estrella, Puerto Rican Raquel Abella, and Luis Mandret. Unfortunately, *La Voz*'s review on October 8 said that the production left much to be desired but that in spite of obvious defects the public was pleased. The unnamed reviewer condescended, noting that the Teatro Hispano was lacking financial and performance resources to support a full-scale production at popular ticket prices. The reviewer also noted that the production was supported by a beautiful chorus line of "temporarily Hispanicized girls." In October the Hispano also featured *Seda y oro*, a revue dedicated to bullfights, and *Soles de Venezuela*, featuring Luis Mandret. A Mexican *pelado*, don Cuco, was also featured.

In October, there were also two extraordinary functions: a performance of Luis Llorens Torres's *El grito de Lares* to raise funds for Puerto Rican political prisoners, at which Gilberto Concepción de García spoke in defense of Albizu Campos; and a benefit performance for Club Cubano Julio A. Mella, with thirty entertainers from all over the city.

In the months and years that followed, numerous revues and an occasional *zarzuela* were staged, always balancing out the Puerto Rican, Cuban, Spanish, Mexican, and Argentine themes and performers. The *negrito* Antonio Rodríguez and the Cuban *negrito* Edelmiro Borras became ubiquitous and especially popular at the Teatro Hispano. The former at times functioned as master of ceremonies at the Hispano, while the latter played the Hispano and every other theatre and club he could get into. Documents in the Elsa Ortiz Robles private collection show that Edelmiro Borras supplemented his theatre income during the Depression by removing snow from the city streets and sidewalks and that his total income before deductions for one of these years was $6,570.

The cast at the Hispano was constantly being reinforced by refugees from the Spanish Civil War, like Rosita Rodrigo, formerly of the Teatro Cómico de Barcelona, and artists from the failing stages of the Southwest, like La Chata Noloesca, Jesús and Netty Rodríguez, Eva Garza, and even Romualdo Tirado, who in 1943 functioned for a while as a master of ceremonies at the Hispano. In a curious reversal, Puerto Rican soprano actress Raquel Abella, formerly of the Tampa stage, became a permanent fixture at the Hispano, while Manuel Aparicio went to Tampa to become the artistic director of the Hispanic Federal Theatre Project there.

By 1940 the Teatro Hispano had fixed its relationship to the predominantly working-class community, which had by now become Puerto Rican in the majority. The ethnic balance of shows was thus tipped in the direction of working-class Puerto Rican music, entertainment, and nationalism, but the other groups and their cultures would continue to be reflected into the 1950s. The Hispano would continue to hold benefits not only for Puerto Rican causes but also for the other groups, notably the Spaniards, as it did in its 1938 benefit for the Spanish Red Cross, in which Marita Reid starred in the *Viva España* revue. During World War II not only would there be benefits but numerous revues and comic skits would elaborate Hispanic support of and participation in the Allied cause.

Of course, topicality continued to be a mainstay of the theatre, which allowed for the reflection and elaboration of New York Hispanic culture in works like the 1938 *Nueva York de noche* and *Sucedió en Harlem,* a comic satire of Puerto Ricans in court, and *De Puerto Rico a Nueva York,* both written and staged in 1939 by Puerto Rican author Frank Martínez. The latter, which was repeated various times, even in church auditoriums into the 1940s, lightheartedly developed the theme of Puerto Rican migration to New York, culture shock, and the acculturation of Pepita, the young daughter of the *jíbaro* (mountain man) family. Predating by almost a decade and a half René Marqués's *La carreta, De Puerto Rico a Nueva York* is divided into three settings as in *La carreta* (in Martínez's play these correspond to two acts and a cuadro) which represent, respectively, the farm in the highlands of Puerto Rico, San Juan, and Harlem. In Martínez's play, the role of oppressing the migrant family befalls the landlord, a Mr. Cohoen. The musical theme for the comedy is provided by the commercial song "Salud, dinero y amor," whose lyrics Martínez changed to reflect the message exhorting Puerto Ricans to stay on the island instead of braving the poverty and extreme cold and heat of New York City:

Tres cosas tiene Niu Yol,
frío, rilif y calor,
el que tenga estas tres cosas,

no le dé gracias a Dios.
Pues con ellas sí se vive
lleno de preocupación.
Por eso pido que aprendan,
el refrán de esta canción.
      Coro
El que tenga un hogar
en Borinquen, que lo cuide,
si se quiere embarcar
que no se tire, que no se tire.
  Hay que pasar,
  pues no conviene,
  un temporal
  de frío y nieve.[16]

And along with topicality at the Hispano there was a waving of the flag, playing to the nationalistic sentiments not only of Puerto Ricans, Cubans, and Spaniards but also the South Americans, as in the birthday celebrations for the Great Liberator Simón Bolívar, at which the revue *Soles de Bolívar* would be staged in honor of Venezuela, Colombia, Ecuador, Bolivia, and Peru. There were also the religious days that called for productions of plays on the life of Jesus or on the patron saints of the Hispanic countries. In all, like the theatres in the Southwest, the Teatro Hispano maintained its own rhythm by monitoring the pulse of the community.

The New York Playwrights

As mentioned at the beginning of this chapter, there was a tradition of Spanish-language publication of plays established in New York City in the late nineteenth century. However, with a few exceptions, the playwrights to be studied below did not write their plays for publication but for production on the commercial stage in the 1920s and 1930s. Many of their works, in fact, were topical and more in the nature of librettos than scripts, more in the tradition of *revistas* and *obras bufas cubanas*. While the dramatic activity was intense in New York City, the Big Apple did not support a downtown center where five or six major Hispanic houses located side by side competed fiercely with each other on a daily basis, as did the theatres in Los Angeles. There was no vying for the Hispanic audiences by promoting play-writing contests. Neither was the community of immigrants and migrants cognizant of a resident Hispanic tradition and history in New York, as were the communities in Los Angeles and San Antonio. Although *El Gráfico* newspaper did support Alberto O'Farrill as editor, there were very few other theatre people or playwrights working for the Spanish-language press in New York, as there were in Los Angeles. Furthermore, the relationship between journalism and play writing had been firmly established in Mexico, but this does not seem to have been the case in Spain, Cuba, and Puerto Rico. Then, too, many playwrights were drawn to Los Angeles to work in the Hispanic film industry. Finally, the New York Hispanic public was not as large as Los Angeles' during the 1920s and thus could not support so large a business as the theatre industry represented in the City of the Angels.

That there were Hispanic playwrights in New York willing to see their works staged there is no doubt. Quality, financial backing, and audience tastes were factors that came into play in the risky business of staging unknown works. The record shows, unfortunately, that the New York impresarios were not risk takers. The desperation of budding authors volunteering their talents to impresarios can be appreciated from this classified advertisement which ran in *La Prensa* on March 25, 1926, when serious drama was still being produced (although the taste for melodrama was definitely waning) on commercial stages:

A todos los Empresarios de Teatros, el que desee obtener una obra teatral, emocionante, católica, en verso, cinco actos, titulada *Los Dos Sepulcros,* aproveche la ocasión; pues como es sabido, los estrenos de obras como la que aquí se ofrece, son de muy fácil venta. No ha sido ya vendida porque el nuevo autor tiene interés en que la referida obra se quede en alguien de su raza. Adviértese que esta obra estará en este país únicamente por un mes. Para informes diríjanse a Mateo Pou, en casa de Valentín Aguirre, 82 Bank St. NYC, hasta el domingo.[17]

Most likely a young Cuban playwright, Mateo Pou, was never heard from again, probably having found out that plays were not sold as easily as stated in his ad, even among his own people.

By far the most productive playwrights and librettists were the Cubans, especially those riding the crest of popularity of the irreverent, baudy, satirical *obras bufas cubanas.* The majority of the librettists, however, were just mentioned briefly by the newspapers as the librettists of works being offered at the Teatro Campoamor, the Apollo, the Hispano. Virtually nothing else is known about such authors as Ruperto Fernández, whose *Un toque en el trigémino (o las curas del Dr. Asuero)* was debuted at the Teatro Apollo in 1930; Cristino R. Inclán (see chapter 5) and his *La reja tapatía* at the Apollo in 1926; Fernando Mendoza and his *Cabo de guardia, siento un tiro* at the Apollo in 1927; Guillermo J. Moreno and his 1927 Apollo works, *Bronca en España* and *De Cuba a Puerto Rico*, and his 1936 Teatro Campoamor work *De la gloria al infierno;* G. Pando's *El negro que tenía el alma blanca* at the Apollo in 1927; and Raúl del Valle's *Garzona y bataclán* at the Apollo in 1927. Besides mentioning the Dominican literary critic and author Pedro Henríquez Ureña and his five-act drama *Dionisios,* published by *Las Novedades* newspaper in 1916, Perrier devotes most attention to two Cuban playwrights that we have seen delighted the theatre world with their comedy: Alberto O'Farrill and Juan C. Rivera.

According to Perrier (1926: 71), Alberto O'Farrill was born in Santa Clara, Cuba, in 1899 and had begun his career as an actor and playwright in Havana in 1921 before emigrating to the United States. In New York O'Farrill was the ubiquitous *negrito* of *obras bufas cubanas* and Cuban *zarzuelas* who made a career playing all the major Hispanic stages in New York's stock and itinerant companies. O'Farrill was also an intensely literate man who had been the editor of *Proteo,* a magazine in Havana, and had become in 1927 the first editor of New York's *Gráfico* newspaper, which he led in becoming the principal organ for the publication and commentary of literature and theatre. In *Gráfico* O'Farrill also published various stories and essays of his own. Despite his literary interests, Perrier confirms that as of 1926 none of O'Farrill's dramatic works had been published. Perrier has also noted that O'Farrill debuted two *zarzuelas* at the Teatro Esmeralda in Havana in 1921: *Un negro misterioso* and *Las pamplinas de Agapito.* His other known works were all debuted at the Apollo Theatre in 1926: one *sainete, Un doctor accidental,* and the four *zarzuelas Los misterios de Changó, Un negro en Andalucía, Una viuda como no hay dos,* and *Kid Chocolate.* In most of these, as in his acting, he seems to have been concerned with Afro-Cuban themes. And, despite Perrier classifying these works as *zarzuelas* and *sainetes,* it is probable that they tended more toward the musical farces of the *bufos cubanos.*

Even less is known about Juan C. Rivera, who quite often teamed up with O'Farrill in *obras bufas cubanas.* Rivera's favorite role in the *bufos* was that of the penny-pinching, cranky *gallego.* Another secondary Cuban actor and playwright who also played the *negrito* role was Jesús Solís; his melodrama, *El negro que tenía la visión clara,* and *revista, La perla de las Antillas,* opened on Friday, October 17, 1941, at the iwo Lodge, performed by El Conjunto de Arte Hispano and directed by Luis Mandret.

While it is true that Cubans and Spaniards made up the majority of theatre artists in New York City and that their works dominated the stages of the times, it is also true that Puerto Rican drama emerged at this time and, it seems, accounts for a more serious and substantial body of literature. Two of these first New York Puerto Rican playwrights appear to be socialists whose dramas supported the Spanish Republican cause and working-class movements: José Enamorado Cuesta (1892–1976) and Franca de Armiño. Of the former, all that we know is that *La Prensa* on May 22, 1937, called him an "escritor revolucionario" when it covered his play *El pueblo en marcha,* staged at the Manhattan Lyceum for the Comité Pro-Democracia Española. It is Nilda González (1979: 44) who claims he was Puerto Rican and who supplies us with his years of birth and death.

Almost nothing is known about the biography of Franca de Armiño, whose name is most certainly a pseudonym. In her published drama *Los hipócritas,* which was issed by Modernistic Editorial Publishing Company in 1937, various other works by Armiño are referred to: a dramatic comedy *Tragedia puertorriqueña,* a book of essays, and a book of poems. All three remain lost. *Los hipócritas,* which was debuted in three performances at the Park Palace Theatre on April 15 and 16, 1933, by the Compañía Manuel Santigosa, is a social drama in four acts and eight scenes which the author dedicated to the oppressed of the world and to those who work for the ideas of social renovation. In the introduction, the author explains that, although the play is set in Spain during the Republic and the Civil War, it is truly an international play that is based on the greatest and most burning issues that humanity faces in this century. The work, which begins with the 1929 stock market crash, deals with a daughter's refusal to marry her father's choice, the son of a duke. Rather, she is romantically involved with a son of the working class, Gerónimo, whom her father calls a communist and who has led her into atheism. Gerónimo works for Gloria's father, who owns a shoe factory that he was hoping the duke's son would help to save from financial ruin. Meantime, Gerónimo organizes the workers for a strike, but Gerónimo's father, worried about the developing fascist dictatorship and the persecutions of Sacco and Vanzetti and Tom Mooney, escapes. In Act Two a corrupt priest tries to arrange for Gloria to become a nun so that the church will get her dowry and an informer and traitor helps organize workers against the strike.

The main marriage triangle is reflected in the comic minor characters' arrangement for marriage. Act Three concerns Gloria's and Gerónimo's devotion to each other. In Act Four the strike takes place, with Gerónimo making an agitating speech to the fledgling union. Gerónimo unmasks the traitor Perico as a strikebreaker and hypocrite. The play ends with the strikers prevailing over the police, who are attacking them brutally.

While full of propaganda, Marxist theory, and stereotyped characters, *Los hipócritas* is a gripping and entertaining play that reflects the tenor of the times, as far as the Depression, labor organizing, and the Spanish Civil War were concerned. As can be seen in the number of leading theatre people that took part in fundraisers for socialist, Puerto Rican nationalist, and Spanish Republican causes, the sentiments expressed by Armiño were not unpopular. Marita Reid, Edelmiro Borras, Alberto O'Farrill, Luis Mandret, and the Apollo and the Hispano, besides the mutualist societies and clubs, all participated in leftist political theatre and fundraising to some degree at one time or another.

While Franca de Armiño and José Enamorado Cuesta were calling for a workers' revolution around the world, Gonzalo O'Neill was championing Puerto Rican nationalism and independence from the United States. Having been born and raised in Puerto Rico, O'Neill came to New York immediately upon graduation from Puerto Rico's Instituto Civil.[18] In New York O'Neill became a successful businessman and somewhat of a protector and godfather to newly arriving Puerto Rican migrants. O'Neill's literary career began as a romantic poet while he was still a young man on the island. There he and a group of writers founded the literary magazine *Palenque de la Juventud*, which published poetry by some of Puerto Rico's leading writers. From his very first published dramatic work, *La indiana borinqueña*,[19] a dialogue in verse issued in 1922, O'Neill revealed himself to be intensely patriotic and interested in Puerto Rican independence. His second published book was the three-act play *Moncho Reyes*, issued by Spanish American Printing in 1923; it was a biting satire of the current colonial government of Puerto Rico in the hands of the United States military. According to Antonia Sáenz (1950: 63), *Moncho Reyes* is interesting for its truthful account of the Mont Reiley rule on the island and of the reaction of Puerto Rican public opinion to it. Although both of these works enjoyed stage productions, it was his third play, *Bajo una sola bandera*, which debuted at the Park Palace Theatre in New York in 1928 and at the Teatro Municipal in San Juan in 1929, that deserves the greatest attention for its artistry and thought, which made it a popular vehicle for the Puerto Rican nationalist cause.

In *Bajo una sola bandera*, the political options facing Puerto Rico are personified in down-to-earth flesh-and-blood characters. The daughter of a middle-class Puerto Rican family residing in New York is directed by her mother toward a young American second lieutenant, the personification of the United States and military rule, and by her father toward a young native Puerto Rican, whom she loves. On a symbolic level, the daughter must choose between two costumes for a masquerade ball: Columbia, representing the United States, and a *jíbara*, or Puerto Rican mountain folk. She chooses the latter and also drapes herself in the Puerto Rican flag. The play ends with sonorous, patriotic verses which underline the theme of independence for Puerto Rico under one flag alone. A glowing review in San Juan's *La Democracia* on April 16, 1929, marveled at O'Neill's conserving perfect Spanish and his Puerto Rican identity, despite having lived in the United States for forty years, during which time he had spoken English and been in intimate contact with a civilization so contrary and exotic to Hispanic culture.

In 1937 Gonzalo O'Neill became an investor in and member of the management of the Teatro Hispano. Besides allowing him to maintain his involvement in theatre, his relationship with the Hispano also translated into his being able to write topical poems and publish them in the playbills of the Hispano and also to see his works staged at this theatre. The only thing that we know about O'Neill's last dramatic work, *Amoríos borincanos*, is that it was announced as upcoming in the playbill for November 25–December 1, 1938. How many other plays he wrote and where and when they were staged is as yet unknown.

The remaining four Puerto Rican writers were for the most part authors of shorter, lighter works:[20] Alberto M. González, Erasmo Vando, Juan Nadal de Santa Coloma, and Frank Martínez. Of the first, all that we know is that he authored the libretto for a published *zarzuela*, *Colegiales*, a *suelta* copy of which is on file at the New York Public Library and is dated May 18, 1928, probably the date of its staging. Set to a score by the famed composer Rafael Hernández, the *zarzuela* is a light three-act romantic comedy dealing with a romance that blooms during the preparations for a play at the college of medicine. The published libretto indicates that actress A. Luciano and actor Erasmo Vando had the leading roles in *Colegiales*, with Luciano's role lightly satirizing the problem of a country bumpkin coming to a school in the big city. The nucleus of the *zarzuela* is an incipient love triangle involving Armando, Rosa, and Juan. The humor in the play is basically provided by a "dirty old man," sexual *double entendres* in the dialogue of an effeminate character, and the rural dialect and customs of Clarita. Local color is provided by allusions to New York streets and landmarks, including Rafael Hernández's record shop, and the roaches and mice in don Robustiano's Brooklyn apartment. In all, *Colegiales* is an enjoyable, lighthearted, and rose-colored view of student life that, set to Rafael Hernández's incomparable music, must have been a success.

Like Alberto O'Farrill and Juan C. Rivera, Erasmo Vando was a talented comic actor. But instead of characterizing the *negrito*, Vando popularized the typical Puerto Rican countryman: the *jibarito*, symbol of Puerto Rican culture and the desire for freedom and independence. Many were the comics who attempted to portray this character type from Puerto Rican life, folklore, and literature. According to Bernardo Vega (1977: 202), except for Vando, most of the others were disgraceful.

Vando lived in New York for thirty years, during which time he directed the Compañía Teatral Puertorriqueña, which was so instrumental in producing works by his countrymen and in fomenting a Puerto Rican national theatre. He also directed the Compañía Alejandro Tapia y Rivera and participated in many of Juan Nadal de Santa Coloma's theatrical initiatives. Pasarell (1967: 196) also notes that Vando founded the Club Artístico de Puerto Rico and the Spanish Musical Company in New York. The works written and staged by Vando in New York all seem to be musical comedy, but because they were never published and are lost there is no knowing whether any of them were more serious, as was his *Amor en el batey*, a three-act comedy that he later staged in Ponce in 1950. Vando's works from the late 1920s through the 1930s were *Cinco minutos más*, performed at the Apollo in 1929; *Los amores de papá; Como en Borinquen; Madre mía; Metamorfosis;* and *De Puerto Rico al Metropolitan o el Caruso Criollo*, which was performed at the Dalys, the Apollo, and various other theatres beginning in 1928 and 1929. By far the latter work, which told the tale of Puerto Rican opera singer Antonio Paoli's rise to fame at the Metropolitan Opera in New York, was Vando's most popular contribution.

Probably the grandest Puerto Rican figure of all was the previously mentioned Juan Nadal de Santa Coloma, who, in a task similar to the one chosen for himself by Mexican Gerardo López del Castillo, set about developing a Puerto Rican national theatre. Part of his labors took place in New York. Nadal left school, San Juan's Instituto Civil, in 1898 to begin a career on the stage, which was especially disconcerting to his mother, who had wanted him to become a priest (Carreras 1935: 37). His first role was a benefit performance at the Teatro Municipal for the Spanish forces during the Spanish-American War. During the next few years he worked his way through various companies, including those of Cristóbal Real, Miguel Leisabasas, and Méndez Medrano, which toured the Spanish Antilles and the coastal areas of South America. With the latter company he became a leading man in Venezuela. According to Sáenz (1950: 175), in 1902 Nadal also directed his own Compañía de Zarzuela Puertorriqueña. Around 1902 he married leading lady Carmen Beltrán, formed his own company, and went to Madrid. Over the years he had the typical ups and downs of the trade—successes in Spain, tours to the Caribbean and South America—and even administered the great Teatro Principal in Mexico City and the Teatro Eslava in Madrid for a while. In Barcelona and Madrid he began working in cinema for Hércules film and in Bogotá, Columbia, he became a professor of speech at the National Conservatory. Back in Madrid Nadal wrote the screenplay for the hit movie *Madrid en el año 2000*. From 1927 to 1929 Nadal was working in Puerto Rico developing the national theatre as the head of several companies. Nadal returned to New York in 1930 and spent four years there acting, forming companies, and working with Spanish dramatist Abelardo Fernández Arias, Puerto Rican actor Erasmo Vando, and composer Rafael Hernández at the Park Palace, Cervantes, Variedades, and other theatres.

It was in 1930 that he wrote and staged his musical comedy *Día de reyes*, with a score by Rafael Hernández, which celebrated Puerto Rican regional customs. According to Carreras (1935: 55), *Día de reyes* had 156 performances in New York City alone. It opened at the Park Palace in May, staged by the Compañía Teatral Puertorriqueña and directed by Erasmo Vando. In 1932 Juan Nadal de Santa Coloma began touring his own company through the theatres of New York, often staging *Día de reyes* and Luis Llorens Torres's patriotic drama *El grito de Lares*. In April 1934, Nadal staged Gonzalo O'Neill's *Bajo una sola bandera* at the Teatro Variedades. Later he would take the play to its San Juan debut.

In 1935 Juan Nadal de Santa Coloma returned to Puerto Rico after what he described as "the cold shower" that was New York. On the island he directed the Compañía Teatral PRERA, a government-sponsored company that was charged with performing plays by Puerto Ricans in San Juan, Río Piedras, and Mayagüez (Pasarell 1967: 31). In 1937 he formed a company in San Juan and another in 1938. After this nothing else is heard from the distinguished actor (ibid.: 169).

One last Puerto Rican playwright, Frank Martínez, was important, for he appeared in the late 1930s as an actor and then as a director in the 1940s to keep Puerto Rican theatre alive through the war years and afterward. Almost nothing else is known about Martínez except the titles of his plays, *La corte del juez peligroso, Un velorio en Harlem,* and *De Puerto Rico a Nueva York,* which was described earlier in the chapter as a curious precedent to René Marqués's *La carreta.* Pasarell (ibid.: 192) notes that *De Puerto Rico a Nueva York* was produced in Puerto Rico on March 18 and April 6, 1945, by the Compañía Artística Ponceña.

The only two resident Spanish playwrights of record in New York City at this time were the *ABC de Madrid* journalist Abelardo Fernández Arias and the actress Marita Reid, who was much more important to the Hispanic stage than were her four one-act plays. Of Arias, all that is known is that Juan Nadal de Santa Coloma produced his two plays, *El clown del Circo Imperial* and *La tragedia del faro,* at the Roerich Theatre in 1932 and that Arias used the pseudonym of El Duende de la Colegiata. Marita Reid, on the other hand, has left us a rich inheritance of over fifty years of work developing Hispanic theatre in New York.

Born in Gibraltar, Spain, to a Spanish mother and an English father, Marita Reid grew up bilingual and began her life on the stage at age seven, according to a short biography on a 1946 playbill for a performance at Casa Galicia. Her early experience was performing on tours in extreme southern Spain. She began performing in New York in the early 1920s in Spanish companies at the National and Belmont theatres. After 1922 she acted in the companies of Pilar Arcos, Narcisín, and others and then formed her own company, which worked for seven years at the Calpe American, the Casa Galicia, the Ateneo, and elsewhere. During the late 1930s and 1940s Reid was responsible for keeping serious Spanish-language drama alive by producing works at numerous halls and mutualist societies as well as in conventional theatres. For nearly three decades she was the leading lady of the Hispanic stage and one of its leading directors, along with Luis Mandret. Because of her English background, Reid was able to cross over to American, English-language mainstream theatre. Her career extended to Broadway, cinema, and television, including live television drama in the "Armstrong Circle Theater," "The U.S. Steel Hour," and "Studio One" (Miller 1978: 41). Reid forever championed liberty for Spain from fascism and tirelessly took part in efforts to support the Spanish Republic.

Marita Reid's four unpublished plays (as of 1946) were *Patio Gibraltareño, Luna de mayo, Sor Piedad,* and *El corazón del hombre es nuestro corazón. Sor Piedad* was debuted in January 1938 at the Centro Libertario. *El corazón,* written in 1933 and reworked in 1939 with the addition of two more characters, was a short comic farce, according to a 1939 broadside. Nothing else is known about the plays, but, as can be appreciated from comments on the same broadside, Reid was very modest about her playwriting. But, like her counterparts in San Antonio and Los Angeles who labored to keep Hispanic theatre alive during the Depression, the war, and postwar years, Reid should have been proud of her tremendous contribution to Hispanic culture in the United States.

5. Tampa

The history of Hispanic theatre in the Tampa area is one of the most interesting when compared with the other centers of professional Spanish-language theatre in the United States. In the late nineteenth century the Tampa area witnessed the transplant of an entire industry from abroad and the development of an Hispanic enclave which chose the theatre as its favorite form of art and culture. In order to remove themselves from the hostilities attendant on the Cuban war for independence from Spain, to come closer to their primary markets and avoid import duties, to try to escape the labor unrest that was endemic to this particular industry, various cigar manufacturers from Cuba began relocating to Tampa. In the swampy, mosquito-infested lands just east of Tampa, Ybor City was founded in 1886. By the 1890s the Spanish and Cuban tobacco workers had begun establishing mutal aid societies and including theatres as the centerpieces for the buildings they constructed to house these societies. Many of the theatres eventually would host professional companies on tour from Cuba and Spain, but, more importantly, they became the forums where both amateurs and resident professionals would entertain the Hispanic community for more than forty years without interruption. These theatres were also the training ground where numerous tobacco workers and other community people developed into professional and semiprofessional artists, some of whom were able to make their way to the Hispanic stages of New York, Havana, and Madrid. Finally, Tampa also played a key role in one of the most exciting chapters of American theatre history: it was the site of the Federal Theatre Project's only Hispanic company under the WPA.

Unlike Los Angeles, San Antonio, and New York, there was very little truly commerical theatrical activity in the Tampa–Ybor City communities. The six most important mutual aid societies—Centro Español, Centro Español de West Tampa, Centro Asturiano, Círculo Cubano, Centro Obrero, and Unión Martí-Maceo—each maintained a *comisión de espectáculos,* or show committee, to govern the use of their theatres, a task which included renting the theatre, scheduling events, hiring professional directors, scenographers, and technicians, and even purchasing performance rights to theatrical works from local representatives of the Sociedad de Autores Españoles. Along with this *comisión,* which obviously took on the theatre management role, most of the societies also supported a *sección de declamación,* or amateur theatrical company, made up mostly of the society's members. For a good part of each year the company would rehearse on weeknights and perform on Sundays. For the most part, the audiences were made up of tobacco workers and their families. The tobacco workers prided themselves on their literary and artistic tastes; they were considered an intellectual or elite labor class that had gained an informal education from the professional *lectores,* or readers, they hired to read aloud to them from literary masterpieces, newspapers, and other matter while they rolled cigars. Neither the demanding audiences nor the managing committees would be satisfied by strictly amateurish renditions, especially since they could compare performances with those of the professional companies that often visited their theatres. The tobacco workers and their families knew the difference between good and mediocre shows and were quite demanding, if newspaper critiques are indicative. It therefore became the custom to recruit and hire professional actors and directors from Havana to train and direct the resident *sección de declamación,* which was paid for its performances. Over the years, numerous professional artists either settled in Tampa or were recruited to become part of the local companies. But Tampa's Hispanic societies also prepared such important actors as Manuel Aparicio, Cristino R. Inclán, and Velia Martínez, who later abandoned the cigar factories to dedicate themselves completely to the world of marquees and footlights. By the 1920s a good number of the local artists considered themselves professionals and demanded reasonable salaries for all their performances. This became such a well-known and widely accepted fact of cultural life that the *Gaceta* theatre critic on November 15, 1922, in a column entitled "Para los Aficionados," recalled nostalgically the good old days when an amateur was an amateur, and thus he attacked the current pseudo-professional actors for always requiring payment.

Centro Español

The oldest and one of the most active of the societies, the Centro Español, was founded in 1891 to offer insurance benefits and social activities to the Spaniards in Ybor City in exchange for twenty-five cents a week (Mormino 1987: 178). Spaniards and Cubans were polarized and antagonistic in the community at this time for two reasons: the war for Cuban independence from Spain was raging and Spaniards occupied the elite positions in the cigar industry while Cubans were at the lower levels (ibid.: 178). To some extent the Centro Español served to insulate the Spaniards from their lower-class Cuban brethren. The charter called for members to be "español de raza y sentimientos, o simpatice lealmente con España y su prestigio en América."[1] In addition, there also seems to have been some local anti-Hispanic sentiments from Anglo-American quarters, further motivating the Spaniards, mainly of Galician and Asturian extraction, to solidify (ibid.: 180). The Centro Español was also a more conservative organization than the Asturian and Cuban ones to be founded later, and its cultural activities and theatre looked almost exclusively to Spain for their base and inspiration. As will be seen below, the Centro Asturiano and the Círculo Cubano were considered to be hotbeds of labor unrest and free thinking and, in the case of the Cubans, more focused on Cuban and New World culture and theatre.

In 1892 the Centro Español finished erecting a sixteen-thousand-dollar wooden structure which contained a cantina, classrooms, and a dance hall–theatre. All of these facilities complied with article one of the Centro Español's constitution: "proporcionar instrucción y honesto recreo a los miembros que la integran." The theatre hall in this first theatre measured fifty-one by twenty-one feet and accommodated five hundred Chicago-manufactured seats which could be removed to create an area for dances.[2]

A second more elegant brick and marble structure replaced the earlier Centro Español headquarters in 1912; the building still stands today, although it is not presently in use. In that same year, another building was constructed to house the West Tampa branch of the society. Both buildings housed large theatres, besides other meeting, game, and instructional rooms. According to the Centro Español fiftieth anniversary album, construction costs for both buildings totaled more than $150,000.[3] On November 11, 1912, the theatre in the new Ybor City center was inaugurated with a gala performance of *La viuda alegre* by a *zarzuela* and operetta company brought in directly from Havana's Payret Theatre. The golden anniversary album states that tickets for the box seats were priced at fifty dollars and regular seating started at ten dollars per ticket, with receipts totaling $6,500 on that first night, all of which supposedly went toward buying furniture for the new building.[4] According to an undated manuscript, "Centro Español Theatre: Restoration and Renovation Project" by René González, director of today's Tampa Little Theatre, the Centro Español has both a raked auditorium and stage, the latter measuring twenty-eight by thirty-five feet, with a proscenium arch twenty-four feet high. The auditorium once included an orchestra pit and 6 bottom box seats; there still remain 6 upper box seats accommodating 5 chairs, 231 seats in the balcony, and 465 in the orchestra.

Very little is known about the theatre productions sponsored by the Centro Español in its first hall. It is certain, at least from reports in newspapers of the turn of the century, that the club's amateur society as well as touring professional companies played the hall. It is also certain that resident professional companies, which also played at such commercial houses as the Teatro Sans Souci, also rented the hall or were hired by the Centro Español's directors to perform there. The earliest indication of theatrical performances comes from the *Tampa Morning Tribune* (June 6, 1892) which mentions the staging of the melodrama *Amor de madre* and a *sainete Slap the Fly* (certainly a translation of the title), starring leading lady Carmen Fernández. As she is designated a *primera actriz* (leading lady), she was most likely considered a professional. It will be seen below that Ms. Fernández and this company resided in Tampa at least into the first decade of the new century.

More regular coverage of the cultural activities at the Centro Español began in 1903 with the founding of *La Revista,* edited by Rafael M. Ybor, son of the cigar magnate. From 1903 to 1905 the magazine enthusiastically covered theatre life at Tampa's mutual aid societies. From 1903 through 1905 the Centro Español supported its own *sección de declamación,* led by a small core of professional actors. The *sección's* director-concertist, Domingo Perdomo, drew upon the members of the society to perform secondary roles. Included in the *sección de declamación* were the first soprano, señora Cristina Caubín de Perdomo, the leading man and artistic director Luciano García, and the leading man and baritone Rodolfo Francisco López. *La Revista* also occasionally mentions the participation of Carmen Fernández, who has already been mentioned. Numerous other amateur actors, including Mrs. Conchita Perdomo, were enlisted for the cast of a theatrical fare that included staple *zarzuelas* such as *El puñao de rosas, El anillo de hierro, Marina,* and *Chateau Margaux,* and occasional melodramas such as *El gran galeoto* and *sainetes* such as *Juan el Perdío.*

On August 21, 1904, *La Revista* noted the debut of a new leading soprano, the young Miss Josefina Rodríguez. It is not certain whether she was a professional who relocated to Tampa or an amateur newly initiated into starring roles; but Rodríguez was to become one of the most popular actresses on the Tampa stages during these early years. On January 29, 1905, *La Revista* announced that the Centro Español had contracted in Cuba the notable artist Jacinto González to become the artistic director of the group. Perdomo and his core of professionals went on by themselves to stage works at local halls and cinemas, such as the Porvenir, El Edén, and Aurora. Under González's direction, the group's offerings seem to have remained the same, but *La Revista* noted numerous performances by this *sección de declamación* at the halls and cinemas as well. This touring in the Tampa–West Tampa area may be another indication of the increased professionalism of the group. But despite this apparently more elevated status, the *sección de declamación* remained an integral part of the Centro Español and the community, as indicated by its production of an original *juguete cómico Los asistentes* by Pablo Parellado, which satirized local personalities known as *el intruso* (the busybody) and *el loco* (the town fool), who had the misfortune of being present in the audience for the debut, according to *La Revista* (February 26, 1905).

The documentary file is again broken from 1905 to 1912, when the two new buildings of the Centro Español were inaugurated, as mentioned above, and a light opera company was contracted from Havana. In 1912 the Centro Español's impresario, Joseph Chamoun, of Lebanese origin but know as El Turco, would go to Havana to contract companies for performances at the Centro Español each day of the week. According to *Tampa Ilustrada* (December 12, 1912), El Turco had succeeded in contracting the Gran Teatro Español, which included the baritone Mardurell, leading soprano Carmen Ramírez, a Mr. Cortés, and a Mr. Escribá to perform operettas and *zarzuelas*. At this time, it seems, the Gran Teatro Español also incorporated into its company Mrs. Conchita Perdomo, formerly of the *sección de declamación*. On January 30, 1913, *Tampa Ilustrada* reported the return of the company to Cuba and its replacement with another Compañía de Opereta, whose business manager was Marco Santiago and leading actors were a señor Mijares, señora Alicia Rico, and tenor Luis Pacheco. According to *Tampa Ilustrada* (February 10, 1913), this company was very well received, except for the lovely leading lady's occasional mispronunciation of Castillian *ce* and *ze*, because she was Cuban; also censured were the Mexican accent of the baritone and the "calamitous" pronunication of the tenor Dori. Nevertheless, the stellar performances of the *catalancita* señora Pascual and the Mexican tenor-baritone señor Santa María were praised to the heavens, especially for being models of diction and grace.

Such was the beginning of the second life of the Centro Español in Ybor City. The theatre continued for years to support its own *sección de declamación* and to host touring companies, but it seems it did not achieve the great artistic and financial success of its two closest rivals, the Centro Asturiano and the Círculo Cubano. Very few performances are covered by the press in the following years, until in 1928 the great Spanish actor who had made a career in the United States, Eduardo Arozamena, settled in Tampa and became associated with the Centro's *sección de declamación*. Along with Carmen and Pilar Ramírez and Chela and Velia Martínez, Arozamena at times directed; other times local stars Manuel Aparicio or Cristino R. Inclán directed. These two had already proven their mettle in New York, Havana, and Madrid. *La Gaceta* on August 15, 1928, proclaimed that the good old days were back at the Centro Theatre with Arozamena in the series of melodramas and comedies staged that year, which included old-time favorites such as *Madam X*, *Papa Lebonard*, *La jaula de la leona*, *Mala ley*, and *El místico*. But the euphoria was short-lived; by July 1929 a Mexican vaudeville and *revista* troupe, Los Charros Mexicanos de Mondragón, had taken over the stage and then the center was closed down. It reopened under new management as an English-language movie house, named the Casino, in November 1929 and remained as such for the rest of its life.

The Centro Español in West Tampa operated much the same as the Ybor City headquarters. Troups that performed at the Ybor City center would also make part of their runs at the West Tampa branch. But the West Tampa center also hosted the stock companies from other mutual aid societies and commercial houses. In fact, during the 1920s the West Tampa theatre seems to have been more active and to have garnered more attention than the Ybor City one, which was showing films. In 1923, for instance, it was the West Tampa center that debuted the Compañía de Dramas y Comedias Carmen Du Molins and, in 1924, the Compañía Cómico-Lírica, directed by Miguel V. Lluch. The Centro Español de West Tampa was also one of Manuel Aparicio's favorite venues whenever he was in town. It was from this West Tampa stage that he stormed off to New York, according to *La Gaceta* (March 5, 1924), complaining of an environment of bad faith ("la mala fe ambiente"), although he was to be found once again on the same stage exactly a year later in 1925.

Centro Asturiano

According to Mormino (1987: 180), the more liberal Asturian members of the Centro Español split off from the Centro to found the Centro Asturiano in 1902 as an auxiliary to Havana's renowned benefit society of the same name. The Asturiano erected a $75,000 center in 1909, which was destroyed by fire in 1912. In 1914 it was replaced by what the *Morning Tribune* on May 15, 1914, called "the most beautiful building in the South," a $110,000 structure which housed a twelve hundred–seat theatre with a twenty-seven-by-eighty-foot stage which is still in operation today. Socially progressive and inclusive of all Latins, including Cubans and Italians (according to ibid.: 181–182), membership rose to 3,618 in 1919 but attracted as many as 6,000 people to some of its social activities. The Centro Asturiano also holds the distinction of housing the only Spanish-language Federal Theatre Project in the nation during the Depression.

The Centro Asturiano's long history of theatrical activity begins in December 1911, when *El Internacional* recorded a performance of the Asturiano's own *sección de declamación* under the direction of a señor Carvajal and with the participation of leading lady Caridad Castillo in programs of *zarzuelas* and *sainetes*. Newspaper files end on December 1, 1916, when *El Internacional* announced the *zarzuela* of a social nature, *El triunfo de Pachín en Pravia*. It is interesting to note, however, that at this time—the period from 1911 to 1915—the Asturiano's troupe was also performing at the Centro Español in West Tampa and out of town at such places as Robert City for the Sociedad de Instrucción y Recreo el Oasis (*El Internacional*, December 20, 1911).

When newspaper coverage picks up again in 1922, the Centro Asturiano's *comisión de espectáculos*, or show committee, was featuring operettas and *zarzuelas* by the *sección de declamación* under the directorship of Luis Rueda and was promising to bring in new artists from Havana. At this point, *La Gaceta* considered the sopranos Isabel Marquet de Rigou and Carmen Ramírez as professionals (the latter had immigrated and settled in Tampa in 1912 when she was a member of the Gran Teatro Español) and the rest of the company as amateurs. Through January 1923, the *sección* staged such standard works as *La trapera, Bohemios, La alegría de la huerta,* and *El soldado de chocolate* each Sunday. In February the Centro Asturiano contracted the Federación Lírica for a season of Italian opera, but this did not curtail the *sección's* performances. Rather, members of the Federación reinforced the *sección* cast; most notably, this was done by the Asturian baritone Augusto Ordóñez. During the next months, the *sección* was also reinforced by Josefina Rodríguez, New York Metropolitan star Manuel Salazar, a Spaniard, and others. Finally in September, new works from Spain were debuted, such as *La montaña* and *La bruja.*

In July 1923, Manuel Aparicio had been denied permission to rent the theatre for his troupe for one night only and was forced to use the Unione Italiana, but later he was contracted from October 11 to November 4 as director and leading man, "courtesy of Luis Rueda," for the dramas *Gloria, La malquerida, Don Juan Tenorio,* and *Malvaloca.* In November Aparicio was replaced in a similar capacity by the baritone from Havana, Jerónimo Galicián, this time for a series of operettas and *zarzuelas.* In December, the Comisión de Espectáculos contracted the baritone actor-director Cristino R. Inclán to star in his own *El dragón millonario* and other operettas and later that month hired the singers Abelardo Galindo and Juan Manuel Díaz for the debut of the popular *La canción del olvido,* which *La Gaceta* on October 22, 1923, claimed cost $100 for performance rights. For this operetta the Asturiano charged $1.25, $1.00, and $.75, as opposed to its usual $.75 for adults and $.25 for children.

Despite these reinforcements, after a steady diet of *zarzuelas* and operetta and the same *sección de declamación,* in *La Gaceta* on March 6, 1924, the theatre critic complained that "el público quiere algo nuevo, está cansado de admirar durante años y años a las estrellas locales. Una buena tiple, un magnífico actor, un gran cantante, llegan a cansar si se les mantiene, como pasa con algunas figuras valiosas del teatro de Nebraska, continuamente en el cartel."[5] In March, therefore, the Asturiano contracted a troupe from New York that included the perennial dame of the Hispanic stage there, Pilar Arcos, and her husband as well as the baritone Pulido, the tenor Moriche, and Abelardo Delgado. For its debut on March 29, ticket prices once again rose to $1.50, $1.25, and $1.00 for the performance of *La canción del olvido*. It is not certain how long the Pilar Arcos troupe continued at the Asturiano, but for at least two months some different lyric titles were offered, including *Benamor*, *El afinador*, and *La reina del fonógrafo*.

In June Miguel V. Lluch took over direction of the *sección de declamación*, reinforcing it with some professionals, perhaps leading the *Tampa Daily Times* to surprisingly comment later on October 3, 1924, that "the Asturian company, directed by Miguel Lluch, is composed of professionals, many of whom have sung in grand opera." Unfortunately the Lluch company was not strong enough for the annual ritual of staging *Don Juan Tenorio* for All Souls' Day; the grand melodrama had to be canceled for inability to cast the play, according to *La Gaceta* (November 8, 1924).

The new year 1925 opened with the Centro Asturiano hosting the Compañía Argentina de Urquiza-Podestá (Malena Urquiza and M. Podestá) with daily performances of Argentine comedies. Unfortunately the troupe was not making any money and *La Gaceta* on January 19 made a special plea of help for these modest artists. The Argentines soon went on their way and were replaced by an American vaudeville company. The *sección de declamación*, however, continued to perform dramas, comedies, and *zarzuelas* on Sundays through May under the direction of Manuel Aparicio. On June 6, *La Gaceta* announced that Aparicio's contract was up and that he was returning to Madrid, where his wife and children were residing.

Following Aparicio's departure, the *sección* continued performing and the Comisión de Espectáculos booked another American burlesque company in August: Desmond New York Roof Garden. In October, the Compañía de Revistas, Operetas y Zarzuelas, directed by comic actor Ramón Reinado, had its debut at the Asturiano, including the Abella sisters, who later became mainstays of the New York Hispanic stage.

In mid October the Asturiano hired a new impresario, Víctor Fernández, who had previously served in that function at the Círculo Cubano; he debuted his new ensemble, Gran Compañía de Zarzuelas y Revistas Renacimiento, and introduced to the Asturiano stage a string of musical revues never before seen there and thus updated the fare to the styles of Hispanic New York and Los Angeles. Nevertheless, with Ramón Reinado as the artistic director, standard *zarzuelas* and operettas continued to dominate the bills.

In April 1926 the Asturiano made Tampa theatre history as the local stop for Spain's María Guerrero company and its offering of the best in contemporary Spanish drama. María Guerrero closed on May 14 and was followed by the Manhattan Grand Opera Association, which ran until June 14. The rest of the year the stock company performed, directed by Manuel Aparicio. In January 1927 the Manhattan Opera Stars Company played the Asturiano, followed in February by the Compañía de Zarzuela y Opereta, directed by Eduardo Arozamena, which included Augusto Ordóñez. In September, Narcisín and his Compañía Hispano-Argentina arrived from Havana and offered a different melodrama each evening until Christmas. On December 29 the Compañía Argentina de Camila Quiroga, in from New York on its way to Havana's Teatro Payret, opened for a short run of five nights of contemporary Argentine drama. At the end of January 1928, the Cianci Grand Opera Company was contracted and by March 9 the stage was back in the hands of the *sección de declamación*, reinforced by the troupe of comic actor Bolito (Roberto Gutiérrez), who Robreño (1961: 46) mentions as important during the late 1920s in touring the *bufo* genre. In October Cristino R. Inclán returned from the New York stage to work with the *sección*. The year closed with the Compañía de Bufos, directed by Rafael Arango (*negrito*), occupying the stage. Incuded in the troupe were Luis Guerra as the *gallego* and Emilia and Alicia Rico. Robreño (ibid.: 74) mentions Alicia Rico as a veteran of the *obras bufas* in Cuba during the early 1930s. The Arango company of *bufos* made the Asturiano its home base while also performing such pieces as *Los líos del santero*, *La revancha de Uzcudua*, and *La revista loca y sin fin* at the Círculo Cubano and at the Centro Español in West Tampa.

In 1929 again the pattern was repeated of Sunday performances by the *sección de declamación* under Miguel V. Lluch and by professional touring companies contracted for long or short runs of nightly performances, including once again Narcisín, Arozamena, and periodic visits by Manuel Aparicio. In April 1930 a new amateur troupe, La Columna, began performing on Sundays. Augusto Ordóñez returned in December at the head of his own professional company. Throughout the 1930s, even during the tenure of the Federal Theatre Project at the Asturiano, the *sección de declamación* continued to have Sunday performances, and various professional troupes were occasionally contracted, although not as frequently as before the Depression. Like the theatres in New York, the Centro Asturiano was also affected by the Spanish Civil War and toward the end of the decade began to host benefit performances for the Republican cause, including, for example, the production of *Los héroes de Madrid* and the dramatic prologue *Libertad o muerte* in September 1937. *Las luchas de hoy* by local playwright and director of the *cuadro* Renovación Antonio Jiménez was staged for the same committee and the

Spanish Red Cross in May 1938. In the early 1940s, the Asturiano began holding benefits to help refugees from the war settle in Tampa. During the 1940s as well the Asturiano continued to receive occasional touring companies from New York and the Southwest, such as Marita Reid's and La Chata Noloesca's.

But it was during the tenure of the Federal Theatre Project (FTP), for eighteen months in 1936 and 1937, that the Teatro Asturiano made American theatre history by housing the only Hispanic unit of the WPA's national project. It is a chapter in which the two theatrical traditions, the Hispanic and the Anglo-American, that had existed side by side for so long finally intersect to produce at times exciting theatre but also examples of cultural misunderstanding. From the start the Federal Theatre Project's attitude seems to have been a model of condescension and, ultimately, the Hispanic unit had to disband because of congressional xenophobia, as will be illustrated below.

It is somewhat ironic, however, that Hispanic units were not founded in Los Angeles or New York where there was far greater Hispanic theatrical activity of a professional nature and more in line with the stated purposes of the WPA. But in all of the documents of the Federal Theatre Project, there is no mention of Hispanic theatre outside of Tampa and there seems to have been no awareness at all of the remarkable activities that are documented in this book. The project's basic objective of creating work-relief theatre of a relevant nature would best have been served where the full-time professionals were suffering unemployment, not in Tampa, where many of the artists still gained a good part of their living rolling cigars (Mardis 1972: 168). As we have seen in earlier chapters, commercial Hispanic companies that were suffering the ravages of the Depression in Los Angeles and San Antonio and New York had to take refuge in mutual aid society halls; Hispanic actors were hungry in these cities and many of them could not even raise the money to return to their homelands.

According to *La Gaceta* (January 25, 1936), it was Juvenile Court judge T. B. Castiglia and Joseph Chamoun (El Turco) who took the initiative to contact the Federal Theatre Project authorities about founding a unit in Tampa, and they then set about recruiting the actors for the unit. Manuel Aparicio was chosen to be the stage director and Máximo Echegaray the concertist and music director of the *zarzuelas* and *comedias bufas cubanas* to be staged under the auspices of the FTP. In truth, the Federal Theatre Project repertoire did not differ greatly from the usual Spanish-language fare that Tampa's Hispanic audiences expected. The greatest difference was

brought about, however, by the infusion of capital for scenery, prop-
erties, and costumes, which were now all first-rate. While the list of
dramatic and lyric material performed did not change much (with
the exception of Sinclair Lewis's *It Can't Happen Here*), the Hispanic actors for the first time became integrated into the English-
language shows of the Tampa FTP vaudeville unit and, in general,
began to associate more and more with non-Hispanic artists and personnel. Manuel Aparicio was even chosen to be sent to a conference
of FTP directors in Poughkeepsie, New York. *La Gaceta* on June 17,
1937, proudly proclaimed that it took strangers in their midst to rec-
ognize the artistry of their own Manuel Aparicio.

Such was the pride of the community, but the Federal Theatre
Project administrators, while taking pride in having successfully
"brought" theatre to the Hispanics, otherwise decried the Spanish
speakers' backwardness or fawned at their quaint habits. The Tampa
project, always referred to by them as "one of the strongest in the
South,"[6] was joked about by state FTP director Dorothea Lynch in
the following terms: "they had the darnedest bunch of flimsy scenery . . . it was paper scenery. All kinds of arabesques and imitation-
looking red velvet stuff (laugh)." Upon meeting the prompter at the
Centro Asturiano, Lynch remarked, "And up came a little man, and
he said, 'I am the puntador!' Well, I tried not to look too ignorant,
but of course he was the one who sat in the little promptor's box . . .
and believe me, he was the king pin."[7] Lynch and others were un-
aware that the custom of the prompter still existed to facilitate the
production of different plays each evening throughout the Hispanic
world, which differed from the English-language custom of running
the same play continuously. Ultimately, because of language differ-
ences and misunderstandings about citizenship, the Hispanic unit
lost twenty-five of its members in 1937 when Congress passed the
ERA Act of 1937, which effectively removed foreigners from the WPA.
Other members like Chela Martínez were lost when they were decer-
tified because their family income was too high (Mardis 1972: 188).
Among the twenty-five actors lost were director Manuel Aparicio and
the important Ramírez sisters, Carmen and Pilar. The remaining
citizens were integrated into the "American" vaudeville company of
the federal project. As Dorothea Lynch and her husband, Larry, explained it, "But we salvaged all the young players from the Latin
company, and then all the vaudevillians. . . . the older Latins had
entered this country for twenty years and had never become citizens.
Nobody paid any particular attention to it in those days. . . . They
considered themselves American citizens. They voted and everything else, and may have held office for all I know. (laugh) . . . They

considered themselves Americans, American citizens. But they had never gone through the formality of becoming—just the first papers."[8] For all intents and purposes, the Hispanic unit had come to an end.

In all, the Hispanic unit of the Federal Theatre Project produced fourteen shows in Spanish. The company received its debut on March 5, 1936, with a *bufo* parody of the operetta *El conde de Luxemburgo*, entitled *El conde de mi puchungo*, featuring stars very familiar to Tampa audiences: Manolita León, Chela Martínez, Matilde López, Serafín Rodríguez, Manuel García, and others. The *obra bufa* was followed by *De parientes hasta los pelos* and variety acts. Admission was twenty-five cents for side boxes and fifteen cents for general seating at the Asturiano. The following were the remainder of the productions: *El método Gorritz, La viejecita, Cuesta abajo,* and *Donde las dan las toman* (April 22–April 26, 1936); *La malquerida* (May 20–May 24); *El niño judío* (June 24–June 28); *Molinos de viento* (July 31–August 2); *Los gavilanes* (September 9–September 16); *Esto no pasará aquí* (October 27–November 2); *Eva* (November 27–December 6); *El rey que rabió* (January 17–January 22, 1937); *El mundo en la mano* (March 14–April 4); *El maestro del ballet* (dance-drama, July 18–July 22). A Federal Theatre Project document states that the Hispanic company held forty-two performances of eleven productions, with a total attendance of 23,401, averaging 280 paid attendance, from January 1936 to September 1937.[9] Obviously this does not reflect the actual enumeration of productions cited above, but it does give an idea of the success of the project. In June 1937 state director Lynch reported the following:

> Although, at the end of the first six months the members of the company gave a very moving performance of "The Passion Flower" [*La malquerida*] it is in musical comedy or extravaganza that their public loves them best. Helped by Art Director Syl, they were gradually weaned away from the "1890" production technique and a slow, but fascinating process of modernization was given a tremendous push forward last October by the Spanish production of "It Can't Happen Here." This play opened a whole new theatre world to the people who took part in it, and although Latin audiences were cold and puzzled, the benefit to producers and actors has been apparent ever since.
>
> The musicals, "The Jewish Child," "The Windmills," "The Hawks," "Eva" and "The King Goes Mad" built up a solid following for the company among the residents of Ybor City. The entire following turned out to cheer "The World in Your Hand,"

a revue completely assembled and presented on the project. Many Latins came twice and three times to make the "trip around the world" which took them from Cuba through Spain, Italy, Mexico, China and back to Cuba again, ringing up a $700.00 profit and the biggest Florida Federal Theatre hit to date.[10]

The only really socially relevant material performed by the Hispanic company was in its indirect participation with the English-language vaudeville company in *O Say Can You Sing*, which criticized the Senate's desire to terminate the Federal Theatre Project, and its production in Spanish of Sinclair Lewis's *It Can't Happen Here*, which was all but forced on the company in an awkwardly literal translation and in an equally awkward attempt to synchronize the production opening with the national debut. Hallie Flanagan, the national director of the Federal Theatre Project, pressured Dorothea Lynch to have the play produced in Spanish. But, as Lynch said, "And, Mrs. Flanagan, I didn't know whether she knew that the thing wasn't ready to be put on, but they did it just the same. And they didn't attract the Spanish people. They didn't know what the heck it was all about, naturally. But, they did it, and they did a beautiful job with it, and it was eternally to their credit."[11]

Thus the Lewis play was the nadir of the experience, while *El mundo en la mano* by Aparicio and the troupe was so popular that additional performances were scheduled and the revue even toured in the area and down to Miami. All the while the company was employed by the WPA its members continued to perform at the other theatres in town and, even using the name of the Federal Theatre Troupe, it held benefit performances at such places as hospitals. When the troupe was officially disbanded as a result of the ERA Act of 1937, it actually stayed together and performed for benefits around town, hoping to be reinstated by the WPA. In 1937, the regional director argued unsuccessfully for the reinstatement of the Hispanic unit on the basis of the theatrical and social importance to the community; the professional status of the company and the need of its members for work relief had always been in question. Thus, the primary goal of the WPA of work relief could not be met. In his dissertation, Mardis argues that in terms of establishing a permanent professional theatre—one of the WPA goals—"the Latin theatre was likewise a failure. Like all units of the Florida Federal Theatre, it could not exist without its federal subsidy" (1972: 201). However, this is unjust and should be qualified. This judgment reveals a lack of awareness that these actors were continuously involved in professional theatre on their own terms before the Federal Theatre Project was instituted in Tampa, and the documentary records shows that they continued to perform at area theatres and mutual aid societies afterwards. In another untitled, unsigned report in the Federal Theatre Project archives at George Mason University Library, the following criticism is stated:

> In any future theatre venture by the federal government, foreign language companies like the Tampa Spanish Unit should be organized along different lines from the beginning. The fact that (although urged to do so in the beginning) so few members of the group had applied for citizenship while working on FTP, indicating a failure on the part of the workers to understand one of the fundamental functions of WPA. In the future, while the traditions of the theatre involved should be preserved, they should be used in the interests of international good will, in this case the heightening of our "Good Neighbor Policy" with South America. Or they should be used to increase the understanding of the finest things in the "Old Country" by young Americans who have not been able to travel.
>
> While the art of the foreign theatre is thus being used constructively, members of the company should participate in an Americanizing process which will help them to get jobs in the American theatre, without losing in any degree the art that is their birthright. This is partly a matter of putting across certain ideas to the foreign born, and partly a matter of adjusting character to the democratic idea.

Thus the Spanish-language theatre was seen as possibly a passport into the melting pot but not as an end in itself.

El Círculo Cubano

Before the Cuban community of Tampa founded the Club Nacional Cubano in 1899, it sponsored classes for its children, housed theatre companies, and held its celebrations at the Liceo Cubano, which ceased to exist after the Círculo opened its doors. The club was also preceded by a number of other clubs which were all revolutionary in nature but that dissolved once the Spanish American War had ended. On October 10, 1899, the Club Nacional Cubano was formed and began functioning by renting a hall on the corner of 14th Street and 9th Avenue. It was not until 1902 that the club organized the Secciones de Instrucción, de Recreo y de Declamación, and the name of the club was changed to Círculo Cubano de Tampa. The Círculo grew and in 1907 found the need to construct its own building with a nine hundred–seat theatre, which served the community well until it burned down in 1916.[12] The Círculo soon built another edifice, despite the hard times brought on by World War I and the influenza epidemic, which was so serious that the Círculo was converted into a hospital and expended over $35,000 in fighting the disease and attending to the afflicted of all nationalities (Mormino 1987: 184). The new building was completed in 1918, cost $60,000, and included a spacious theatre, a *cantina*, a pharmacy, a library, and a dance hall (ibid.: 185). Later, the Círculo added on a school and a gymnasium. According to its *Album-Exposición*, the Círculo Cubano, besides offering insurance, savings, and first aid, served social functions similar to those of the Mexican mutual aid societies in the Southwest.[13]

Many of these social objectives—patriotism, instruction, culture—were fulfilled by the *sección de declamación* and by hosting professional companies on tour. But even more they were carried out through the Círculo's own children's theatre, directed for many years by Víctor Fernández and made up of the young sons and daughters of the tobacco workers. Not only did the children's theatre reinforce the values referred to in the *Album-Exposición*, it also served the purpose of training fine actors for a period of almost thirty years, many of whom went on to become important in Tampa theatrical companies.

As early as August 12, 1892, the *Tampa Morning Tribune* reported that the Liceo Cubano was hosting a Spanish opera company, which had come up from Cuba via Key West. In a *La Gaceta* interview of old-timer Cecilio Castillo on August 6, 1954, Castillo affirmed that the Liceo Cubano was the first theatre in Ybor City. Be that as it may, the *Tribune* reference to the 1892 performance is virtually the only one that survives today. More consistent coverage of theatre at the Cuban societies has survived, beginning with Rafael M. Ybor's *La Revista*, which noted in 1903 through 1905 performances of *zarzuelas, juguetes,* and *sainetes,* mostly by the *sección de declamación*, it must be assumed, at the Círculo Cubano. The Círculo's theatrical activities at this time were far behind those of the Centro Español, the Porvenir hall, and the Teatro Aurora. In 1904, the *sección de declamación* seems to have been directed by professional actor and leading man Antonio Rodeiro de Mirat, who *La Revista* on December 8, 1904, claimed had enjoyed success throughout the Americas. Under Rodeiro de Mirat's guidance, the *sección* successfully presented standard *zarzuelas* and melodramas and even Rodeiro's own comic parody *Echar la llave*. In 1905 the Círculo began hosting the performance by the professional *zarzuela* troupe led by Cristina Caubín and Domingo Perdomo, which was also perform-ing at the Centro Español. In July 1905 the Círculo Cubano re-inforced its own *sección de declamación* by hiring the professional Compañía de Molina to become a part of it. The Molina company immediately added *obras bufas* such as *Un varón enamorado o ataques de nervios* to the regular fare of *zarzuelas*. In September 1905, the Círculo added the character actress Angela Vásquez, newly arrived from Cuba.

From 1905 to 1911 information is sketchy. We know that the *sec-ción de declamación* was functioning consistently and that an occa-sional troupe, such as the Terrados company in 1908, was booked in from Cuba. In 1911 and 1912 a professional actor, a señor Miyares, was serving as the director of the *sección de declamación*, when, according to *El Diario de Tampa* (March 13, 1911), a young man named Manuel Aparicio became a part of the company; he would later develop into a leading man and director on stages from New York to Madrid. Miyares, assisted by the veteran actress Froilán García, led the troupe in weekly *zarzuelas*, including some that were composed locally. In the May 29, 1911, edition of *El Diario de Tampa*, Miyares and company were soundly censured for their "terrible zarzuelicidio" upon debuting *El monoplano de Pepita* by a señor Valdespino. The newspaper commented that even Miyares drowned, that someone should tell him not to take singing roles. The critic continued to pan performances in 1911, which included such frivolous *zarzuelas* and *sainetes* as *Si yo fuera hombre, Para eso paga, La hija del barba, El muñeco,* and many others. The Círculo at this time was still open to hosting professionals on tour, such as Blanquita Becerra and Guillermo Pardo in December and the Com-pañía Soledad Castillo in November 1912, in daily shows of full-length Spanish dramas. From the Círculo Cubano, the company's manager, Agustín Cosgaya, booked the Compañía Castillo for a run at the Teatro San Souci in Tampa.

Newspaper documentation of the theatrical activities at the Cír-culo Cubano resume again in November 1922, when the young pro-fessional actress from Cuba, Carmen du Molins, was performing with the *sección de declamación,* which included two actors that *La Gaceta* on November 8 insisted should be considered profes-sionals: Víctor Fernández and Arturo Morán. And on November 21, *La Gaceta* remarked that Arturo Morán was "un 'aficionado' mejor que muchos profesionales" (an amateur better than many profes-sionals). Víctor Fernández was also the director of the children's company at the Círculo Cubano, which drew the criticism of *La Gaceta* in January 1923 for exploiting the young actors, who were performing a different *zarzuela* each Sunday. *La Gaceta* argued that the children should have been free to spend time studying or playing rather than rehearsing. Perhaps in response to these charges, on December 14, 1922, a public show was made of dividing proceeds of ticket sales among the child actors. And on December 22, 1923, a special function was held in which $1,034.40 from box office sales was divided among the youngsters. Despite these unsavory overtones to the children's theatre, under Fernández the group continued to be a highlight of Tampa culture and Fernández prospered and went on to become one of the most important actors, directors, and impresarios in Tampa.

From December 1922 through the year 1923, the Círculo Cubano hosted productions by the *sección de declamación*, with Víctor Fernández, Carmen du Molins, Manuel Aparicio, and at times Cristino R. Inclán. The year was ushered in with the Compañía de Bufos Cubanos de Baby-Colina and such musical farces as *Las vacas flacas* and Armando Bronca's *Lo que puede el amor*, but for the most part the stage was dominated by the local companies.

The Círculo Cubano, always more liberal than the other ethnic societies and a hotbed of labor unrest, was an appropriate place on January 22, 1924, for Cristino R. Inclán to recite the monologue "Un tabaquero huelguista" at performances in his honor. Throughout the year 1924 and into 1925 Víctor Fernández attempted to secure a run by the famous *bufo* Arquímedes Pous and his company, but despite a cash deposit of five hundred dollars and repeated trips to Havana, the comic troupe never arrived. The repeated advance publicity, photos and extended stories in the newspapers converted the canceled trip into a tremendous embarrassment for the Círculo Cubano. In March 1925, Fernández was successful, however, in securing a run from the Compañía de Bufos Cubanos Arango-Moreno, directed by Guillermo Moreno, which featured the "famous" *negrito* Roberto Garrido and an all-black cast unusual for the *bufo* companies, which customarily acted in blackface. Robreño states that the Moreno company in Cuba did not really understand the *bufo* genre and lowered its picaresque humor to poor taste (1961: 48). When they returned for a run in October, *La Gaceta* on October 8 reported that the Círculo's expenses in hiring the company were more than two hundred dollars a day but that seats were sold out for each show. Their two daily shows included such farces as *Pobre Alfredo*, *Un conde negro*, *Pobre pura*, *El espiritista*, *Moreno en el convento*, and Arquímides Pous's famous *Boda de Papá Montero* for ticket prices that ran at thirty-five and forty cents.

The year 1926 opened with the Desmond Company, an American

vaudeville troupe. In March Manuel Aparicio's company took to the stage with *zarzuelas,* comedies, and melodramas. In May the Empresa Ramón Fernández was booked in for more of the same. But the hit of the year was scored by the Compañía de Revistas y Zarzuelas de Roberto Gutiérrez, a troupe of *bufos cubanos* that featured the comic Bolito (Roberto Gutiérrez), the follower and imitator of Arquímides Pous. Robreño states that both Bolito's and Roberto Garrido's companies continuously toured Cuba and were responsible for bringing theatre to the most out-of-the-way places (ibid.: 46–47). The troupe was substantial and formal enough to advertise the authorship of its farces and plays, many of which were written by the then-deceased Pous: *El tabaquero, Amor tirano, El lechonero, Las mulatas de Bombay, La loca de la casa, La clave de oro,* and *La honradez de un obrero.* Other farces were written by Bolito and other members of the troupe: *Bolito en Tampa* and *El chévere Cantúa.*

The Gutiérrez repertoire also included such farces as Armando Bronca's *En la calle y sin llavín, Lo que puede el amor,* and *Filigranas . . . no más,* G. Pardo's *Lolita,* César Ocampo's *Molde de suegra,* Sergio Acebal's *Pastora y borrego,* Agustín Rodríguez and Gonzalo Roig's *Los amores de Clara,* and Guillermo Ankermann's *El novio de la rumba, La mulata del día,* and *La conquista de Alucemas,* among others. According to Robreño, Ankermann was a comic in the stock company of Havana's Teatro Alhambra who had great success as a *bufo* author (ibid.: 64). Bronca (also known as Cacharrito), Pardo, Rodríguez, and Roig were also well-known authors in the *bufo* genre and of *sainetes* in Havana. Roig was a musical composer and scenographer. Sergio Acebal, according to Robreño, was one of the greatest creators and interpreters of the *negrito* character type; his celebrated career as the leading comic of the Teatro Alhambra stock company stretched from 1912 to 1935 (ibid.: 59). On December 15, Bolito's troupe staged a patriotic play based on the Cuban war of independence, *Con todos y para todos,* by Ramón S. Varona. During November and December Gutiérrez's company was also performing regularly at the Centro Español de West Tampa and occasionally at the Centro Asturiano.

In January 1927 a new company, directed by Felo Ramos, occupied the Círculo Cubano stage. It was followed in April by the return of Bolito's Compañía de Zarzuelas y Revistas Cubanas. Besides the usual *bufo* fare, this time with many farces by Armando Bronca, newspaper announcements heavily promoted a novelty: Bolito was to appear in *La niña de los besos* as a white man. In May Bolito's company was reinforced by Pilar Ramírez and local actors and became the Compañía Hispano Cubana, presenting melodramas such as *Doña Diabla,* and *zarzuelas* such as *Los corsarios* along with *obras bufas.* In June the company produced a topical *revista, Cosas de Tampa o la historia habla* by local newspaperman and playwright Leopoldo González, a member of the *sección de declamación.* On Labor Day Bolito's company staged the appropriate melodrama *El capital y el trabajo.* Bolito remained at the Círculo Cubano until October, competing against Narcisín's company at the Centro Español and Manuel Aparicio's company at the Centro Obrero. In October the *sección de declamación* once again became the sole attraction on the Círculo Cubano stage and remained as such until Bolito returned briefly in June 1928 after a run at he Centro Asturiano. In the following months the *sección de declamación* alternated runs with the Manuel Aparicio company, which produced mostly dramas and *zarzuelas.*

The year 1929 opened with the Compañía de Bufos de Rafael Arango, featuring Alicia Rico, which had just finished a run at the Centro Español. Included in the Arango company's repertoire were several topical farces, including *Babe Ruth en Ybor, Paula Romero en Ybor City, La despalilladora,* and *Las máquinas torcedoras o la muerte de la industria* by Luis Guerra, the latter two protesting and satirizing the introduction of machines into cigar rolling and the displacement of workers. Also included in Arango's repertoire was a *revista, El Niño Fidencio,* based on the northern Mexico and southwestern United States folk character of that name which had a considerable impact on the working-class stages of the Southwest. By the end of January the Arango company had finished its run, transferred briefly to the Centro Asturiano, and then left Tampa. For almost the entire year, the Círculo Cubano featured its *sección de declamación,* directed by Víctor Fernández. The *sección* occasionally produced works by its member Leopoldo González, such as its July 27 debut of the *sainete La picada de la mosca o el pánico de los bancos,* which was based on the stock market crash that year. In December the Compañía de Bufos Cubanos de Guillermo Moreno returned to the Círculo Cubano and produced, among other works, the grandiose drama *El garrote* by Cuban poet and composer Gustavo Sánchez Garralaga.

The following year, 1930, saw Manuel Aparicio's new Compañía Renacimiento occupy the stage at the Círculo Cubano from February through September, with Aparicio's usual mix of *zarzuelas* and Spanish melodramas, but also including such Cuban plays as Alberto

Insúa's *El negro que tenía el alma blanca*. Aparicio also produced a Leopoldo González *zarzuela* in two acts, *El escapulario o el huérfano de Ybor*. The rest of the year and throughout the Depression, in spite of the hard financial times referred to by the president of the *sección de declamación* in the newsletter *El Cubano* in January 1931, the *sección de declamación* continued to be active, as was the Compañía Juvenil, now directed by retired actor Miguel V. Lluch. However, fewer and fewer professional companies on tour were hosted at the Círculo Cubano. By 1938, the void left by the *bufo* companies especially was in part filled by the creation of a resident Compañía de Bufos Cubanos, directed by and starring Gilberto Delfino and co-starring his wife, Estelita Echezabal. Besides presenting the usual type of musical comedy, such as *Los tormentos de un soltero* and *Maldita bebida*, the company also produced works in support of the Republican cause in the Spanish Civil War. In conjunction with fundraisers of the Comité Popular Democrático de Socorro a España, for example, the company produced such works as *Bajo el cielo de Cuba* and the dramatic sketch *Lo que puede pasar*, written by Cuban poet Manuel de Sánchez de León, followed by a recitation of the poem "A España" by Marisol Alba on September 27, 1938. On November 4 of the same year, the company produced Ramón Bermúdez Blanco's two-act drama *Huelga general*, followed by León's *Lo que puede pasar*, to raise funds for the Popular Front in Spain. How long this company was active and how long the *sección de declamación* survived at the Círculo Cubano is uncertain, but judging from the Círculo's dynamism in the late 1930s, it must be assumed that theatre was still an important community function during the years of World War II.

Sociedad La Unión Martí-Maceo

It is estimated that 15 percent of the Cuban immigrants to relocate to Tampa in the late 1880s were Afro-Cubans (Greenbaum 1986: 1). Black-white racial solidarity was promoted by leaders of the Cuban war for independence such as José Martí and the black general Antonio Maceo and was said to be the rule of the day in the forty or so mainly prorevolution Cuban clubs in the Tampa area before the end of the Spanish-American War. However, racial divisions were still generally strong in Cuban society, which had recently emerged from slavery, and the postindependence period in Tampa coincided with the Jim Crow era in Florida. In Ybor City, as in the rest of the state, segregation in public services and facilities was instituted following the Plessy *vs.* Ferguson Supreme Court ruling in 1896; all theatres, parks, churches, and schools were racially segregated and served to divide the black Cubans from the other Hispanic immigrants (ibid.: 8). Both white and black Cubans formerly were members of the same clubs and societies, including the Liceo Cubano and even later the Club Nacional Cubano, founded in 1899. However, a racial dispute soon arose and black members of the Club Nacional Cubano were either ejected or they withdrew (ibid.: 7) and on October 26, 1900, founded their own organization, Los Libres Pensadores de Martí y Maceo, honoring both revolutionary leaders who had been the proponents of racial solidarity. Greenbaum has suggested that "it seems likely that this name was chosen partly as a reminder to the white Cubans that they were violating basic principles of the revolution" (ibid.: 7). Like the other ethnic societies, the Martí-Maceo offered mutual aid, cultural (and racial) solidarity, and even medical and economic benefits beginning in 1904 when it merged with La Unión, an Afro-Cuban organization in West Tampa. In 1908 La Unión Martí-Maceo was chartered by the state of Florida and it initiated construction of the two-story building which was to be its headquarters until it was razed for urban renewal in 1965. La Unión Martí-Maceo offered some shelter from the rigors of Jim Crow, including the type of medical and economic benefits other blacks in the South rarely enjoyed. The Afro-Cubans, with 90 percent of the men and 15 percent of the women employed in the cigar factories, also enjoyed employment in skilled jobs with good pay where southern blacks were often less fortunate. Their hall also offered a realistic and viable alternative to the social effects of Jim Crow, for, as in the other ethnic halls and theatres, plays were staged and dances and other celebrations were held. The club also included a game area, a *cantina*, and a library, and a school was set up next to the building to teach the Spanish language and Cuban history to the children.

There are very few vestiges left of the cultural and theatrical life at La Unión Martí-Maceo. Practically none of the Spanish-language newspapers that reported on the theatre at the other societies ever reported on the activities at the Martí-Maceo. On occasion, however, *La Gaceta* did document the tours of local and foreign groups to the Martí-Maceo, including a run by the Círculo Cubano's *sección de declamación* in August 1924. On August 9, *La Gaceta* assured the Tampa public that everyone was welcome to attend, "sin distinción de razas" (regardless of race). Following the week-long performances of *obras bufas* by the Círculo's *sección de declamación*, *La Gaceta* on August 15 announced the performances of a Compañía de Variedades, Dramas y Zarzuelas directed by the "notable actor" A. Saavedra.

In addition to these few mentions in *La Gaceta*, the archives of the Sociedad la Unión Martí-Maceo in Special Collections of the University of South Florida Library include a notebook or a prompt-book with hand-copied versions of a previously unknown one-act play, *Hambre*, and the last ten scenes of an *obra bufa*, *Los novios*. Both works are notable for their relevance to the social and economic ambience of the Martí-Maceo. *Hambre* is a gripping and angry social drama that protests the poverty and hunger suffered by the working class while the rich enjoy a frivolous life of luxury. Probably written locally and staged during the Depression, *Hambre* may be an indication of the liberal, even socialistic ideology prevalent at the club during hard times and labor unrest.

Bound together in the same notebook with *Hambre* was the *obra bufa Los novios*, a much lighter and more entertaining play, structured much like the Spanish *sainetes* of the beginning of the nineteenth century, which relied on mistaken identities and ridiculously complex love triangles. What further complicates matters in *Los novios* is the supposed trespassing of race and class barriers and miscegenation, as a buffoon of a Galician servant and a *negrito* spread mistaken information about the landowner having illicitly fathered a mulatta, the landowner's daughter being caught embracing a black, and the *gallego* being mistaken for his gallant master. To spice up the *double entendres* and extremely complicated mistaken identities and mismatched partners, the play also includes numerous asides that elaborate on race relations, such as the *negrito* Elio Tropo commenting on the gallant Rafael, "Qué blanco más sucio" (What a dirty white man); the landowner don Pepe commenting on the forwardness of the *negrito*, "Este negro ha sido siempre muy confianzudo" (This black has always been too forward); and again the *negrito*, "En todos estos líos, el negro es el que coge los golpes" (In all of these involvements, it is always the black who takes the beating). In the end, order is restored when everyone finds his rightful place and his rightful partner to marry, but throughout it is the *negrito* and the *mulata* who have maintained the greatest dignity in the play, with the upper-class whites shown to be the most bungling and prejudiced. The work ends with the characters calling for music from the orchestra for the dancing and singing of a rumba, the customary ending for most *obras bufas*.

Centro Obrero

From before 1900 and throughout the entire period that is of interest to our study, the Centro Obrero was the headquarters of the Union of Tampa Cigarmakers and served as a gathering place for workers and workers' culture. Through its various classes, workshops, publications, and theatrical activities, the Centro Obrero promoted unionism and, quite often, socialism. From the beginning of the twentieth century throughout the Depression, it served as a forum for the concerns of the tobacco workers and raised funds to support their positions vis-à-vis management. In its newspapers, newsletters, and magazines, such as the *Federación, Federal, El Internacional,* and *Boletín Obrero,* were to be found not only coverage of local and international workers' issues and movements but also locally written poems and even one-act plays expressing their politics and social needs.

Among the plays and excerpts of plays published by El Centro Obrero is "Julia y Carlota," a scene from an unpublished drama *El nuevo régimen,* which appeared in *La Federación* on November 2, 1911. In this dialogue Julia exhorts Carlota to break the bonds of family and religion that are meant to keep women in their place, oppressed and divorced from politics so that they do not reform evil laws. Julia's ideology is consonant with Pedro's in *Hambre,* as she attacks the opiate of religion.

Another play in three short acts, *¡Vivan las caenas!,* published August 24, 1917, in *El Internacional,* was set in a tobacco factory and dealt with union elections that would be taking place at the Centro Obrero. Like many indoctrinating, agitation, and propaganda works, *¡Vivan las caenas!* attempted to inspire workers to assume the responsibilities of leadership in their union. But here the argument is presented humorously as a group of tobacco workers is depicted playing cards, ogling the girls, and wasting time rather than pitching in and helping with the union. Noteworthy in the publication of the play is the attempted use of Cuban working-class dialect, with appropriate written transcription of *r* and *l* confusion, added and dropped consonants, and folkspeak, as in the following: "Dísmelo a mí, que lo conosco desde chiquito! Ese no tiene un pelo de tonto. Es como la mosca que no se arrima más que aonde hay asuquita" (Tell it to me, 'cause I know him since he was a kid. He doesn't have a dumb hair on his head. He's like the fly who doesn't go anyplace that doesn't have a little sugar).

The short play ends with a bitter piece of agitation, delivered by El Hada Infernal (an infernal spirit), that once again reveals the socialist sympathies of the tobacco workers and their union:

¡Serviles, serviles, carne de esclavitud, sentís en vuestras espaldas las nostalgias del látigo! Vuestros sufrimientos son pocos comparados con los que merecéis. Mentecato será quien trate de romper vuestras cadenas; porque le golpearéis con los eslabones. La burguesía está en lo cierto, ella sabe que amaréis al tirano y os tiraniza; sabe que odiáis a los libertadores y se hace amar por vosotros, remachando vuestras cadenas. Esclavos, vuestra esclavitud cesará el día en que las nieves de ambos polos, saludándose en el Ecuador, extingan con su frialdad la vida del último amo en el momento de azotar al poste al esclavo.[14]

Another piece, a short comic one-act in blank verse entitled *Nada entre dos platos*, was written by Edmundo Bohemio (certainly a pseudonym) of Tampa and published in the March 31, 1916, issue of *El Internacional*. *Nada entre dos platos*, which is subtitled *Mítin popular*, was successfully staged numerous times at tobacco workers' meetings, according to *El Internacional*, and, in fact, the subject of the sketch is a typical union meeting at which the problem of rising prices for consumer goods is on the table for discussion. But this is just an excuse; the real issue of the sketch is the disorder and chaos that reign at meetings and that cause workers to lose interest and nothing to get accomplished. What, in effect, *Nada entre dos platos* does is comically dramatize the disorder with everyone speaking at the same time, various workers making ridiculous interjections, and the large meeting dwindling down to a few hardy souls while others leave disgusted.

But the Centro Obrero's publications were not the only forum for drama; its hall served to house many workers' skits as well as plays produced by professionals. As early as November 2, 1900, there is news in *La Federación* of the performance of a play, *Rodo y envenenamiento*, at the Centro Obrero. But the most active period at the center seems to have been the late 1920s and early 1930s when such companies as Manuel Aparicio's, Chela Martínez's, and Leopoldo González's performed there regularly.

On February 9, 1928, *La Gaceta* reported on *Alma guajira*, an original work by Marcelo Salinas, a Cuban tobacco worker residing in Cuba and author of some fifty plays. On November 27 of the same year the workers at Manuel Valle's workshop performed short comic pieces *Marido y mujer* and *Sin dinero* with the assistance of professionals Manuel Gutiérrez and Pilar Ramírez. For May Day 1929, *La fragua* was staged and, beginning in September the same year and lasting well into 1931, local playwright-journalist Leopoldo González and his troupe of *bufos cubanos* performed regularly at the Centro Obrero. Besides staging standard farces by Armando Bronca and Agustín Rodríguez, the playwright González also staged a number of his own creations: *Borinquen, El cambio de niños* (based on local events), *La columna y el círculo* (based on his newspaper column and its criticism of the Círculo Cubano), and *El huérfano de Ybor*. In March another local playwright-journalist, Francisco José Descartes, had his work *Libertad sin honor* staged by González's group in honor of the young amateur actor Benito Ochart, a member of the troupe. In 1931, a company directed by the local professional actress Chela Martínez began performing dramas and *zarzuelas* every Sunday. Interspersed with their presentations of such standards as Jacinto Benavente's *La malquerida* were other titles more appropriate to the aims of the Centro Obrero which *La Gaceta* on November 7, 1931, referred to as "el teatro del proletariado (the proletariat theatre): *Lucha de clases, Alma de jíbaro,* and *La real gana;* the latter was staged to raise funds for arrested strikers and featured stellar performances by the two local professionals Carmen and Pilar Ramírez.

Another period of intense theatrical activity at the Centro Obrero was the late 1930s, when the Republican effort in the Spanish Civil War was supported at the center through dramatic performances. Particularly noteworthy were the numerous fundraising performances of *Milicianos al frente* in 1937, co-sponsored by such organizations as the Comité de Defensa Frente Popular Español, Comité Femenino de Socorro a España, Sección de Damas y la de Recreo del Centro Obrero, and Agrupación Benéfica del Centro Obrero. According to *La Gaceta* (October 1, 1927), *Milicianos al frente* dealt with Spain and how peaceful people were obligated to take up arms to defend themselves against fascism. Other plays of a similar nature that were presented were *Abajo Franco, Los tocayos,* and *Las luchas de hoy.* All of this serious political organizing and fundraising for the Spanish Republicans did not stop the Centro Obrero from being at the same time the theatre house for a company of *bufos cubanos* which featured actors moonlighting from the Federal Theatre Project. And this company, starring Salvador Toledo, Manuel García as *negrito,* and Serafín Rodríguez, continued to use the Centro Obrero well into 1939 to perform such *obras* as *¿De quién será?*, written by Toledo, *Se vende una mula, Chico tropical, De Cuba a Estados Unidos,* and, ironically, *Por meterse en la política.*

Other Theatres

When all of the theatres at the Hispanic societies were occupied, touring companies rented theatres and halls which belonged to the Italian community of Tampa, a community which heavily identified and even intermarried with the Hispanics and subscribed to Hispanic theatre, especially *zarzuela* and operetta. The period of greatest Hispanic activity at the Unione Italiana occurred in 1923 and 1924, when such professional troupes as the Compañía Carmen du Molins, the Compañía de Zarzuela y Opereta Internacional, and the Compañía Miguel V. Lluch regularly staged *zarzuelas,* operettas and melodramas there. The *sección de declamación* of the Círculo Cubano also performed on occasion at the Unione Italiana. Conversely, the Spanish-language newspapers regularly reviewed and advertised Italian opera at the Unione Italiana, the Federazione Lírica, and the Centro Asturiano, and Hispanic performers were quite often members of the casts of Italian operas, sponsored by the Italian community. A typical confluence of both traditions, for example, was the February 10, 1923, program at the Federazione Lírica, at which Hispanic singers performed selections from *zarzuelas* in between the acts of an opera. Throughout 1923, Juan Manuel Díaz was the star tenor at the Federazione.

As one can readily see from the foregoing in this chapter, Tampa differed from the New York and southwestern Hispanic experiences in that the major theatrical activity and the best theatrical facilities were to be found in the Hispanic mutual aid societies. Tampa did not support a booming commercial stage, with the whole infrastructure of impresarios, investors, private theatre owners, etc. Most of the professional companies that toured to Tampa from Cuba, Key West, New York, or Spain had to perform at the pleasure of the committees of tobacco workers who were elected or appointed to operate the stage at the mutual aid societies. There apparently was no need for the entrepreneurial leadership that was exerted in Los Angeles, New York, and San Antonio by such men as Sam Lucchese, Frank Fouce, and Manuel Noriega. Theatre was the business of the Hispanic community at large; in Tampa it was more of a shared communal responsibility than in any other city we have studied.

At the turn of the century, when the Hispanic societies were just developing, there were, however, nascent private theatrical enterprises, but they were short-lived. The most dynamic entrepreneur in this regard was Domingo Perdomo who, with a small core of professionals, started out as the director of the *sección de declamación* of the Centro Español in 1903 but also began booking his company into the Sociedad Porvenir and La Aurora halls in West Tampa, which were often rented by other companies as well. With his talented wife, Cristina Caubín, in leading roles, his company achieved reasonable success in *zarzuelas* and melodramas at that time, especially when performing such well-known and beloved material as the *zarzuelas Verbena de la paloma, Marina,* and *El puñao de rosas.* But by 1911, it seems, Perdomo decided to go on to bigger and better things and greater stability and to have entered upon a partnership with a Mr. Ortagus to lease or purchase the San Souci Theatre, primarily a movie house, in Tampa. From the beginning, it seems, Perdomo decided to play to the working class by booking in *bufos cubanos,* such as Caricatos Cubanos, directed by a Mr. Herrera, for two performances each day. While reviews were initally favorable in *El Diario de Tampa* in May, they began to become more mixed in June, with the critic Chalo, although enjoying the *obra bufa La duquesa de Haití,* stating on June 24, 1911, that the work was a *mamarracho,* or totally ludicrous, and "lo más estrafalario que pueda pedirse; pero es del género catedrático y tiene cosas que reír, precisamente por lo absurdas, grotescas, por lo disparatadas."[15] On December 8, 1911, *El Internacional* congratulated Ortagus and Perdomo for presenting to the community "el rico manjar de arte" (the delicious meal of art) in the form of the *zarzuela* company then engaged at the theatre; but in the same breath, the critic went on to bemoan the fact that the San Souci was a cinema house, run like a cinema house:

> ¡Lástima que aún repercuten en nuestros oídos, los gritos cinematográficos de: —¡Soda fría! . . . ¡Ponche!— dados, de vez en cuando, en los pasillos del San Souci! ¡Lástima que se haya destinado la orquesta para "las grandes solemnidades"! ¡Lástima que el decorado no haya salido aún de las arcas donde se conserva! Pero . . . Todo se andará poco a poco: desaparecerán esos gritos de . . . verano; volverá la orquesta y admiraremos el decorado de que se nos habló.
> ¿Verdad, querido maestro? ¿Verdad, señor Ortagus?[16]

It seems that after awhile the Teatro San Souci solved its problem of insufficient capital to support an orchestra and sport scenery, for on March 15, 1915, *El Internacional* commented that the San Souci possessed a grand and magnificent repertoire of scenery. Continuing to host *bufos cubanos* and *zarzuela* companies, the San Souci functioned at least into 1916, when Paul Pizzo (who was also connected to the Círculo Cubano) was serving as its impresario. It is not clear whether he had been hired by Ortagus and Perdomo or he had replaced them. After 1916 there are no more notices in the newspapers of Hispanic performances at the San Souci.

Two other theatres, probably movie houses as well, also housed *zarzuela* companies and *bufos cubanos* in 1911: Teatro El Edén in Tampa and the Howard Theatre in West Tampa. The most notable thing about these theatres and their catering to the *bufos cubanos* crowd was the attack leveled at the genre by the critic of *El Diario de Tampa* on June 16, 1911, an attack somewhat reminiscent of the at times snobbish censure of the *peladito* and the *revista* genre, so beloved of Mexican working-class audiences in the Southwest. After commenting on the colossal full house at the Teatro El Edén for Herrera's production of the *obra bufa Mefistófeles,* the critic launched into the following tirade:

> *Mefistófeles* es lo más típico del repertorio bufo cubano, lo que quiere decir que es de lo más ridículo, de lo más estrafalario, de lo más grotesco y de lo más extravagante que pueda concebir la fantasía.
>
> Es una desgracia: casi todos los autores cubanos creen que al escribir para el teatro en ese género bufo, deben prescindir del sentido común y violar las leyes del buen gusto.
>
> Juzgando ese género, en general, puede decirse que esos autores no han hecho en ella uso del pincel sino de la brocha más gorda y más ordinaria.
>
> De ahí el que el género no prospere y sólo tenga aceptación en cierta parte del público, aquella precisamente que puesta a escoger entre *La Caricatura y El Fígaro* se deduciría sin vacilación por la primera.[17]

After stating that *Mefistófeles* did not even have "pies ni cabeza" (beginning nor ending), the critic went on to blame the failure of more serious theatre in Tampa on the public's preference for the *bufos!*

That this passionate attack on the taste of working-class audiences should emanate from a theatre critic is no surprise, given similar responses by elitist commentators in Hispanic communities throughout the United States. It is surprising, however, that the forum for such snobbery was *El Internacional,* the newspaper of the Centro Obrero, the protector of working-class culture. But it must be remembered that, in general, the tobacco workers considered themselves an elite among workers, the best read, the most politically astute, and the most cultured. Much of the support for theatre arts in Hispanic Tampa was, in part, attributable to those proud sentiments.

In summarizing, then, many parallels can be drawn with the Hispanic theatre as it flourished in the Southwest and in New York: the relationship of the theatre to politics and immigration patterns; the dominance of Spanish *zarzuela* and melodrama, eventually ceding to more popular forms, such as the *obra bufa cubana;* the effects of the Depression; the role theatre played in protecting Hispanic cultural values and the Spanish language and in the education of the youth; the isolation of Hispanic culture and theatre from the larger society, etc. But Tampa's Hispanic theatrical experience was unique in more than one regard. First of all, it provided a successful example of deep and lasting community support for theatre arts, so deep and so strong that private enterprise could not compete with the efforts of the mutual aid societies. And because the Hispanic stage had become such a symbol of proud achievement, the necessary political and organizing steps were taken to make Tampa the site of the only Hispanic company in the Federal Theatre Project. The fate of the project itself revealed the current level of misunderstanding of Hispanics by official societal structures and the impossibility at that time of meaningful integration and assimilation of Hispanics in Florida. Finally, although documentation is tragically incomplete, Tampa was also unique in its at least partial support of Afro-Hispanic culture and theatre, despite the fact that that very theatre and the Sociedad la Unión Martí-Maceo may have pointed to very real indictments of racism and segregation, not only in the Jim Crow South but also within the Hispanic community itself.

6. On the Road: Hispanic Theatre outside Its Major Centers

As has been seen up to now, Los Angeles, San Antonio, New York, and Tampa were centers of intense Hispanic theatrical activity. They were centers that constantly attracted companies touring from abroad and from within the United States, and they were also centers where touring companies were assembled to head out into the less densely populated areas where Hispanics lived in small, agricultural communities, as in the Rio Grande Valley, and manufacturing communities, as in the port cities of northeastern New Jersey. With the exceptions of Laredo and El Paso, very few other cities sustained their own resident professional companies. Rather, they supported numerous theatre houses, cinemas, and halls which housed the road shows and they also developed numerous amateur companies that placed their hobby at the service of community and religious charities while presenting wholesome entertainment and cultural education to their Hispanic neighborhoods and colonies. Although there was considerable activity in between the points of San Antonio and Los Angeles, New York and Chicago, taken as a whole it would never equal the commercial and professional levels achieved in Los Angeles alone, not to mention the other three centers. It is also true that the big city houses were often the exclusive domain of the larger, more sophisticated theatrical and vaudeville companies, thus leaving the small towns of the Rio Grande Valley and New Mexico, for instance, to the smaller itinerant companies and tent-theatres. It is also true that when first vaudeville and later the Depression and cinema pushed serious drama and *zarzuela* out of the big city houses, numerous serious artists were able to continue their profession by touring to small towns and cities.

Texas

In Texas, most communities from Dallas southward that had a substantial Mexican-origin population supported, at one time or another, amateur or professional theatrical productions. The area of greatest activity, however, outside of the major Mexican population centers of San Antonio, El Paso, and Laredo was the lower Rio Grande Valley. At least since the last decade of the nineteenth century, the communities of the Valley and the nearby communities of Corpus Christi and San Diego were consistently visited by small itinerant theatrical companies and tent shows, even up into the 1950s. The tale of *puebleando* in the Valley was largely told in chapter 3.

What is left to be said is that since at least 1910 the Valley also relied on theatre performances for fundraising and that this fundraising was accomplished by resident companies of amateurs who were at times directed by professional actors. The year 1910 is an appropriate starting point because, besides being the date of the Mexican Revolution that was to result in numerous refugees moving to the Valley, it also marks the centenary of Mexican Independence. According to *La Crónica* (July 2, 1910), it was the theatrical group of the Altamirano School in Hebbronville that was performing patriotic plays and allegories such as *El mártir de Chihuahua* and *Sangre azteca* to raise funds for the centennial celebration to take place that September. And as the expatriate community in Texas grew larger and larger, the reason for raising funds shifted to constructing Mexican schools to accommodate the larger school-age population. Again one of the favorite means to reach this end was through dramatic performances. In August 1921, for instance, an unnamed amateur company performed throughout the Valley—at the Teatro Juárez in San Benito, at the Dittman in Brownsville, at the Casino in Del Rio—under the banner of Beneficio Centenario Escolar, raising funds for Mexican schools. The company, supported by the Comisión Honorífica Mexicana, presented such works as José Espronceda's romantic three-act drama *Hojas caídas*, as well as *sainetes, juguetes cómicos,* and comedies. The school crusade continued into the Depression but became somewhat overshadowed by other needy charities. In the late 1920s and the 1930s the Dreamland Theatre in Rio Grande City, the Park Theatre and the Junior High auditorium in Harlingen, Roosevelt School auditorium in Mission, the Instituto del Valle in Pharr, and the Stephen F. Austin School auditorium in Edinburg, among others, sponsored fundraisers for church schools and charities with the production of secular comedies and religious dramas by local amateurs such as the Jóvenes de la Sociedad Católica and the Antiguos Alumnos de la Escuela Parroquial. Again, the most popular works for these events were the humorous one-act *sainetes* and comedies by Spain's Alvarez Quintero brothers.

During the early 1930s two somewhat stable and long-lived amateur groups were active in the lower Rio Grande Valley. The first of these was the Cuadro Artístico Harlingen, directed by J. A. Moreno, which always performed to raise funds for such charities as the Mexican Clinic in San Antonio, the high school in Matamoros, Mexico, and even for the director when he became stricken with typhoid fever in 1933, according to *La Prensa* (June 18). The group, which included Moreno's wife and various other community people from Harlingen, periodically performed *revistas, zarzuelas, juguetes cómicos,* and even original comedies: *Jeremías* by Moreno himself, and *Así es Mercedes* (probably referring to the town Mercedes) by the local *La Prensa* correspondent José Díaz. The group, which performed variety acts as well, also included the comic duo, supposedly favored by Valley audiences, of doña Sinforoso and don Pancitas, who probably represented *peladitos.* The usual ticket prices for the Moreno shows were twenty cents for adults and ten cents for children. Unlike the professional companies that toured the Valley and performed at such commercial establishments as the Teatro Chapultepec in East Donna and the Teatro Nacional in Weslaco, Moreno's group had to be content with performing in such places as the Hidalgo Hall in Brownsville.

The second group was somewhat more substantial, producing three-act melodramas such as Miguel Ramos Carrión's *Levantar muertos* and Constantino S. Pérez's *Caridad y redención,* along with lighter pieces. From 1933 to 1935 San Antonio's *La Prensa* documents performances by the Grupo Ildefonso Mireles every few months at the Roosevelt High School auditorium in Mission. Mireles's group, which included local firemen, Explorer Scouts, and other community people, is similar to the Círculo de Obreros Católicos San José of East Chicago, Indiana, to be studied below. Like the

Círculo, the Mireles group was an official secular arm of the church, which was charged with providing wholesome entertainment for the young people while raising money for the church. The Mireles group was part of the Asociación Católica José y María of Mission. The Asociación had other branches in the neighboring Valley towns, with the McAllen branch supporting its Anacleto González theatrical group and the Brownsville one sponsoring its Luis Segura Vilches group. It is not known how many other similar groups existed, but at least once the Diocese of Corpus Christi brought them together, on March 1, 1935, for performances at the McAllen school auditorium.

Two cities on the border developed a significant theatre culture of their own in Texas. The first of these, Laredo, was visited by Mexican touring companies in the late nineteenth and early twentieth centuries because it was the principal port of entry into Texas and the central United States from central Mexico. The other, El Paso, situated just across the border from a major Mexican urban center, Ciudad Juárez, became the destination of thousands of refugees from the Mexican Revolution who were not anxious to get too far from their homeland; they brought their taste for the dramatic arts with them. With San Antonio, these cities became the extreme ends of a triangle on direct railroad lines that meant lucrative tours for the large dramatic companies traveling up from central and northern Mexico. Of course, runs in San Antonio were the longest, and San Antonio also received more defectors from the touring companies who stayed on in the Alamo City to form the backbone of its resident Hispanic theatre. But Laredo and El Paso could each lay claim to artistic glories: first Laredo as the earliest Hispanic theatre town in Texas and later during the Depression El Paso, which continued to attract large companies from Mexico City even when San Antonio and Los Angeles did not.

As mentioned in chapter 3, during the period 1890 to 1910 there seem to have been more Mexican troupes touring to Laredo than San Antonio and also more theatre construction and earlier establishment of resident companies than in San Antonio. During this time, the two most active companies in Laredo were the Compañía Dramática Solsona and the Compañía Solórzano, both of which probably used Laredo as a base from which to venture forth to San Antonio, Corpus Christi, San Diego, and other points along the way. As mentioned in chapter 3, the Solsona company moved up to make San Antonio its base, but the Compañía Dramática Solórzano continued to perform in and around Laredo and in 1910 settled there definitively when director Francisco Solórzano leased and opened the

Teatro Solórzano, at which his troupe began service as the stock company in 1911. Solórzano had bought the theatre outright by mid 1911, according to *La Crónica* (September 14, 1911). Not only did Solórzano's company become one of the first resident Mexican theatres in Texas, but it also represented the founding of a Texas theatrical family, as in the cases of the Villalongín, the Astol, and the Noloesca-Areu families, for Solórzano's daughter Berta also developed a fruitful acting career with the F. Díaz de León company and many major companies that performed in the Southwest.

By the end of 1910 there were various theatres in Laredo offering silent films and dramas, *zarzuelas* and/or variety acts: Solórzano, Alarcón, Eléctrico (advertising American vaudeville), Palacio Eléctrico, Dreamland, and Hidalgo (in Nuevo Laredo). At times the fierce competition came down to which theatre could offer the coolest auditorium; on July 2, 1910, for instance, the Solórzano announced its installation of an electric fan. That first year the Solórzano featured the Señores Valdez Hermanos y Compañía and other unnamed performers of *zarzuelas* and *sainetes*, while the Hidalgo and the Dreamland featured variety acts. The Dreamland presented *sainetes* and *juguetes*, directed by leading man José Albelo. But it was the Palacio Eléctrico, with Francisco Fierros as impresario, that *La Crónica* on November 19, 1910, classified as the favorite of Laredo aristocracy, where the most select segment of the society would meet.

Things soon changed in 1911 when Solórzano installed his troupe as the stock company at the Teatro Solórzano. With prices of ten cents for adults and five cents for children and a fare that included *zarzuela*, melodrama, and high comedy, the Solórzano became a profitable venture indeed. So much so, in fact, that Francisco Solórzano was soon able to buy the theatre and later another in 1916: Teatro Principal. By May 5, 1911, another theatre opened, the Royal, and was registering full houses, just like the other six, according to *La Crónica*. By December the Electric began to give the Solórzano more competition by offering *zarzuelas, sainetes,* and comedies performed by local artists. The Solórzano, meantime, had standardized its fare: dramas and comedies on Saturday, Sunday, and Thursday, *juguetes cómicos* the rest of the week. Such was the beginning of Laredo becoming an obligatory stop for road companies. During the next twenty years, the doors to other theatres would open here: Teatro Iris, Teatro García, Teatro Strand, Teatro Independencia, Teatro Variedades, Teatro Iturbide (later Teatro Nacional).

El Paso, probably the first city in the United States to have the distinction of receiving the grand company of Virginia Fábregas as early

as 1899, continued through the 1930s to be a profitable town for Hispanic touring companies. It benefited doubly because of its geo-
graphic location: it was not only visited by companies coming up
from Mexico but also those en route from San Antonio to Los Angeles. Furthermore, the happenstance that it was located just across
the border from a large Mexican city, Ciudad Juárez, also meant that
Mexican companies touring the northern border during the Depression could also play Juárez without adding to their food, lodging, and
travel expenses, as they certainly would be in going to Los Angeles
and San Antonio with their companies, which numbered from thirty
to fifty members; according to *El Continental* (May 1, 1935), Toña la
Negra traveled with fifty. Because of this, such large companies as
Roberto Soto's, Joaquín Pardavé's and Toña la Negra's played El Paso's
Teatro Colón and Liberty Hall without going on to the other two
cities in 1935 and 1936. In fact, the Teatro Colón from 1935 to 1937
hosted one large company after another, including even Virginia
Fábregas.

Manuel Gamio surveyed the movie houses, most of which also accommodated touring Mexican and Spanish companies in the 1920s
(Colón, Alcahazar, Paris, Alhambra, Eureka, Rex), and noted that
they were cleaner than those of San Antonio.[1] Whether this was true
or not, he overlooked other theatres: the Hidalgo and Estrella. Judging from newspaper articles, El Paso was very proud of all its theatres but most proud of the Teatro Colón, whose history *El Continental* summarized on August 29, 1937, its twenty-first anniversary.
In fact, as a functioning theatre house the Colón was only outlived
by San Antonio's Teatro Nacional in the Southwest. *El Continental's*
article reviewed how El Paso grew so rapidly with the flood of refugees from the Maderist Revolution that, to meet the cultural needs
of the large and prosperous community, Silvio Lacoma constructed
the theatre in 1916 and baptized it Colón, despite criticism in the
English-language newspapers that preferred the theatre be named
Christopher Columbus, especially since *colon* in English is the large
intestine.

The theatre was inaugurated with a performance by the Familia
Bell and in the years to come housed performances by some of
the greatest names in Hispanic theatre: Virginia Fábregas, Amelia
Wilhemy, Esperanza Iris, María Conesa, Leopoldo Beristáin, Dorita
Ceprano, Los Hermanos Areu, don Catarino, María Teresa Montoya,
Beatriz Noloesca, Nelly Fernández, Romualdo Tirado, etc. In 1924
the theatre was purchased and remodeled by a Mexican entertain-
ment company which was still administering the Colón in 1937; the

owners were José U. Calderón, Juan Salas Porras, and Rafael Calderón and the general manager Alberto Salas Porras. Later the same company also founded a distributing company for Mexican films, Azteca Distributing, and made the Teatro Colón the headquarters for this effort, which also supported offices in Los Angeles and San Antonio. Azteca Films still exists today.

During the Depression El Paso is of interest not only because it was able to continue to attract the large touring companies from Mexico but for various other reasons as well: despite the success of the Teatro Colón and Liberty Hall during the 1930s, numerous community theatre groups appeared to raise funds for the church and for those suffering the most from the Depression; among the community theatres, one group seems to have foreshadowed the not-for-profit structure of today's community theatres: Teatro Intimo.

As did the other cities we have studied, El Paso, too, developed numerous community and church theatre groups that set about raising funds by presenting dramas, *zarzuelas,* and shorter pieces. Such names as Cuadro Dramático del Santo Angel, directed by Roberto Rechy, Cuadro Artístico de la Parroquia de la Sagrada Familia, Cuadro Buena Voluntad, and Los Luises de la Parroquia Sagrado Corazón de Jesús were active for years in raising funds for church-related charities with performances of standard dramas and comedies by such authors as the Alvarez Quintero brothers and Tamayo y Baus and also in presenting typical works that related to the Depression, as in *La crisis,* for instance, which was staged at Our Lady of Guadalupe Church in January 1938 by an unnamed group. The Mexican Protestants also supported theatre groups, but these quite often staged religious plays translated from English originals, such as Grave Sloane Overton's *El ensueño de la maternidad,* performed at the Iglesia Presbiteriana del Divino Salvador.

Along with the church-backed theatre groups, there also existed various secular groups that would use school auditoriums, mutualist societies, and church halls for performances. One of the most prominent of these was the Cuadro Bárcena, which included the Bárcena brothers and sisters and various other members of the community and performed *zarzuelas* and *sainetes* at the Lydia Patterson Institute and the San Ignacio Church hall. Another group which seems to have been more professional, for it counted among its members professional actors and scenographers and would even play Liberty Hall, was the Grupo Margarita Hernández, directed by Pedro Meneses, Jr. There was also the Cuadro Alianza, directed by Gustavo Rodríguez, of the Patria lodge of the Alianza Hispano Americana, which performed melodramas at Liberty Hall. There were Juárez-based amateur groups that also performed in El Paso such as Tespis, which performed at Liberty Hall and Teatro Alcázar in 1935. But one personality stands out among all for his tireless development of theatre arts during the Depression, acting with and directing numerous groups on both sides of the border in settings that ran the gamut from Liberty Hall in El Paso to the Club Piloto in Juárez: Fernando Navarro. From 1934 to 1938 *El Continental* documented Navarro as leading man and/or director of the Club Rosicler's (a women's organization) drama group, the Brigada Cultural of the Partido Nacional Revolucionario in Juárez, Club Tardes de Martes, Grupo de Damas de Ciudad Juárez, UFCM de Ciudad Juárez, the Comité Pro-Damnificados de Guadalupe, and numerous ad hoc groups.

One final interesting note about the El Paso theatre culture involves the appearance of a theatre, Teatro Intimo, whose relationship with the community was somewhat similar to the not-for-profit theatres of today. The Teatro Intimo's stock company maintained a membership of over two hundred as a means of supporting itself, according to *El Continental* (December 29, 1936). The members were entitled to come to private previews of plays before they were opened to the general public. The Teatro Intimo also attempted to attract both Anglo and Mexican audiences and alternated plays in English and Spanish. Noted from 1935 to 1937 by *El Continental* were *Michael and Mary, Doña Clarines, Cobardías, Tomorrow and Tomorrow,* and *La marcha de Cádiz,* a *zarzuela*. For the 1936 staging of *Doña Clarines* the artistic director was H. G. Partearroyo and the leading lady was Carolina Velarde. There is no way to know if Partearroyo was the permanent director of the stock company, but the production of *Tomorrow and Tomorrow* involved an Anglo cast, according to *El Continental* (September 28, 1937).

New Mexico

There have been more scholarly studies on the folk theatre of New Mexico than any other aspect of Hispanic theatre.[2] So much has appeared that a clear impression was created in scholarly circles that the only theatre Mexicans of the Southwest had was a folk theatre whose origin can be traced to the first colonizers from interior Mexico in 1598. The religious folk theatre represented by the annual *pastorela,* or Mexican shepherd's play,[3] and the early secular, historical folk dramas of *Los tejanos, Los comanches,* and *Moros y cristianos*[4] are beyond the scope of this book, which is dedicated to the study of the professional stage and the amateur theatre influenced by the professional stage.

There is one phase of the New Mexican folk theatre that does interest us, however, because it illustrates how drama from the professional stages of Mexico City was integrated into folk culture. John E. Englekirk uncovered and brought to light the history of various New Mexican families of performers that operated from 1885 until the late 1920s in the Santa Fe and Las Vegas areas of New Mexico for a public he described as poor, unlettered, isolated from Hispanic culture, but nostalgic for it (1941: 230).

Englekirk (ibid.: 232–288) described how two immigrants from Mexico, Félix Tenorio and Manuel Prada, during the early 1880s brought with them a collection of *sainetes*—*El roto, El tambor mágico, El sordo zapatero,* etc.—and plays—*Hernán o la vuelta del cruzado* and *La inocente Dorotea*—that would become the basis of their own itinerant company, which performed from 1885 to 1910, and then the property of a new Compañía de Aficionados de Santa Fe, directed by Manuel L. Romero until its dissolution in the late 1920s. Another itinerant company also got its start from this initial repertoire of works imported by Tenorio and Prada. Próspero S. Baca, a carpenter born in Las Vegas in 1875 and an actor in school plays at the Jesuit School there, became the copyist for some of these plays; in 1896 he founded his own company, made up of his four younger brothers, his sister, and his wife, and performed for years at the San José Hall in Las Vegas, as well as in Taos, Mora, San José, and Villanueva (ibid.: 239). Writing in 1940, Englekirk concluded that it was the silent screen that put an end to his folk theatre.[5]

Whether this is true folk theatre or not is for folklorists to answer. The fact is that these itinerant players did supplement their income through their performances, but for the most part they were unstudied amateurs, as their title, *aficionados* (amateurs), clearly indicates. What differentiates the Baca and Romero families, as well as the players that joined Tenorio and Prada, from their San Antonio amateur counterparts is that they were not immigrants, not intellectuals taking refuge from the Revolution, not using theatre as a wholesome and moral entertainment to preserve the culture from the threat of assimilation. They were performing without models and stimulation from the professional stage, at least until the late teens, when professional companies began touring southern New Mexico regularly.

Other than these manifestations of folk theatre, New Mexico supported halls and small theatres that housed the smaller touring com-

panies, especially in southern New Mexico. The state was also a lucrative area for tours by tent shows and circus and became a regular
part of the circuit of the great Circo Escalante and the Ortiz Brothers,
both mentioned in chapter 3.

Arizona

After the setback suffered by Hispanic theatre in the late nineteenth
century in Tucson, due to a combination of the arrival of the railroad
and the growth of the Anglo-American community, it was not until
the mid teens of the twentieth century that the Spanish-language
stage reconstituted itself and then surpassed the levels of activity
and professionalism of the past. The rebirth of the Hispanic stage in
Tucson and the further development of the touring circuit in Arizona was due principally to the influx of refugees from the Mexican
Revolution, so that Tucson's Mexican-origin population rose to
15,000, or 50 percent of the entire city. From the 1880s to 1915, itinerant companies continued to tour to Tucson following the original
circuit through the state of Sonora in northern Mexico to Tucson
and then to Los Angeles. But in the 1900s and possibly as early as
1893, companies also began coming to Tucson from Texas via El
Paso and points in New Mexico. *El Fronterizo* on April 15, 1893,
noted performances in Tucson by a Compañía Dramática Solórzano Figueroa. It is possible that this was the company of the same
Francisco Solórzano who was actively touring south Texas during
this time and who in 1910 founded the Teatro Solórzano in Laredo.
By 1915 the Clifton Theatre, the Royal Theatre, which was owned
by the Aros sisters, the Opera House, and the Elysean Grove were
housing companies touring vaudeville, drama, and *zarzuela*, although it was the two latter houses that offered drama most often.
But Tucson was in need of a major theatre to house larger dramatic
companies which were now accessible, especially for the middle-
class Mexican immigrant and Mexican American families.

In 1915, Carmen Soto Vázquez constructed a first-class theatre,
Tucson's largest to date, which seated fourteen hundred people (Miguélez 1983: 54). From 1915 until 1922, the Carmen hosted some of
the most important touring companies, including Virginia Fábregas,
María del Carmen Martínez, María Teresa Montoya, the Cuadro
Novel, and numerous others. When a touring show was not at the
Carmen, its own stock company, made up in 1915 of defectors from
the Compañía Nacional and the Compañía Turich, performed along
with the showing of silent movies. True to custom, the Carmen be-

came the pride, joy, and center of cultural life for the Mexican community and even served as the forum for political candidates wish-
ing to win the Mexican vote. According to Thomas E. Sheridan,

> to the Mexican elite of Tucson, Teatro Carmen was a powerful
> symbol of self-identity, living proof of the depth, power, and
> beauty of their culture. They were the ones who supported the
> most vigorous cultural institution in town, a theatre whose works
> were in Spanish, not English. Such an institution destroyed once
> and for all the image of Tucson as a crude little frontier town.
> In the face of increasing discrimination, Teatro Carmen also re-
> assured these cultivated ranchers, merchants, and professional
> men and women that they belonged to a society equal or superior
> to that of their Anglo neighbors. The dramas of Spain's Golden
> Age or the contemporary works of Mexico's finest playwrights
> and composers gave lie to the derogatory stereotypes of Mexicans
> so prevalent in the Southwest.[6]

Unfortunately, by 1919 the Carmen was on the decline and the
Spanish-language newspapers were continuously exhorting the public to attend functions (ibid.: 57). In 1920 the theatre closed up for
six months, until in December the Compañía César Sánchez leased
it for a very successful run of melodramas. Probably in an effort to
avoid paying the rent of the theatre, on December 29 the Sánchez
company moved to a tent on the west side of the city and began presenting *zarzuelas* there (ibid.: 58). In 1921, besides serving as a theatre, the Carmen also became a boxing ring and was closed by city
authorities, supposedly because it lacked accommodations and emer-
gency exits for large crowds, to which *El Tucsonense* on March 26,
1921, responded, decrying discrimination. After a poor showing for
the María Teresa Montoya company in 1922, the Teatro Carmen became a dance hall and later a boxing ring and in 1927 a garage; the
building still stands today (ibid.: 59).

During the 1920s through the early 1930s the Teatro Royal continued where the Teatro Carmen had left off. But, according to *El
Tucsonense* (March 16, 1926), the Royal was too small to accommodate sizable audiences and to render a profit for large companies. It
was joined later by the Lyric Theatre, the Temple of Music and Art,
and the Rialto in occasionally housing touring professional companies. It was the latter, in fact, that received the Virginia Fábregas
company in 1927. But toward the end of the decade and into the
1930s, fewer and fewer touring companies made calls on Tucson and
those that did were mostly vaudeville groups. At the same time, to

compensate for the loss of the Teatro Carmen and the waning of serious theatrical fare, the community responded with numerous amateur groups, many of them related to the churches or to the sociocivic Alianza Hispano Americana. Whether church-related or not, the common repertoire for these amateurs consisted of secular *sainetes, zarzuelas,* and dramas, and the San Agustín cathedral auditorium was the preferred forum. Among the numerous charitable purposes addressed by these theatrical groups, one political function stands out, the same one mentioned in chapter 3, which the Circo Escalante was supporting in 1927: the defense fund for accused murderer Alfredo Grijalva. At the San Agustín auditorium on June 17, 1927, the Cuadro Artístico Pedro Mena García performed *El difunto Nicolás* to raise funds for the Comité Pro-Grijalva. The most active of these amateur groups, however, was the Club de Aficionados de la Sagrada Familia, which, numerous times each year at Sagrada Familia Church auditorium, performed a wide range of comedies, *sainetes,* and *zarzuelas* from 1928 through 1932.

The Alianza Hispano Americana was founded in Tucson in 1894 by prominent members of Tucson's Mexican middle class to promote their ethnic interests and protect themselves from the growing Anglo population, which was gaining in political and economic power and was even supporting such nativist anti-Mexican groups as the American Protective Association.[7] The Alianza grew to embrace working-class Mexicans and its membership spread until it became the most widespread mutualist society in the Southwest. By the time of the Depression, the Tucson area supported various politically active Alianza lodges. The lodge halls themselves were often used for productions by amateur companies, and some lodges, such as the Lodge No. 1 of Florence, Arizona, supported their own theatrical groups. Los Angeles playwright Brígido Caro, who had become active in the Alianza in Los Angeles, had various of his plays performed at Alianza lodges in southern California. But it was in the Tucson area, the heart of the Alianza, that his nationalistic works gained their greatest popularity. It is difficult to estimate just how many of Caro's works were performed and how many times, but from 1929 through 1931 his *La gloria de la raza* was performed at least once a year at area lodges and his work in honor of the Alianza itself, *La bandera de la Alianza,* was performed at least once.[8]

The whole of Arizona attracted touring companies and tent shows. Tucson itself, in addition to being a site for more established theatrical institutions, was also considered part of the standard tent show and circus route dating back to the 1870s (Gipson 1972: 238). In 1925 alone, four tent shows visited Tucson: Circo Escalante,

Circo Pérez, Compañía Azteca de los Hermanos Olvera, and Carpa Rosete-Aranda. *El Tucsonense* on July 15 and August 15 recorded *zarzuela* performances at the Olvera show and numerous allegories and dramas at the Rosete-Aranda: *La Guerra Ruso-Japonesa, El grito de independencia, Las rosas del Tepeyac,* and *Las cuatro apariciones de la Virgen de Guadalupe* (two standard Virgin of Guadalupe plays), among others. The Circo Escalante, which also provided stage shows and *zarzuelas,* was a perennial presence in Arizona during the 1920s and the Depression.

The Midwest

Tours by itinerant companies to the Mexican communities of the Midwest from 1910 through the Depression were few and far between. Except for Chicago, the Mexican communities in the Midwest did not develop their own resident companies either. However, from Detroit to St. Paul the amateur theatre was plentiful and intense and in some communities could rival the professional companies for quality. During the 1930s such places as the Lithuanian Hall in Detroit, which housed the Cuadro Artístico Anahuac, directed by professional actor Tigrio Vargas; the Nuestra Señora de Guadalupe Church auditorium in Kansas City, housing the Club Tepeyac; the Neighborhood House in St. Paul, sponsoring the Sociedad Anahuac; and Chicago's Hull House, Aiken Institute (housing the Primera Iglesia Bautista), and Nuestra Señora de Guadalupe housed performances not only to celebrate Mexican and religious holidays but also just to provide the wholesome, cultural entertainment in the mother tongue that the community needed for enjoyment and a sense of cultural and ethnic solidarity in enclaves that were seen as far from home indeed.

It would seem that nowhere would Mexicans feel more out of place than on the southern border of Lake Michigan, where the snowy and icy-cold winters only provided stark contrast to the open hearths of the steel mills where many of them had to work. It is in the Indiana Harbor section of East Chicago, Indiana, that one of the most interesting Mexican community theatres developed.

Dating from the second decade of the twentieth century, the urban industrial complex of East Chicago, Indiana, attracted large-scale immigration from Mexico and Mexican American migration from Texas. In particular, the economic security that derived from the fast-growing steel industry along Lake Michigan was a prime motivation for the settlement of Mexicans in the area. Furthermore, the economic and social turmoil produced by the Mexican Revolution, in combination with the shortage of manpower in the United States during World War I, among other factors, explains the influx of Mexicans to East Chicago. To be sure, the majority of the population consisted of laborers, many of whom came from rural areas, but intellectuals and professional people also made up a considerable portion of the community. Many of the intellectuals were political and religious refugees from Mexico, who, underemployed in the United States as manual laborers because of linguistic and social barriers, sought to preserve their cultural and religious identity in their new land. They also desired to approximate their former middle-class and aristocratic lives, if not in the economic sense at least in the cultural, by sponsoring and participating in many educational, religious, and social activities. It is this sector of the community, through its various religious and mutualist societies, that created and sponsored theatre productions for the Mexican community as a whole.

Of the three or four societies sponsoring plays in East Chicago during the twenties, the most active was the Círculo de Obreros Católicos "San José" with its Cuadro Dramático. The Círculo de Obreros Católicos "San José" was founded on April 12, 1925, for the express purposes of raising funds for the construction of a church, promoting the welfare of fellow Mexicans and working for the education of their children, raising funds for a library, and providing wholesome forms of recreation for the members.[9] In accordance with these goals, the Cuadro Dramático was created to provide "wholesome recreation" and raise funds for the construction of Our Lady of Guadalupe Church.

According to the weekly newspaper and official organ of the Círculo de Obreros, *El Amigo del Hogar*, published from 1925 to 1930, nine plays were presented by the Cuadro Dramático from March 1927 until May 1928.[10] It is most likely that the Cuadro Dramático fulfilled more the recreational than the financial goals of the Círculo, since after the $35.00 to $59.00 for rental of Auditorium Hall and the costs of refreshments, programs, transportation, musicians, and scenery were paid for, the net profits usually totaled only from $12.00 to $60.00 per program. The tickets were usually priced as follows: reserved seats at seventy-five cents, general admission at fifty cents, and amphitheatre at forty cents.

It is not safe to assume that the presentations were only of an amateur nature. Rather, it must be emphasized that along with the *aficionados*, former professionals from the Mexico City stage took part. Such was the case of J. Jesús Cabrera, who directed all of the plays of the Cuadro Dramático and who brought the scripts from Mexico.[11] Furthermore, the quality of the productions must have been good, not only because of the professionalism, but also because of the extensive preparation of the plays and the enthusiasm exhibited by both the participants and the community.

In most cases the Cuadro's plays were full length and their authors were clearly identified on the playbills and programs. Moreover, the only *sainete* (*El que nace para ochavo*) by the Cuadro Dramático was presented on the same bill with a full-length play, Jacinto Benavente's *El nido ajeno*. In fact, the Cuadro Dramático even accomplished the tremendous feat of producing the prologue and five acts of the Spanish play *El juez de su sangre* by Eduardo Vidal y Valencia and José Roca y Roca. The plays in their chronological order of presentation were: *El nido ajeno* by Jacinto Benavente and *El que nace para ochavo* (March 13, 1927); *Hernán o la vuelta del cruzado* by Fernando Calderón (April 3, 1927); *El Conde de Monte-Cristo* (April 30, 1927); *El caudal de los hijos; La Mujer X* (November 19, 1927); *El juez de su sangre* by Eduardo Vidal y Valencia and José Roca y Roca (February 19, 1928); *Los pobres de Madrid* by Manuel Ortiz de Pinedo (February 4, 1928); and *Santa Inés,* a Silesian play (May 1928). There is news of other plays directed by J. Jesús Cabrera but performed by groups other than the Cuadro Dramático: *El herrero o Felipe Derblay* by Ohnet (January 1926); *La muerte civil* by Giacometti (March 1927); *Para mentir las mujeres* and *Levantar muertos* (October 1928); and *La nuza* (August 1929). The Cuadro Dramático of the Círculo de Obreros Católicos "San José" was not the only Mexican theatrical group in the area. There are announcements and reviews in *El Amigo del Hogar* of plays produced by Cruz Azul Mexicana, Cuadro de Aficionados de Gary, the Arcos family, Sociedad Fraternal de Chicago, as well as *zarzuelas* and *cuadros de variedades* by professional companies on tour.

Chicago had the Asociación Católica de Juventud Mexicana of the San Francisco de Asís Church, Cuadro Artístico Adalís, Cuadro Dramático Olimpia, and other groups similar to East Chicago's Cuadro, but none of them were really so elaborate as to have their own statutes, newspapers, professional director, and even critics to take the work of the group seriously. But during the Depression the Chicago Mexican community, according to San Antonio's *La Prensa* (April 18, 1931), was organizing cultural functions, including theatre, dances and civic and literary meetings, at the rate of one every two weeks. And then, too, Chicago's large Mexican community did support a resident professional company, which struggled long and hard to survive. In Los Angeles' *La Opinión* on March 18, 1931, the Chicago correspondent published a report that various professional artists of the Mexican community had gotten together to form a *zarzuela* and operetta company to be directed by dance teacher and actor Paco Perafán and composer-singer Silvano R. Ramos, with its orchestra to be led and concertized by Maestro D. Justino Sánchez. From artists that had settled in Chicago from touring companies and those that had been performing at cabarets, the manager, Ignacio M. Valle, and the director were able to assemble a considerable group that included four singers, two female comic chorines, a male and a female character actors, two leading dancers, a publicity director, and a public relations specialist, each one named in the article. Despite one of the actors being mugged on the way to rehearsal by two men of "Italian nationality," reported on May 9 by *La Opinión,* preparations continued and on June 6, 1931, the new Artistas Unidos Mexicanos debuted at the Eighteenth Street Theatre with a program of two *zarzuelas:* the Spanish *Gigantes y cabezudos* and the Mexican *Chin chun chan.* During the next few months the group performed at various auditoriums, including Hull House, according to the Chicago newspaper *El Nacional* (August 29, 1931).

By October 1931, the Artistas Unidos Mexicanos had leased a permanent performance space at 1107 South Halsted and were giving regular performances there, followed by socials and dances. By June 1932, however, Paco Perafán and some of his company signed a contract to combine with American vaudeville artists and tour the Orpheum Circuit, according to *La Prensa* (June 8). After this there is only word of Paco Perafán and consorts in occasional performances of *zarzuelas* by them in Chicago at West Side Auditorium. Then a May 13, 1934, *La Prensa* article reported that they had returned to Chicago after touring Illinois, Indiana, and Kentucky in a vaudeville company named Old Mexico. Of course, Old Mexico staged songs and dances "typical" of Mexico for Anglo-Americans of the Midwest and, according to *La Prensa* of this date, the tour was very successful and lucrative.

In an article published on August 24, 1932, for *La Opinión,* J. Xavier Mondragón complained that Chicago was where Mexican performers had suffered the most. He states that numerous stage artists had been out of work and that there had been various unsuccessful attempts to establish companies. A few days earlier, groups like New York's Compañía Santigosa had come through Chicago, but the Mexican community was in dire economic straits and did not support the show. Therefore, various artists were forced to join American vaudeville companies. Also various great performers had to leave Chicago, including Silvano R. Ramos of Artistas Unidos Mexicanos whose performances at the Eighteenth Street theatre were attended by more Americans than Mexicans. Ramos and his family of singers were currently touring the Southwest. As noted above, Paco Perafán was soon to sign with an American vaudeville company and hit the Midwest circuits. After naming various other performers who were in dire circumstances, Mondragón went on to describe how Mexican artists have to play up to Anglo audiences. Later in the decade and in the early 1940s, Paco Perafán resurfaced in New York City to play the Hispanic vaudeville circuits and the mutualist societies with Marita Reid and Luis Mandret.

To partially address the hiatus left by the failure of Hispanic professional theater in Chicago, amateur groups similar to Indiana Harbor's Cuadro Dramático del Círculo de Obreros Católicos "San José" stepped up their activities. The most noteworthy of these was the company associated with the San Francisco de Asís Church, whose artistic director was leading man Pepe Luis, who had been very active on southwestern stages. From 1933 to 1935, Luis's group performed plays, *zarzuelas*, and *sainetes* regularly at the San Francisco de Asís auditorium and occasionally at other sites, such as McCormick Hall. With his wife, members of the Rangel family, and other leading families of the diocese, Luis kept serious drama alive in Chicago for the Mexican community, at least for a while.

California

Los Angeles was the site of the greatest flowering of Hispanic theatre in the United States and, of course, it was the theatrical and entertainment center for Hispanics in California. From here radiated numerous dramatic, lyric, and vaudeville companies which traveled south to San Diego, Mexicali, and Tijuana and north to San Francisco. The many cities and towns with substantial Mexican populations that were close to Los Angeles all benefited from numerous companies which included them on their itineraries. The San Francisco area functioned for the most part as the northern terminus of the southwestern circuits. San Francisco was a good show town that offered numerous theatres for short- and long-term leasing and one house, the Liberty Theatre, which regularly housed Hispanic shows for more than a decade.

From 1915 through 1919 a resident company, which included professionals and amateurs, performed drama, *zarzuela*, and light comedy at the Liberty on a regular basis. According to *La Crónica* (October 30, 1915), one of the plays performed by the company was a locally written play, perhaps about events that had taken place in nearby San Jose, California, *San José, 90* by a señor Quintero. By 1919 this Círculo Cómico Dramático, directed by a señor Vico and

starring leading man Romero Malpica, had became so profession-
alized that it began to venture out for tours to surrounding cities.
Later it performed at other San Francisco houses such as the Teatro
República. The Liberty, which was charging fifty cents for adults and
thirty cents for children, offered variety acts when the company was
not performing there.

After the Liberty changed its name to the Crescent in 1922, Romualdo Tirado's Compañía de Opereta y Zarzuela Española came up
from Los Angeles for a month's run. *La Crónica* on February 4, 1922,
praised the morality of Tirado's repertoire and its appropriateness for
families and also praised the qualities of the scenery, which supposedly Tirado had brought from Mexico. The *Hispano América*
(formerly *La Crónica*) newspaper commentator, who had all along
been praising Tirado's work, stating that it had been a long time
since a dramatic company had visited San Francisco, waxed elo-
quent on March 18, 1922: "Es un consuelo muy grande al par que
grato, encontrar un rincón en donde se puede escuchar la sonoridad
de nuestro idioma, saborear sus chistes, escuchar sus músicas."[12] Because of the great audience reception, Tirado stayed on at the Crescent; by April 29 he had given eighty shows, changing the program
each night of the week. On June 3, 1922, Tirado gave his last performance for free to thank the community for its support; his company
staged the popular operetta *La viuda alegre* and sponsored a dance
after the performance at Eagles Auditorium in San Francisco. He and
his company then left town, announcing that they were headed for
the Teatro Fábregas in Mexico City. In September, the Tirado company returned to San Francisco but did not play the Crescent. Instead, it played Native Sons Hall and California Hall, where Tirado
debuted his original *revista, De México a California.*

Unfortunately, in the pages of the *Hispano América* there is no
coverage of the Crescent Theatre for the next three and a half years;
however, coverage resumes in March 1926 and finds Hispanic theatrical activity at the theatre, once again named Liberty. Once again it
is Tirado's company that is packing in audiences for drama, *zarzuela,*
and operetta. On April 17, 1926, Tirado debuted his specially written *revista, San Francisco en camisa,* which included characters
named for and based on members of the audience who frequented
the shows. Once again newspaper coverage becomes spotty, without
showing when Tirado left, but by September the theatre hosted the
Compañía Artística Vásquez, which had toured from El Paso, Texas.
Shortly after the Vásquez troupe arrived, Tirado and his wife came
up from Los Angeles and joined the troupe, providing various *revistas* written by and starring Tirado. In August the famed Mexican

comic Leopoldo Beristáin joined the company for some two weeks, after which he left to return to Mexico with an insult on his lips for Mexican Americans. He said that he was sick of *pocherías,* according to the *Hispano América* (October 23, 1926). The company now known as Vásquez-Tirado stayed at the Liberty until December, when it shut its doors for the cold weather and because the artists' contracts were up. The dramatic company then went on tour of the northern California region.

In March 1927, the Virginia Fábregas company performed primarily European drama for two months, followed in June by the Compañía de Operetas, Zarzuelas y Revistas of the famed Mexican composer Luis Mendoza López. Promoted as the former assistant director of New York's Metropolitan Opera House orchestra, Mendoza López proceeded to perform a repertoire in which predominated operettas, many of them composed by himself, such as *Jugando al amor, Salomé, El as de los ases, El tigre real, César Imperator,* and *La esclava Nara.* In October the Compañía de Novedades Bell-Areu, with the Bell Family, the Areus, and La Chata Noloesca, occupied the stage. They were followed by the magician Justiniani and the Cuadro de Variedades Multicolor, which seems to have played through February. The Cuadro was followed in February by the Compañía de Revistas Argentinas for ten days. The last word we have of the Liberty concerns the Cuadro Frívolo, with Dorita Ceprano and Enrique Areu, who just arrived at the Liberty in May from a tour originating in Cuba. Thus ends the history of San Francisco's most important and long-lived (rather short when compared to houses in Los Angeles, San Francisco, El Paso, New York, and Tampa) house for Hispanic theatre.

Companies that toured to San Francisco played the Liberty and/or a number of other houses: Washington Theatre, Eagles Auditorium, California House, Fugazi Hall, Native Sons Hall, Dante Theatre, and Corran Theater. It was quite common for a company to move from one to another of these houses during their San Francisco visits. Of the above-named houses, Eagles Auditorium was favored by the Hispanic community as a place to hold fundraisers, besides hosting professional companies. It is also a house worthy of note because it was here that resident author Benjamín Padilla saw his *zarzuela Sangre azul* staged. Written in 1906, debuted at the Teatro Principal when Padilla still resided in his native Guadalajara (Monterde 1970: 256), and published in 1907 by the newspaper edited by Padilla,[13] *Sangre azul* in one act and two scenes ran for more than one hundred consecutive nights at the Principal in Guadalajara, according to *Hispano América* (November 17, 1923). Padilla lived in San Francisco as

a political refugee and from here edited a satirical newspaper column under the pseudonym of Kaskabel which was sindicated to
Spanish-language newspapers throughout the Southwest.[14] It seems
that Padilla's political commentary, as evidenced in *Sangre azul*, was
a contributing factor to his exile. According to *Hispano América*, this
comic *zarzuela* criticizes certain morbid sectors of society whose
only merit is having been born into the nobility and who are shown
to be less worthy than those of humble birth that are of greater use
to society. Monterde (1970: 256) lists another *zarzuela* by Padilla
which was debuted at Guadalajara's Principal and published in 1907
through his newspaper *El Kaskabel: Así es la vida* in one act and
three scenes. The score for both *zarzuelas* was composed by Fernández Méndez Velásquez. There is no documentation to show that
Así es la vida was ever staged in the Southwest or to show that
Padilla continued to write for the stage, although both possibly did
occur.

As in the other cities and towns that did not benefit from the high
level of professional theatrical activity, the Hispanic community of
San Francisco supported numerous amateur groups from the mid
teens through the 1930s. These groups performed at such halls and
auditoriums as the Nuestra Señora de Guadalupe Church auditorium, the Knights of Columbus Hall, the Sociedad Mexicana Ignacio
Allende, the Golden Gate Commandery Hall, the Knights of Pythias
Hall, the Centro Hispano Americano, and the Club Ibérico, besides
Eagles Auditorium. One of the most active groups, performing *zarzuelas* and operettas from 1918 through 1921, was the Compañía de
Aficionados de Opereta y Opera, directed by Jesús Amable. Very
little is known about the group, except that one of its benefit performances in Oakland was to raise funds for a headstone for the leading
lady who had died: señora Concepción Amable. An original *juguete
cómico* by a member of the group, Martín Solís, was staged in her
honor: *Marizoltzin*.

One can trace the map of the United States from Calexico to
Buffalo and discover similar Hispanic theatrical manifestations. All
along the tour routes, through Pennsylvania and Ohio, northern
New Mexico and Colorado, even Louisiana, similar community institutions developed to accommodate the dauntless itinerant companies which forged ahead, at times through snow and ice, as F. Díaz
de León reported from Detroit, through insults at border crossings
and Arizona movie houses featuring films denigrating Mexicans.
And these communities, in their fervor to preserve their native
tongue and the culture it represented, in order to provide a Catholic
and moral upbringing for their children, relied upon theatre as a

model of the highest levels of language and culture. If vaudeville and its lower and more risqué humor usurped the stages or if the professional companies did not often visit, the communities supported their own neighbors, really pillars of their enclave, in amateur companies. These companies performed, as in the Círculo de Obreros Católicos "San José," with a moral and cultural fervor, with a sense of mission that was indeed similar to that of their sponsoring organizations, the churches. The mutualist societies and political organizations also relied upon theatre to consolidate the Hispanic enclaves and to insulate them from cultural encroachment by the broader Anglo-American society. Hispanic theatre in communities large and small served needs far beyond those of the homeland. Hispanic theatre, beyond entertaining and enlightening audiences, had to assume patriotic and moralistic missions, had to take the lead in the fight for cultural preservation—the preservation of identity—in a foreign land.

7. Conclusion

This has been a somewhat incomplete survey, filled with the gaps left by too many missing documents, due largely to the minority or "foreign" nature of the subject vis-à-vis mainstream Anglo-American interests. Newspapers, plays, and theatre records were not preserved by the official educational and informational agencies of the society, libraries and universities. The English-language media, the history books, the offical records simply ignored this dynamic and vibrant cultural history we have here attempted to begin to document. But that minority and foreign status, on the other hand, also had its role in shaping Hispanic theatre in the United States: its importance as a community institution, its nationalism, its service as an alternative to the mainstream. The Hispanic stage thus served to ameliorate minority and foreign status, the contradictory pressures of separatism and assimilation, and racial and class oppression. In summary, being outside the official national culture furthered the market potential for the Hispanic stage; it helped to define and solidify the market.

At its most elevated (high drama as interpreted by Virginia Fábregas or María Guerrero), the stage was a temple of culture at which the community could pay homage to the glories of Hispanic culture and mores and the language of Cervantes. At its most down-to-earth (the *revista*, the *obra bufa cubana*, vaudeville), the stage and tent-theatres were arenas for psychodrama where the immigrants and Hispanic citizens of the United States could vent their frustrations vicariously, laugh at the oppressor and at themselves, and forge a new Mexican American, a mainland Puerto Rican, or a Cuban American identity.

The origins of the professional Hispanic theatre in the United States are to be found in California during the mid-nineteenth century, a period when the Southwest was making the transition from Mexican to U.S. rule. For the most part, the theatre of the times continued the Spanish dramatic tradition in content and style; it is in the social context and in the public life of its purveyors, like Gerardo López del Castillo, that a model is created for the social and political functioning of Hispanic theatres in the United States—the protection of language, culture, nationality, and community interests.

By the turn of the century, professional companies were actively touring the Southwest and to Tampa, a little later to New York, with various companies and individual artists putting down roots and becoming residents. But the touring tradition continued to thrive into the beginnings of the Depression, with the railroads facilitating the linkages between Mexico City, San Antonio, and Los Angeles, the steamships carrying troupes back and forth between Cuba, Key West, Tampa, and New York.

It is not until the late 1920s, furthermore, that the Hispanic stage sees its greatest flourishing in the United States, with Los Angeles becoming its Mecca, reinforced by that city's large Mexican population and the growth of the Hispanic motion picture industry in Hollywood. The magnitude of the Hispanic theatrical and entertainment business in Los Angeles was unheralded: more than thirty practicing playwrights; numerous commercial theatre houses, some of which changed their attractions daily; ongoing formation of companies to go on tour throughout the Southwest and even as far east as New York; a direct and financially rewarding relationship with other information and entertainment enterprises, such as newspaper and book publishing and the movies.

While Los Angeles and San Antonio rode the crest of this wave of success, the undertow brought on by the Depression and Repatriation was devastating. But despite the Depression, New York was able to maintain Hispanic vaudeville and some serious theatre, due mostly to the growing influx of Hispanics, mainly Puerto Ricans and Spanish expatriates. Tampa, which had developed the stage as a non-commercial enterprise, also was able to maintain Hispanic theatre during the economic cataclysm. Hispanics in both these cities were not subjected to the push for deportation by the social welfare and legal authorities, as was the case in the Southwest and Midwest.

In style, content, and genre, the Hispanic stage in the United States during the nineteenth and early twentieth centuries was almost completely dominated by the Spanish tradition. Not only were Spanish plays and *zarzuelas* most frequently produced, but there was also a disproportionate number of directors, actors, and impresarios from Spain. During the first two decades of this century, however, Mexico and Cuba (somewhat later Puerto Rico) were just developing their own national theatres and slowly beginning to complement Spanish theatre with their own dramas based on regional life (including the life and culture of the Southwest) and their own genres, like the Mexican, Cuban, and Puerto Rican *zarzuelas*. But it was the *revista* and the *obra bufa cubana* that came closest to expressing their national character, customs, music, and ideology. These appealed directly to the working classes, forging archetypes of working-class culture—the *peladito, negrito/mulata,* and *jíbaro*— and in the large cities finally displacing more elite and refined theatrical genres, like drama and operetta.

Political and economic events directly influenced the stage, not only by determining immigration and demographic patterns as well as immigrant and resident status but also by becoming community concerns that found expression in dramatic material. The Mexican Revolution, the war for Cuban independence from Spain, the Puerto Rican independence movement, U.S. and Mexican immigration policies and foreign relations, the Depression and Repatriation, labor organizing, all became issues to be discussed in high art and low humor, depending on the genre and audience. Economic realities, especially those created by the Depression, contributed directly to the popularity of vaudeville and its displacement of serious theatre. As entrepreneurs bought up theatre chains and converted them to the less costly operation of showing talking films, live performance was further reduced in these establishments to a few stock vaudevillians and musicians performing between the showing of films. On the other hand, the Depression gave birth to numerous charities and community needs that could be addressed, in part, by using serious theatre for fundraising at mutual aid societies and churches.

In fact, there has always been a mission or a cause associated with Hispanic theatre in the United States, even in its most commercial manifestations. To the stage befell the lot of protecting the home culture and language in exile, educating the youth in the traditional customs and mores, providing the ideological and spiritual leadership that was needed to fend off the threat of assimilation to Anglo-American culture. In a word, the stage was a primary weapon of Mexican, Cuban, Puerto Rican, even Spanish nationalism. It promoted cultural and group solidarity, not only through the content and language of the material presented but through promoting family, community, and national activities, celebrations, and holidays; by taking on the roles often reserved for themselves by the churches and mutual aid societies; by impresarios and owners assuming the role of cultural and community leader, at times to nurture their financial investments. But the larger society, on the other hand, was not open to Hispanic entrepreneurship or to Hispanic culture. Even the more liberal Federal Theatre Project—an expression of government and society—did not succeed in getting Anglo-American audiences to attend even the English-language plays at the Centro Asturiano simply because it was located in the Hispanic side of town, nor did it succeed in salvaging its most successful project in the South—the Hispanic unit of the FTP. Race and class discrimination were barriers maintained by the larger society to keep Hispanics in their enclaves. That Hispanics enjoyed such a sophisticated and artistic cultural vehicle as theatre, even where and when Anglo-Americans did not, was inconceivable and completely ignored by the larger society, except in the one case of the Federal Theatre Project and except for the few Hispanic performers that were able to sing and dance their way into American vaudeville.

But in the cities of large Hispanic populations, nationalism was not destructive within the group. General Hispanic solidarity was promoted; Hispanics of all national backgrounds were seen as related and they worked together, although it was more often the Spanish and the wealthier, more educated Mexicans, Cubans, and Puerto Ricans who found themselves on top as community leaders and theatrical entrepreneurs. While, for instance, most of the playwrights in Los Angeles were of Mexican origin, a sprinkling of Spaniards, Salvadorans, Cubans, and South Americans was also represented. Among the actors and impresarios in Los Angeles and New York, two Spaniards—Romualdo Tirado and Manuel Noriega—had by far the greatest following and success. And even at the level of vaudeville, song and dance, and *revistas*, it was the Spanish-Cuban Hermanos Areu that had an illustrious career in the Southwest, that recruited and trained the great Beatriz (La Chata) Noloesca, and that produced the succeeding generation, the Mexican-Cuban Belia Areu. While the theatre personnel and audiences in the Southwest were overwhelmingly Mexican, they were cosmopolitan in their theatrical tastes and they subscribed to an international Hispanicity.

The very dominance and ubiquitousness of the Spanish theatrical tradition reinforced Hispanicity in these communities. But it was the Teatro Hispano in New York that became the emblem of this Hispanicity by openly advertising and reinforcing the diversity of nationalities represented in its casts and theatrical offerings, in attempts to mirror the diversity of its audiences and their community. While New York audiences were the most diverse and cosmopolitan, San Antonio and Tampa audiences were probably the purest in their respective Mexican and Cuban-Spanish identities. But even in these two cities there was always an awareness of a Hispanicity that united their cultural endeavors within the United States and the Hispanic world in general. This Hispanicity was another face of their nationalism; it made it stronger. They may have been minorities and/or foreigners within the political boundaries of the United States, but on the international level their culture was as broad as the distance from Spain to the Americas and the Philippines, as imperial and marvelous as the Aztecs, as worthy as Cervantes. True, this ideology was fomented by elites to promote their class and business interests, but it also made for a culture and information business with a coast-to-coast marketing potential and, as we are realizing today, a type of political and economic power that can reshape the national identity of the United States.

Notes

1. Origins

1. See the manuscript copy with stage directions written in the margin (Document C-E 120) and a covering letter (C-E 120: 2) at the Bancroft Collection of the University of California-Berkely.

2. DeWitt Bodeen, *The Story of the Great Southwest*, cited in Hazel Vineyard, "Trails of the Trouper: A Historical Study of the Theatre in New Mexico 1880–1910" (University of New Mexico, master's thesis, 1941).

3. See the José Abrego archive, Document C-D 86 v.2, the Bancroft Collection, which makes reference to his "tienda y junto a ella un salón con dos mesas de villar" (store and next to it a hall with two billiard tables).

4. See his extensive article on entertainment in Los Angeles in the April 15, 29, and May 13, 1855, editions.

5. See the *pastorela Sueño de Luzbel* written and performed for the benefit of San Vicente College, dated 1861, in the Antonio Coronel Collection. There are various other untitled *pastorela* manuscripts and one entitled *Canto a Luzbel* in the collection. Other plays in the collection are *El hijo pródigo; Norma*, printed in Valparaíso in 1815; *Semiramis*, printed in Mexico City in 1832; *Condestable de Chester*, printed in Mexico in 1836; *Oedipus Tyrannus* (in English), printed in Piqua, Ohio, in 1880; and an undated, printed dialogue, *Diálogo entre un labrador y un soldado*.

6. William Andrew Spalding, *Los Angeles Newspaperman. An Autobio-*

graphical Account (San Marino, Calif.: Huntington Library, 1911), p. 23.

7. At least two other professional companies were performing in the San Francisco area at this time. There is no way to ascertain if San Francisco was also their home base. According to *La Voz de Méjico* (July 9, 1864), the Compañía Salazar performed *Vivir loco y morir más* and *El puñal del godo* by Zorrilla at Tucker's Academy. *La Voz del Nuevo Mundo* followed the Compañía Española de Drama, Canto y Baile de Mariano Luque rather closely noting on June 16, 1874, the performance of Juan Polán y Coll's *La campana de la almudaina* in three acts and the *sainete Casa del campo* and on June 17 *La campana* in two acts and *Maruja* at the Opera House on Bush Street. The newspaper stated that the company performed a different play every night, with an additional play on Saturdays. Like the Estrella company, the nucleus of the troupe was the Luque family, with Francisca A. de Luque as leading lady and the children Enrique and Adolfo also acting, along with Mariano's brother Julio and Julio's wife, Soledad Alva de Luque. Unfortunately, the issues from June 17 until July 17, 1864, are missing. We hear of the Luque company again on July 17, 1874, now at the Teatro California. On July 19, *La cabaña de Tom*, translated by Ramón Saavedra, and the *juguete Los parvalillos* were performed and on September 27, now at Maguire's Theatre, *El terremoto de la Martinica*, in four acts, and the one-act *zarzuela La castañera*.

8. A promptbook for this unknown play is included in the Hernández-Villalongín archives of the Benson Collection of the University of Texas.

9. *Diccionario Porrúa de historia, biografía y geografía de México* (Mexico City: Porrúa, 1964), p. 910.

10. Gipson notes that the company's performances in Hermosillo included the following: *Una lágrima y un beso, La gracia de Dios, Guzmán el bueno, Traidor, inconfeso y mártir, Don Juan Tenorio, La razón de un bandido, Un voto sacrílego, Dios, mi brazo y mi derecho, Hércules III, El pilluelo de París,* and *La hija de las flores.*

11. In *La Voz de Méjico* (June 30, 1863), in an announcement of the performance signed Gerardo López del Castillo, the following revealing statement is made: "Invitado por varios de mis amigos y demás personas amantes de las Bellas Artes, y como tal, protectores del ilustrado Arte Dramático, para dar una función de teatro en nuestro hermoso idioma español, no he vacilado un momento en obsequiar sus deseos, sin embargo de los mil inconvenientes con que lucha en este país todo artista español. Al efecto, y aprovechando la oportunidad de la llegada a este puerto por el vapor 'Orizava' del artista mexicano, D. José de Jesús Díaz, he arreglado para la noche de este día un escogido espectáculo" (Invited by various of my friends and other persons who love the Fine Arts, and as such, are protectors of Dramatic Arts, to give a theatrical performance in our beautiful Spanish language, I have not hesitated a moment to fulfill their wishes, in spite of the thousand and one inconveniences that each Spanish artist has to deal with in this country. To that end, and taking advantage of the opportunity provided by the arrival at this port of the Mexican artist don José de Jesús Díaz on the steamship *Orizava*, I have arranged a select spectacle for tonight).

12. See Edmund M. Cagey, *The San Francisco Stage. A History* (New York: Columbia University Press, 1950), pp. 10–11.

13. Rodolfo Usigli, *Mexico in the Theater* (University, Miss.: Romance Monographs, 1976), p. 102.

14. The audience gave our comic, nationalist actor ovations on and off the stage; he had a following in his time and he died poor, but without abandoning the national stage for which he lived, hoping that it would be understood for what it was and what it was worth. His gallant attitude drew laughter, in spite of his good intentions and patriotism. He sought what was most noble and just, a Mexico for the Mexicans (María y Campos 1964: 22–23).

15. Item 1425 (8) from the Antonio F. Coronel Collection.

> To Laura Morales de Mollá
> At Her Benefit Performance
> Oh, bewitching Laura, who taught you to make us enjoy such serene happiness?
> Who granted you the delicate artistry in which you make us laugh and sigh?
> From whom, moving free on stage, have you learned to move us to piety, and after storming hard and furiously, whisper the name of your loves?
> You make happy or you sadden, as you please; you inflame passions, as you please; you move, calm, agitate, harden, and melt all tender hearts.
> Whoever hears you with sensitivity appreciates the prodigiousness of your marvellous art, becomes ecstatic, is delighted, is fooled, and enjoys the sweetest repose.

16. We have been informed that various young people of our city are presently making the necessary arrangements for establishing a new theatre. The large size of our population and the lack of public entertainment have been demanding an establishment of that type for a long time; but although this may be true, it hurts to see that some other improvements of a more pressing nature have been unattended for the sake of other secondary ones. I believe that the money that is going to be invested in that theatre could be better spent on the construction of a hospital, which is certainly needed by our poor and disabled citizens.

17. For a complete description of the staging of this melodrama, see John C. Bourke, *On the Border with Crook* (New York: Charles Scribner's Sons, 1891), pp. 85–86.

18. At least one author has argued for the priority of Texas as the site where the Hispanic stage finds its origins in the Southwest, drawing conclusions, I am sure, from information too limited and from insufficient research. See Brokaw 1977.

2. Los Angeles

1. Despite the severity of the winter, the Hispanic Americans attend the daily functions offered by the Compañía Díaz de León, being that it is such a

rare opportunity for these enclaves to see shows that represent their customs and in which actors of their own culture take part.

2. See Virginia Fábregas, *Virginia Fábregas. Su tournée por la América Latina 1911–1914* (Mexico City: Grandes Almacenes "Ciudad de Londres," 1914).

3. For a while in this city we have felt the overwhelming need for shows of high culture and morality in our language.

4. One night they put on a play, the next night a *zarzuela*, after that a drama and later an operetta . . . those who work like that are "students" of everything and experts in nothing.

5. The theme of the work is the painful theme of the Revolution. Through its scenes parade the disenchanted, those who had adapted themselves to an environment of comforts abroad, who now see themselves living a precarious life in their homeland, struggling to readapt to the new environment. (See Juan Bustillo Oro, *Tres dramas mexicanos: Los que vuelven, Masas, Justicia, S.A.* [Mexico City: Editorial Cenit, 1933].)

6. Rafael Carrasco, in *Hemerografía de Zacatecas 1825–1950* (Mexico City: Secretaría de Relaciones Exteriores, 1951), p. 142, asserts that Alfonso Busson Lodoza (1890–1929, editor of *El Eco de México*) was the founder of the Teatro México. This may be a contradiction of the newspaper record or simply indicate a partnership with Tirado and González Jiménez.

7. To present shows in Spanish for our own cultural community (*La Opinión*, February 3, 1931).

8. Now the ancient name of those six almost sacred letters [Mexico] again shining in incandescent characters over the door of the "Grand." Once again the Aztec calendars adorn the lobby, and in its passageways can be heard the soft and musical inflections of our language. Soon only the remembrance of those lubricious dances, the swinging of hips and the stridency of jazz music will remain, substituted now by languid Mexican songs, by shows that are modesty and art, by the Hispanic culture which, despite everything, survives in this corner of the United States.

9. I interviewed Mr. Trujillo on June 22 and 23, 1981, at his home in Los Angeles.

10. At the Capitol Theatre they are beginning to convince themselves that our public doesn't want dramas, operettas and *zarzuelas*. It wants *revistas.* . . . It's because our audiences have become frivolous. They want to enjoy the times. Now those cape and sword plays, those melodramas of tears and shrill screams, those old and worn-out *zarzuelas* that we know by heart are no longer wanted by our public. It wants to laugh. Enjoy. See the festival of lights. Of color. Of song. . . . The people want to laugh. They want variety. Sensation after sensation. Polychromy.

11. My informant on this matter is the deceased Rosalinda Meléndez's son, William Lanceford, who was a child actor and worked with his mother, Francisco Vega, Romualdo Tirado, and Frank Fouce. I interviewed him on June 21, 1981, at his home in Marina del Rey, California.

12. Leonardo García Astol, or, as he is popularly known, Lalo Astol, was

an actor and vaudevillian who was hired by Fouce. I have interviewed Mr. Astol over a period of six years, beginning in April 1979.

13. María Teresa Montoya, *El teatro en mi vida* (Mexico City: Ediciones Botas, 1956), p. 55: The run was good, although the audiences did not satisfy me; our compatriots are not Mexican anymore, nor Americans . . . and naturally, with that type of public . . . Comic theatre and by all means with music and dance, that's what was the greatest success; they understand it better.

14. . . . enthusiastic about the preservation of our Hispanic culture and united now out of the necessity to counter the influence of theatre which is foreign to our customs.

15. . . . the Hispanic community . . . also has the duty to patronize shows out of love for our agonizing culture.

16. We need theatre . . . even if it's just to counter the influence of Saxon letters, customs and tendencies that surround us at times.

17. Since the Repatriation started, the Mexican and Hispanic American ambience has not been very favorable, shall we say, to all types of artists. First of all, there's only one theatre for the community, and not even this one sells out for functions that are well prepared ahead of time and in which the major actors are those who in earlier times were real attractions. Then, the conditions that we are going through are difficult not only for us, but also for the Americans. One proof of that is that the movie houses, well appointed and with film debuts, have even had to lower their prices to practically nothing, and even then they don't sell out as they used to in earlier days (Fidel Murillo, *La Opinión*, August 1, 1933).

18. It shakes one to think about the truth. What's missing is the audiences. A few years ago, any insignificant motive was enough to pull in the masses to the theatres. Three full houses on Saturday, Sunday, and Monday was the rule. The rest of the week, when some special attraction was added, or any debut they got along fine. Now, not even with great attractions— unless it's José Mojica, Dolores del Río, or Lupe Vélez—can the theatre fill up. The excuses given are the heat, the poor economic conditions of the community, etc. The bare truth, as disagreeable as all of the truths that hurt, is what I said before: there no longer are audiences for our theatres.

And it's that for some time now they have been returning to Mexico in great streams of repatriates, officially or privately. The ones who stay in Los Angeles are those that have not been able to leave the city or those who don't want to. The former are trying to deal with their most pressing problem, rather than with entertainment. The latter frankly prefer American spectacles.

The old people are few. The young people have learned English and can go to a first-class theatre that offers first-class variety, plus a movie, an orchestra, etc., for a minuscule charge, something that our theatres cannot do, because they don't have a larger patronage than our local Spanish-speaking community.

19. For instance, *La Opinión* (August 12, 1933) reports that Esteban V.

Escalante was about to debut a *revista* on a Mexico City stage on the theme of the Mexicans in the United States.

20. Tomás Ybarra-Frausto, "El Teatro Libertad: Antecedents and Actuality," in *Teatro Libertad* (Tucson: Teatro Libertad, 1978), p. xiv, reports his interview of Marcos Glodel, a former actor, who remembered that his company, Cuadro México-España, would enter the audience after performances of this play to collect signatures on petitions to the governor of California for redress of the injustices perpetrated against Pompa. It seems that this was not an isolated practice; for instance, the Circo Escalante Hermanos Compañía de Baile y Variedades, which presented *zarzuela* and variety and circus acts, in March 1927, in efforts to raise funds in Phoenix for the defense of Alfredo Grijalva, accused of murdering an American official, gave a benefit performance. See the Escalante broadside in the Manuel Gamio Folkloric Materials file of the Bancroft Collection. Regardless of the use of *El proceso de Aurelio Pompa* or any other play for raising defense funds, it is important to note that plays based on topics like the struggle of Aurelio Pompa were commodities that the Los Angeles audiences continued to pursue for the human drama, relevance, and even sensationalism that they promised. In fact, after Aurelio Pompa was executed (this too was incorporated into the play), Carrillo's play continued to be financially successful, so much so that a drama critic from *El Heraldo de México* (December 2, 1925) editorialized that the dead should be left to rest and that impresarios should not be so greedy for profits at the expense of the deceased.

21. Virginia Fábregas made arrangements to buy the rights of González's works, and she actually produced them, but it seems she never paid the author for his works. This led him to threaten to sue her for usurpation and for even ascribing his play *Ramona* to a fictitious Italian writer, Alfredo D. Cavaletti (see *La Opinión*, January 2, 1920). The first movie version of his play *Sangre yaqui* opened at the Capitol Theatre, according to *El Heraldo de México* (October 22, 1926). According to *El Heraldo de México* (October 27, 1927), *La degradación de los pobres* was translated into English by an American writer.

22. Monterde, *Bibliografía*, p. 163, shows that *Nido de cuervos* was published by the Sonora Printing Company in 1924. Being that González hailed from Sonora, this may have been a self-published effort, which has been lost.

23. See Document I/131/(02)/2718 "Solicitud de Empleo" in the Adalberto Elías González file in the archives of the Secretaría de Relaciones Exteriores, Mexico City.

24. See Documents III/139(S-1)/1 and III-274-9 in the Adalberto Elías González file in the archives of the Secretaría de Relaciones Exteriores.

25. Manuscript copy on file at the Sociedad de Escritores, No. NT 0227.

26. Manuscript copy on file at the Sociedad de Escritores, No. NT 3909.

27. For an account of the real-life drama of Aurelio Pompa, see Ricardo Romo, *East Los Angeles: History of a Barrio* (Austin: University of Texas Press, 1983), pp. 158–159.

28. See Nos. NT 0105 and NT 0154 under Carrillo's name.

29. San Diego: Sociedad Editora Mexicana, 1925. Printed at Talleres Gráfi-

cos de "El Hispano Americano." According to the last page of the book, the novel was finished in Coronado, California, in 1925.

30. *El homenaje lírico a la raza* and *Las falsas apariencias* also are part of *Uno más. Prosa y verso.*

31. The undated *suelta* can be found in the library of the Instituto de Cooperación Iberoamericana, Madrid.

32. See Armando I. Lelevier, *Historia del periodismo y la imprenta en el Territorio Norte de Baja California* (Mexico: Gobierno del Territorio Norte de la Baja California, 1943).

33. See file numbers 241.2/728.4, 16-24-144, and III-628-12 under Gustavo Solano at the Secretaría de Relaciones Exteriores.

34. According to Monterde, *Bibliografía*, p. 95, the play was debuted at the Teatro Alvarez in Guaymas, Sonora, on February 26, 1888, and was published by *El Sonorense* in January 1894. See *Diccionario Porrúa de historia, biografía y geografía* (Mexico City: Porrúa, 1965), pp. 287–288.

35. See Miguel Angel Ponce, *Diccionario biográfico mexicano* (Mexico City: Editorial PAC, 1944), pp. 160–161.

36. Two of his works were known to have been staged in Los Angeles: *El gran recurso,* a drama in three acts, and *El proceso del mal humor,* both on file at the Sociedad de Escritores (Nos. NT 3879 and 1276). *Luz de estrellas* (Mexico City: Editorial Río, 1913–1915) and *Aquiles Serdán* (Puebla, 1949) are two of his plays that exist in published versions. Page 64 of *Luz de estrellas* seems to indicate that *El gran recurso* was also staged in Mexico City in 1929.

37. See his file, No. I/131/3007, at the Secretaría de Relaciones Exteriores.

38. Alfredo Bussón, who died in Los Angeles on December 18, 1929, was a journalist and author of *La vendetta* and the librettoes for two *revistas, Su majestad Tiraklán* and *Ya mi' anda;* according to *El Heraldo de México* (June 9, 1926), the Teatro Hidalgo was going to contract Jorge Loyo, a writer for Mexico City's *El Universal Ilustrado,* to write a series of *revistas;* Max Cervantes, author of the drama *El puñal del yaqui;* Arturo Chacel, author of *Se solicita un marido;* Juan N. Chavarrí, author of *Cuando ellas sean ellos;* Margot, pseudonym of an *Heraldo de México* journalist who wrote *Un viejo drama;* Margarita Robles, founder and director of a school for Mexicans in Los Angeles and author of *Corazón ciego;* Pezantes Ganoza, a Peruvian writer and author of *La sinfonía incompleta, Media noche,* and *El coyote;* Daniel L. Cosío, author of *El porqué de nuestras guerras;* Ramón Méndez del Río, also a Mexican journalist and author of *Los repatriados;* María de Jesús Olazábel, also a journalist for *La Opinión* and author of *El presunto suicida;* actress Eugenia Torres, author of *En torno a la quimera* in three acts; and Miguel de Zárraga, author of *La vuelta del muerto.*

39. This and much of the following information was obtained during my personal interviews of Trujillo at his home in Los Angeles on June 22 and 23, 1981.

40. Mr. Trujillo allowed me to copy his manuscript of "El derecho de la fuerza," signed by Virginia Fábregas and her company on the night of its debut, May 1, 1940, at the Mason Theatre.

41. See Armando María y Campos, *El teatro de género chico en la Revolución Mexicana* (Mexico City: Biblioteca del Instituo Nacional de Estudios Históricos de la Revolución Mexicana, 1956) and Antonio Magaña Esquivel and Ruth S. Lamb, *Breve historia del teatro mexicano* (Mexico City: Ediciones de Andrea, 1958), p. 99.

42. María y Campos, *El teatro de género chico*, p. 50.

43. See John B. Noland, *Teatro mexicano contemporáneo (1900–1950)* (Mexico City: Instituto Nacional de Bellas Artes, 1967), pp. 127–182.

44. Miguel Covarrubias, "Slapstick and Venom," *Theatre Arts Monthly* 22/8 (August 1938): 588.

45. In this comedy you can savor the humorous tribulations of the repatriated.

46. A well-established Mexico City tailor, already aging, has frequently heard about the greatness and progress of the United States, and particularly (because that's what interests him) of things referring to his trade. Enthused by the fabulous news that he receives and with the ambition of learning and becoming rich, he comes to the United States without anything but a little notebook in which someone wrote down some English phrases, and because of which he believes that he has covered all the ground he needs in learning the language; but it turns out that from the very moment he arrives he becomes convinced that his little scribbled notebook isn't worth anything and, after receiving some hostile reactions from some "types," a gendarme, whom he praises, comparing him to our policemen, drags him off and sticks him in a hotel in which his misfortunes continue because of his inability to understand English. At last he arrives at a Mexican(?) restaurant where he thinks he'll be safe from being bothered, but it turns out that he gets hit hard by a "settlement" he has to pay to an American individual to whose wife he has offered a modest ice cream soda. Our hero goes to the Venice beach and becomes delighted; but in spite of everything, more impressed by the disagreeable encounters than by the beauty of the beach, he decides to return to Mexico without even learning a new system for threading needles.

47. See Abraham Hoffman, *Unwanted Mexicans in the Great Depression: Repatriation Pressures, 1929–1939* (Tucson: University of Arizona Press, 1974).

48. There is no doubt that Tirado remained a Spanish citizen, at least until 1931. In the files of the Secretaría de Relaciones Exteriores (IV/553/73-27/195) Tirado mentions his citizenship in a cablegram requesting permission to tour Mexico with his theatre company.

49. Interviewed and transcribed by Manuel Gamio. See Manuel Gamio Notes, ZR-5, "Observations, Notes and an Itinerary or Diary of a Trip to Mexico," Bancroft Library, University of California, Berkeley.

You go around sporting
A big automobile.
You call me unfortunate
And dying of hunger.

And it's because you don't recall
When you were on my farm
Going around almost naked
And without huaraches.
That's what's happened to a lot
Of people that I know here,
Who have learned a little
About American ways
And they dress up like dandies
And go dancing.
But he who negates his culture
Doesn't even have a mother,
'Cause there's nothing worse
Nor more dirty
Than that horrible figure of the renegade.
And although far from you,
My beloved homeland,
I have been thrown out
By continuous revolutions.
A good Mexican
Will never negate
His beloved fatherland.

In real life Tirado seems to have been prejudiced against the *agringado* and the *pocho*. After a short season in San Francisco, the *Hispano América* on October 23, 1926, quoted him as saying that he was returning directly to Mexico City because he was fed up with *pocherías* ("enfermo de pocherías").

50. María y Campos, *El teatro de género chico*, p. 232.

51. Ibid., p. 248. This one is more responsible than the generals that I have just shot, because I also believe that his pen can do more damage than a military sword.

52. Miguel Angel Peral, *Diccionario biográfico mexicano* (Mexico City: Editorial PAC, 1944), p. 157.

53. At the Sociedad de Escritores, see *El proceso de Cupido*, *Los tres mosqueteros* (NT 3634), *Los tres pistoleros* (NT 3941), *El colmo del Tenorio* (NT 0057), *La chacha Micaela* (NT 0604), *Hijos de Pancho Villa* (NT 4195). In addition, Noland, *Teatro mexicano contemporáneo*, p. 320, lists four works at the Instituto Nacional de Bellas Artes: *Bizcochería nacional*, *El candidato agrarista*, *La chacha Micaela*, and *Mujeres de México*. Also see Lamb, *Bibliografía*, p. 63, for the numerous titles of Guz Aguila's works.

54. See *El proceso de Cupido* manuscript, which shows extensive rewriting and a change of title from *Los amores eternos*.

55. There's money, lovely works, pretty women, good costumes, scenery and, over all, plenty, but I mean plenty of good will and good faith.

56. Roberto el Diablo (Roberto Núñez y Domínguez), *Cincuenta Close-ups* (Mexico City: Ediciones Botas, 1935), pp. 98–99.

57. Interview with Douglas Landsford.

58. First published in 1928 by *El Heraldo de México* but reissued in Mexico City in 1984 by SEP, with my introduction.

59. So much has been written about these two comedians whose names are synonymous with the *revista* in Mexico. See María y Campos, *El teatro de género chico;* Covarrubias, "Slapstick and Venom," pp. 587–596; Noland, *Teatro mexicano contemporáneo,* pp. 151, 157, 169, 173–174; Armando María y Campos, "Homenaje a Leopoldo Beristáin y un Recuerdo de sus Mejores Tiempos" and "El Beneficio de Soto," in *Archivo de teatro* (Mexico City: Ediciones Populares, 1946), pp. 59–61, 71–72.

60. My informant was his daughter Margarita Mendoza López, who accompanied him in his voluntary exile in the United States. I interviewed her at her home in Mexico City in March 1983.

3. San Antonio

1. *La Fe Católica,* May 14, 21, 28; June 4, 11, 18; July 2, 9.

2. In Laredo's *La Crónica* (December 17, 1910) is published a poem by Rafael Téllez Girón; this may be an indication that he was a resident of Laredo. No other information about him has surfaced.

3. The life drama in which the characters acquire Shakespearean and apocalyptic proportions, and in which the horror, a tormenting horror, shakes the stupefied audience, like a hurricane shaking a palm tree. In that tragic ocean a colossal duel of infinitely human passions is unleashed.

4. The Mexican community was very sensitive about Hollywood movies and the ugly stereotypes of Mexicans that appeared in them from the very beginnings of the industry. This same month, *La Prensa* on August 22, 1919, reported on a motion picture firm that had been founded in San Antonio. It assured the readers that the company would portray Mexicans as they were, that it was important that on American screens "no se ofenda ni se calumnie a México" (Mexico not be offended or calumniated). The theatrical artists themselves were also sensitive about the insulting stereotypes of Mexicans in American cinema. The Familia Bell walked out of its sold-out engagement at the Teatro Ramona in Phoenix and Teatro Rialto in Tucson, owned by Rilard and Company, in protest of Rilart showing *The Patriot,* in which Mexicans were allegedly portrayed as savages, according to a Guadalajara theatrical publication, *Respetable Público* (February 6, 1921).

The attack on the *peladito* and working-class entertainments at Los Angeles theatres by *El Heraldo de México* also took the form of defending the community against stereotypes of "greasers" popularized in Hollywood movies and blaming the creation of these steroetypes on the characters and customs portrayed on the Mexican stages there. See *El Heraldo de México* (July 30, 1925).

5. See *La Prensa,* February 6, 13, October 5, 7, 1917; July 21, and November 1, 1922.

6. *La Prensa* (April 26, 1916): a truly artistic, cultured and moral spectacle. On the other hand, it may be considered a patriotic act and one of cul-

tural solidarity to attend the evenings of art at the Teatro Juárez, where a modest group of Mexican actors struggle for their lives on foreign soil so that we may become acquainted with the most valued gems of contemporary theatre in our mother tongue, that is, the sweet and sonorous language of Cervantes.

7. See Monterde, *Bibliografía*, p. 149. He noted that the first edition of this play was published in Washington, D.C., in 1904, with later editions in Guatemala City, San Salvador, and Mexico City, in 1907.

8. *La Prensa* (May 23, 1916): who is national spirit, who is of Aztec tint; who is the eagle of Tenochtitlán.

9. My informant on these matters was Mr. Gaetano Lucchese in an interview at his real estate business office on August 28, 1980.

10. Prida, . . . *Y se levanta el telón*, p. 162.

11. This issue is part of the Manuel Gamio Notes ZR-5, collection of newspapers entitled "Prensa Mexicana Editada en Texas," at the Bancroft Collection of the University of California-Berkeley.

12. They start drooling as soon as they see Juanito Suárez and Manuel Tiesta, but especially the former when he comes out all dressed up as a charro from Puebla and he belts out some Mexican song.

13. Carcachas rolls her eyeballs blank, gives the ground three little stomps, places one hand over her heart and with the other lifts her skirts up to her knees so that they don't get dusty and answers in a passionate accent: "I shall keep it safe here for the rest of my life."

14. See "Cabristea o te ahorcas," recording and transcription reproduced on *The Chicano Experience*, Folkloric Records 9021 (El Cerrito, Calif.: Arhoolie Records).

15. The troupe is not very big, nor does it rely on that overused resource of lots of legs and spicy jokes, and precisely because of this it triumphs.

16. See *La Prensa* (September 4, 1922): the showing of the shirtless and foul-mouthed *peladito* that once again is on stage at the Nacional as a symbol of our so-called "national artistic production" that would not be recognized without the *mecapalero*, the "lottery ticket vendor," or the barrio don Juan with long moustaches and rebellious cowlick whose vocabulary is a litany of disrespect and whose appearance discredits Mexico in the eyes of those who don't know her.

17. From my interview with him at his home in San Antonio on August 28, 1980.

18. From my interview on August 29, 1980, of Rudy Diamond García in San Antonio, a descendant of the Carpa García family.

19. In *La Prensa* (February 7, 1924) a section of that dialogue is reproduced.

20. For details concerning the arrangement with Lucchese and the transit from Tampico to Laredo and San Antonio, see Prida, . . . *y se levanta el telón*, pp. 153–157.

21. See the interview with Luis Felipe Recinos and the "Lista de Nombres de Restaurantes de Propiedad de Mexicanos o México-Texanos" in Manuel Gamio Notes Z-R5 at the Bancroft Collection, University of California-Berkeley.

22. My informant on this matter was Diego Arturo Pino, who performed as an amateur actor in San Antonio from 1924 to 1927 and as a professional in Cotera's company from 1927 to 1936. I interviewed him in Houston on February 26, 1986.

23. It is not as John Brokaw has stated in "Teatro Chicano," pp. 541–542, that this theatre "stopped suddenly" in the late 1920s nor that "the teatros ceased and theatrical production in the Spanish language was left in the hands of the church and its annual productions of *Los pastoreles* [*sic*]." As I have shown in the text, production continued well into the 1930s and the repertoire almost never included *pastorelas* (religious *folk* drama) and only occasionally included a religious play.

24. This biography of Leonardo García Astol comes from my interviews with him and from his manuscript "Mis memorias," on file at the Mexican American Library Project of the Nettie Lee Benson Latin American Collection at the University of Texas.

25. My sources for the biography of La Chata Noloesca are my interviews with her daughter Belia Areu on March 6, 1982, and an interview done by Lupita Fernández of Belia Areu on file in the Chata Noloesca archive of the San Antonio Conservation Society.

26. See Armando Miguélez, "El Teatro Carmen (1915–1923): Centro de Arte Escénico Hispano en Tucson," in *Mexican American Theatre: Then and Now,* ed. Nicolás Kanellos (Houston: Arte Publico Press, 1983), p. 55. According to *La Prensa* (May 20, 1917), Alberto M. Alvarado had contracted the Areu brothers to do variety acts at his movie house, Teatro México, in San Antonio.

27. See Tomás Ybarra-Frausto, "La Chata Noloesca: *Figura del Donaire*," in *Mexican American Theatre: Then and Now,* pp. 41–51.

28. *Maroma* was a term derived from the rope tied to flyers or acrobats of a pre-Columbian ritual which became a circus act. By extension small, *mestizo* circuses were called *maromas.*

29. "La Carpa: El teatro popular de México," *Norte: Revista Continental* (May 1945): 22.

30. Ibid. The fine humor of the people, their critical spirit, their complaints and desires; and the people, in turn, upon seeing their own existence portrayed on the stage, cooperate directly with the comics, conversing with them, proposing problems for their inventive spirit to solve, rewarding and punishing them, with crude sincerity.

31. John Steven McGroaty, *Los Angeles from the Mountains to the Sea,* vol. 1 (Chicago and New York: American Historical Society, 1921), p. 79.

32. See "Gran Circo-Teatro Orrin-City of Mexico" in the Townsend-Walsh Collection Scrapbooks of the Hertzberg Circus Collection of the San Antonio Public Library.

33. From an interview of Consuelo García, published in the *San Antonio Style* magazine of the *San Antonio Express-News* (July 26, 1981).

34. From a broadside in the "Folkloric Materials" file of the Manuel Gamio papers at the Bancroft Collection, University of California-Berkeley.

35. See "Final Curtain/Mariano Escalante" in *Amusement Business,* Au-

gust 14, 1961, p. 42, and *Billboard,* May 27, 1950, p. 54.

36. *El Heraldo de México* (December 16, 1917): If you haven't gone to the circus, get ready to do so today, bearing in mind that it's a Mexican spectacle, that in many senses, as in its order and the cleanliness of its acts, is superior to the large American circuses.

37. From a letter to me from Arturo Mantecón, a resident of Sacramento, California, dated October 6, 1987.

38. María y Campos, *Los payasos poetas del pueblo,* p. 231 mentions a Circo Progresista with horse, dance, and variety acts as having performed briefly in Mexico City in 1907.

39. As reported to me by Rodolfo's son Rudy ("Diamond") García in an interview on August 29, 1980.

40. See "El Fotógrafo," in *Mexican American Theatre: Then and Now,* pp. 15–16.

41. Interview of Consuelo García.

42. In an undated photo of the "Banquet for Emmanuel King" in the Hertzberg Circus Collection, José Abreu is identified as a slack-rope walker of "The Cuban Show" and is said to be a cousin of the famous Codonas.

43. According to a former member of the company, Dolores de Arratia, in an August 1981 interview on file at the San Antonio Conservation Society.

4. New York City

1. "325 Aniversario de la Sinagoga Hispano-Portuguesa de Nueva York," *Nuestro Encuentro* 2 (Summer 1981): 3.

2. See *El Mensajero Semanal* (February 7, 1829) for Act Two of *Tello de Neira* by Spanish playwright Dionisio Solís and the May 16, 1829, issue for a scene from the eighteenth-century Spaniard Leandro Fernández de Moratín's *Comedia nueva.*

3. See José Luis Perrier, *Bibliografía dramática cubana* (New York: Phos, 1926) for information on these nineteenth-century plays mentioned in the text, except for those by Diez de la Cortina. Copies of Diez's plays are at the New York Public Library. The date 1893 is for the second edition of Diez's *El indiano;* the year of first publication is unknown. That this second edition was published in a bilingual format may indicate that the author (he claimed to have a master's degree from the University of Madrid) may have desired to achieve (perhaps he had already done so) an English-language production. There are no indications, however, that either play was ever staged.

4. *La Prensa* (November 12, 1918): We hardly need to speak of Mr. Noriega. He is the hero of the party and it's for him that almost all of the audience goes to the theatre. An educated man and admirable artist, he only has to appear on stage and the audience begins to celebrate his talents and applaud him enthusiastically.

5. Carl Van Vechten, in *The Music of Spain* (New York: Alfred A. Knopf, 1918), p. 94, offers this account of Quinito Valverde's opening at the Park: "A few nights ago a Spanish company, unheralded, unsung, indeed almost

unwelcomed by such reviewers as had to trudge to the out-of-the way Park Theatre, came to New York, in a musical revue entitled *The Land of Joy.* The score was written by Quinito Valverde, *fils,* whose music is not unknown to us, and the company included La Argentina, a Spanish dancer who had given matinees here in the past season without arousing more than mild enthusiasm. The theatrical impresarii, the song publishers, and the Broadway rabble stayed away on the first night. It was all very well, they might have reasoned, to read about the goings on in Spain, but they would never do in America." But according to the critic at *El Heraldo* (November 14, 1917), the performance was well received by both Spanish- and English-language reviewers and, for the first time in New York for Spanish theatre, hats were thrown onto the stage in a show of enthusiastic appreciation.

6. For a complete description of the interesting opening night playbill and the complete repertoire as announced therein, see Prida, . . . *y se levanta el telón,* pp. 82–83.

7. César Andreu Iglesias, ed., *Memorias de Bernardo Vega: Una contribución a la historia de la comunidad puertorriqueña de Nueva York* (San Juan: Ediciones Huracán, 1977), pp. 160–161.

8. For a detailed history of the *bufos cubanos* and the life of Arquímides Pous, see Eduardo Robreño, *Historia del teatro popular cubano* (Havana: Oficina del Historiador de la Ciudad de la Habana, 1961).

9. From a playbill in the private collection of Elsa Ortiz Robles. Ms. Ortiz Robles and Pablo Figueroa assembled the archive when creating an exhibition, Teatro: Hispanic Theatre in New York City, 1902–1976, for the Museo del Barrio. They in turn made copies of numerous documents from Marita Reid's personal files.

10. The Cuadro Artístico Proletario is carrying out a positive labor of art and propaganda. Included in its repertoire are various works written specifically about the tragic and moving present-day Spain.

11. J. Miranda Brothers is mentioned as the impresario repeatedly during 1926 in *La Prensa;* however, the April 17, 1926, *La Prensa* stated that the Apollo impresario was Clemente Giglio.

12. Antonia Saenz, in *El Teatro de Puerto Rico (Notas para su historia)* (Río Piedras: Editorial Universitaria, 1950), pp. 111, 178, claims that *No toque usted el trigémino* was written by Puerto Rican playwright Antonio Nicolás Blanco and debuted in San Juan at the Teatro Municipal in 1929 by Juan Nadal de Santa Coloma.

13. "Harlem Arrabalero" is a description of a night in the Latin barrio of New York with a *farrago* of marihuana, *bolita,* muggings, knifings, women, men, misery, police, whistles, *bolita,* and blood. Very rarely has anyone succeeded in collecting and presenting in one show a more vivid description of what supposedly is the Harlem ghetto.

14. Nilda González, *Bibliografía del teatro puertorriqueño* (Río Piedras: Editorial Universitaria, 1979), p. 54.

15. Aguadilla, Puerto Rico: Tip. La Libertad, 1927, 120 pp. The most recent edition is San Juan: Editorial Cordillera, 1973.

16.

New York has three things
cold, the relief and heat,
he who has these three
should not thank God.
Because with these
one lives in constant worry.
That's why I ask you all
to learn the refrain of this song.
 Chorus
He who has a home
in Puerto Rico, care for it.
If he wants to go away,
don't go, don't go.
 It's not easy
 to get through
 a season
 of cold and snow.

17. To all Theatre Impresarios who would like to obtain an emotion-filled, Catholic, five-act play in verse, entitled *Two Graves*, take advantage of this opportunity; because as is well known, the debuts of plays of the sort offered here are easily sold. The play has not as yet been sold because its novice author is interested in having the referred play taken by one of his people. Be it known that this play shall remain in this country only for one month. For information, see Mateo Pou, at the home of Valentín Aguirre, 82 Bank St., NYC, until Sunday.

18. See don Manuel Quevedo Báez, "Prólogo," in Gustavo O'Neill, *Sonoras bagatelas o sicilianas* (New York: s.d., 1924), p. 9.

19. This first book is lost; however, the complete poetic dialogue is included in *Sonoras bagatelas o sicilianas*, pp. 117–125.

20. In his autobiography, Bernardo Vega refers to an Alfonso Dieppa, who supposedly did write serious drama which was never published, although it had been staged successfully at the Círculo de Trabajadores in Brooklyn in 1922. Vega says that his most successful play was a Spanish-language version of Chekov's *Uncle Vanya* entitled *El tío Juanito* (Iglesias, *Memorias*, p. 174).

5. Tampa

1. Of Spanish race and sentiments, or be loyal to Spain and her prestige in the Americas. In *Centro Español de Tampa: Bodas de Ora* (Tampa: Centro Español, 1941), p. 10, Special Collections Library, University of South Florida.

2. Provide instruction and honest recreation for the members. Ibid., pp. 8, 14.

3. Ibid., p. 78.

4. Ibid., p. 38.

5. The public wants something new, it is tired of looking at the same local stars for years and years. A good soprano, a magnificent actor, a great singer, become tiring when they are kept on the bill, as is the case with some valuable figures of the Nebraska Street theatre.

6. "It Is Happening Here," *Federal One* 3/1 (April 1978): 6.

7. Transcript of an interview of Dorothea Lynch, pp. 60, 5, Federal Theatre Project Archives, George Mason University Library.

8. Ibid., p. 14.

9. Unsigned report entitled *Florida Federal Theatre: "The Show Must Go On,"* in the Federal Theatre Project Archives, George Mason University, p. 6.

10. Ibid., p. 7.

11. Lynch Transcript, pp. 52, 53.

12. *Album-Exposición* (Tampa: Directiva del Círculo Cubano, s.d.), pages not numbered. This album is part of the Tony Pizzo Collection at the University of South Florida Library.

13. Ibid.

14. You servile, servile slaves, you miss the whip on your backs! Your suffering is nothing compared to what you deserve. Anyone would be stupid to try to break your chains; because you'd beat him with them. The bourgeoisie is right; it knows that you love the tyrant who oppresses you; it knows that you hate your liberators and it makes you love it by strengthening your chains. You slaves, your slavery will only end on the day that the ice of both poles meets at the equator and extinguishes the life of the last boss as he beats the slave at the post.

15. The most ludicrous that one can ask for, but it is of that professorial genre and has laughable things, precisely because they are so absurd, grotesque, so incongruous.

16. What a shame that still resounding in our ears are the cinematographic cries of "Cold Soda! . . . Punch!" given time and again in the aisles of the San Souci! What a shame that the orchestra performances have been designated only for "great solemn occasions"! What a shame that the scenery has not been unpacked from the trunks where it is stored! But . . . all will progress little by little: those cries of . . . summer will disappear; the orchestra will return and we shall be able to admire the scenery that they have talked about. Right, dear maestro? Right, Mr. Ortagus?

17. *Mefistófeles* is most typical of the *bufo cubano* repertoire, which means that it is the most ridiculous, the most ludicrous, the most grotesque, and the most extravagant that fantasy can conceive.

It is a disgrace: almost all Cuban authors believe that upon writing for the theatre in that farcical genre they should forget about common sense and violate the laws of good taste.

Judging that genre, in general, it can be said that those authors have not made use of the artist's brush but instead the housepainter's with the broadest and most common of strokes.

And that is why the genre does not succeed and only has a following of certain audiences, those that if they had to choose between *The Caricature* and *Figaro* would choose the former without hesitation.

6. On the Road

1. Manuel Gamio Notes, "Nombre de Establecimientos Comerciales en El Paso, Texas," in the "Various Mexican Periodicals and Sample Copies" file at the Bancroft Collection.

2. See Bonnie Stowell, "Folk Drama Scholarship in the United States: A Selective Survey," *Folkdrama Annual* 2 (1970): 51–66.

3. See Juan B. Rael, *The Sources and Diffusion of the Mexican Shepherd's Play* (Guadalajara: Librería La Joyita, 1965).

4. See Mary Austin, "Folk Plays of the Southwest," *Theatre Arts Monthly* 17 (1933): 437–440.

5. "Notes on the Repertoire of the New Mexican Folktheatre," *Southern Folklore Quarterly* 4/4 (December 1940): 237.

6. Thomas E. Sheridan, *Los Tucsonenses. The Mexican Community in Tucson, 1854–1941* (Tucson: University of Arizona Press, 1986), p. 201.

7. Ibid., p. 111.

8. *El Tucsonense,* October 22, 1929; July 31, 1930; February 10, 1931; October 10, 1931.

9. *Estatutos del Círculo de Obreros Católicos "San José"* (Indiana Harbor, 1925), p. 16.

10. For a list of the plays of the Círculo de Obreros Católicos "San José" and of other groups in the East Chicago–Gary area plus other background information, see my article, "Mexican Community Theatre in a Midwestern City," *Latin American Theatre Review* (Fall 1973): 43–48. The first sixteen issues of *El Amigo del Hogar* are missing; thus, there may have been plays produced by the Cuadro Dramático prior to March 1927.

11. Mrs. Consuelo C. de Figueroa, who acted in many of the Cuadro Dramático's productions, was my informant in this matter. She is also the widow of Francisco M. de Figueroa, editor of *El Amigo del Hogar,* and one of the founders of the Obreros Católicos "San José."

12. It is a great and pleasant consolation to find a corner in which one can hear our sonorous language, enjoy its jokes, hear its music.

13. Guadalajara: Edición de *El Kaskabel,* Imprenta y Encuadernación de J. A. Rodríguez, 1907, 31 pp. Monterde states that another undated edition of this *zarzuela* exists (*Bibliografía,* p. 256).

14. Padilla published a compilation of his columns, some of which were written and published in San Francisco, after he had returned to Guadalajara sometime in the 1930s: *Un puñado de artículos* (Barcelona: Casa Edit Maucci, s.d.). A copy exists at the National Library in Mexico City.

Glossary

agringado: Americanized, gringoized.

boceto cómico: Comic sketch.

bufos cubanos/compañía de bufos cubanos: Performers of Cuban farce, a specialized genre similar to *revistas* but employing Cuban humor, dialects, regional and racial character types, and Afro-Cuban music.

carpa: From Quechua, meaning "awning" or "covering." A circus tent in which actors of modest circumstances and means perform (Santamaría 1978).

china poblana: A folkloric and dramatic type based on a beautiful mestiza exhibiting the dress, customs, and music of Puebla, Mexico (Santamaría 1978).

comedia: Drama, play; not necessarily a comedy.

comedia de costumbres: A play of manners, dealing with social conflict.

corrido: Mexican folk ballad, usually made up of twenty or more quatrains of octosyllables with end-rhyme in the even-numbered verses.

couplet flamenco: Couplets sung in the style of Spanish flamenco music.

coupletista: A singer of couplets, quite often a comedienne who sings couplets.

couplets: Songs of *double entendre* employing rhymes; from the French vaudeville tradition.

cuadro: A theatrical or vaudeville group of modest size and means; not a full-fledged company.

cuadro de declamación: An amateur theatrical group quite often made up of members of a mutualist society.

entremés: "A one-act, humorous or satirical play, skit or character sketch, generally with songs and dances, presented between the acts of a longer play" (Newmark).

género chico: "A term used in reference to short, popular dramatic or dramatico-musical playlets, skits, or operettas, generally one act in length" (Newmark).

género grande: "Major dramatic genre, *e.g.*, tragedy, comedy, grand opera" (Newmark).

gracioso: "The buffoon or comic character of Spanish classical drama. . . . Usually a servant or squire, he served as a kind of parody of the principal character . . . At his best he was gay, witty and even tragicomical, supplying a realistic or cynical counterpoint that enhanced the theme of the major character" (Newmark).

juguete cómico: "A short, dramatic skit in a light vein" (Newmark).

maroma: A tumble or somersault made by an acrobat or flyer; of pre-Columbian origin. By extension, the circus.

pastorela: The Mexican shepherd's folk play.

payaso: Clown.

peladito: Literally, a person without resources, specifically money. Figuratively, a poorly educated person who has obscene habits and language. The typical Mexican comic hobo of the vaudeville stage.

pochería: (See *pocho.*) Pertaining to *pochos* or *pocho* speech.

pocho(a): (1) A somewhat derogatory name for descendants of Mexicans living or raised in the United States. (2) A corrupted Spanish, a mixing of English and a poor form of Spanish spoken by Mexican residents of the United States (Santamaría 1978).

redondeles: A circus structure even more modest than the *carpa* for which a canvas was stretched around poles, forming an enclosed circular space for the performance.

renegado: Originally, the person who renounces the law of Jesus Christ (*Real Academia* 1980). In Mexican culture, he who renounces or is ashamed of his Mexican identity and assimilates Anglo-American customs.

revista/revista de actualidad: A theatrical spectacle consisting of a series of loose scenes usually inspired by current affairs (*Real Academia* 1980).

revista política: A revue touching upon political themes. (See *revista.*)

sainete: "A one-act, comic dramatic sketch" (Newmark). (See *género chico.*)

sección de declamación: (See *cuadro.*)

suelto: "'Broadside'. A printed sheet of an actor's script" (Newmark).

tanda: Each one of the groups in which men or beasts are employed at work, a turn (*Real Academia*). The turns or shows of live performances during a day in the theatre, often in between various film showings in movie houses.

tiple: Soprano (*primera tiple,* first soprano, leading chorine).

tiple cómica: A stock comic soprano in *revistas, zarzuelas,* vaudeville, etc.

variedades: Variety acts or show, vaudeville.

zarzuela: A musical comedy or a play in which spoken parts alternate with song. A forerunner of the opera, the *zarzuela* was first enacted in the Buen Retiro Palace, Madrid, in the 1630s (Newmark).

Sources

Diccionario de la Real Academia Española. Madrid: Real Academia Española, 1980.

Newmark, Maxim. *Dictionary of Spanish Literature.* New York: Philosophical Library.

Santamaría, Francisco J. *Diccionario de mejicanismos.* 3rd edition. Mexico City: Editorial Porrúa, 1978.

References

Brokaw, John W. "A Mexican American Acting Company, 1849–1924." *Educational Theatre Journal* 27/1 (March 1975): 23–29.

———. "The Repertory of a Mexican American Theatrical Troupe, 1849–1924." *Latin American Theatre Review* 8/1 (Fall 1974): 25–35.

———. "Teatro Chicano: Some Reflections." *Educational Theatre Journal* 29/4 (December 1977): 535–544.

Cagey, E. M. *The San Francisco Stage.* New York: Columbia University Press, 1950.

Carreras, Carlos N. "La vida de un actor puertorriqueño." *Puerto Rico Ilustrado*, January 19, 1935, pp. 36–38, 54–55.

Earnest, Sue Wolfer. "An Historical Study of the Growth of the Theatre in Southern California, 1848–1894." Ph.D. dissertation, University of Southern California, 1947.

Englekirk, John E. "Fernando Calderón en el Teatro Popular Nuevomexicano." *Memoria del Segundo Congreso del Instituto Internacional de Literatura Iberoamericana* (1941): 220–240.

———. "Notes on the Repertoire of the New Mexican Folktheatre." *Southern Folklore Quarterly* 4/4 (December 1940): 227–237.

Figueroa, Pablo. *Teatro: Hispanic Theatre in New York City, 1920–1976.* New York: El Museo del Barrio, 1977.

Gipson, Rosemary. "The Beginning of the Theatre in Sonora." *Arizona and the West* 9/4 (Winter 1967): 349–364.

———. "The Mexican Performers." *Journal of Arizona History* 13/4 (Winter 1972): 235–252.

González, Nilda. *Bibliografía del teatro puertorriqueño.* Río Piedras: Editorial Universitaria, 1979.

Greenbaum, Susan D. *Afro-Cubans in Ybor City.* Tampa: University of South Florida and Sociedad la Unión Martí-Maceo, 1986.

Kanellos, Nicolás. *Mexican American Theatre: Legacy and Reality.* Pittsburgh: Latin American Literary Review Press, 1987.

Kanellos, Nicolás, ed. *Hispanic Theatre in the United States.* Houston: Arte Publico Press, 1984.

———, ed. *Mexican American Theatre: Then and Now.* Houston: Arte Publico Press, 1983.

Mañón, Manuel. *Historia del teatro popular de México.* Mexico City: Editorial Cultura, 1932.

Manry, Joe. "A History of the Theatre in Austin." PhD. dissertation, University of Texas at Austin, 1979.

María y Campos, Armando. *La dramática mexicana durante el gobierno del Presidente Lerdo de Tejada.* Mexico City: Compañía de Ediciones Populares, 1964.

———. *Los payasos, poetas del pueblo.* Mexico City: Ediciones Botas, 1939.

Mardis, Robert Francis. "Federal Theatre in Florida." Ph.D. dissertation, University of Florida, 1972.

Miguélez, Armando. "El Teatro Carmen (1915–1923): Centro del arte escénico hispano en Tucson." In *Mexican American Theatre: Then and Now,* ed. Nicolás Kanellos. Houston: Arte Publico Press, 1983, pp. 48–67.

Miller, John C. "Hispanic Theatre in New York, 1965–1977." *Revista Chicano-Riqueña* 9/1 (Winter 1978): 40–59.

Monterde, Francisco. *Bibliografía del teatro mexicano.* New York: Lenox Hill, 1970.

Mormino, Gary. *The Immigrant World of Ybor City.* New York: Statue of Liberty, Ellis Island Centennial Series, 1987.

Pasarell, Emilio J. *Orígenes y desarrollo de la afición teatral en Puerto Rico—Siglo XX,* vol. 2. Río Piedras: Editorial Universitaria, 1967.

Perrier, José Luis. *Bibliografía dramática cubana.* New York: Phos Press, 1926.

Prida Santicilia, Pablo. . . . *Y se levanta el telón.* Mexico City: Ediciones Botas, 1960.

Ramírez Cantú, Elizabeth. "A History of Mexican American Professional Theatre in Texas, 1875–1935." Ph.D. dissertation, University of Texas, 1983.

Robreño, Eduardo. *Historia del teatro popular cubano.* Havana: Oficina del Historiador de la Ciudad de la Habana, 1961.

Sáenz, Antonia. *El teatro de Puerto Rico (Notas para su historia).* Río Piedras: Editorial Universitaria, 1950.

Vega, Bernardo. *Memorias de Bernardo Vega: Una contribución a la historia de la comunidad puertorriqueña,* ed. Andreu Iglesias. San Juan: Ediciones Huracán, 1977.

Vineyard, Hazel. "Trails of the Trouper: A Historical Study of the Theatre in New Mexico, 1880–1910." Master's thesis, University of New Mexico, 1941.

Ybarra-Frausto, Tomás. "La Chata Noloesca: Figura del Donaire." In *Mexican American Theatre: Then and Now,* ed. Nicolás Kanellos. Houston: Arte Publico Press, 1983, pp. 41–51.

Index